# SUPERYACHT MASTER

## Other Titles of Interest

*Bridge Procedures*
Captain Michael and Frances Howorth
ISBN 0 7136 7394 X
This essential manual for every large-yacht captain outlines the correct protocol for keeping watch to STCW-95 standards and the procedures to be followed on the bridge of every superyacht. Fully compliant with ISM procedures, this handbook is packed with essential information and useful checklists.

*Reeds Professional Logbook*
Captain Michael and Frances Howorth
ISBN 0 7136 7399 0
Customised especially for the large yacht market, this logbook covers a three-month period and is recommended and approved by the Maritime Coastguard Agency. Divided into two sections: 'on passage' and 'in harbour', and including logs for tests, drills and inspections, crew lists, load lines and helicopter operations, this book will be welcomed by all skippers and crews of large yachts.

*Reeds Maritime Meteorology 3rd edition*
Maurice Cornish and Elaine Ives
ISBN 0 7136 7635 3
This clear and authoritative introduction to maritime meteorology is ideal for serving and trainee deck officers, fishermen, and those studying for certificates of competency in merchant ships. Including descriptions of the elements and forces that contribute to maritime meteorology, this comprehensive book covers topics ranging from weather forecasting at sea to passage planning, and includes a fold out chart of ocean currents.

*The Sea Survival Manual*
ISBN 0 7136 7052 5
Captain Michael and Frances Howorth
The definitive book on sea survival for anyone aboard a yacht of any size, this manual is aimed at the seafarer who is likely to proceed of sight of land. Fully compliant with the IMO resolutions and MCA regulations and including chapters on safety and survival equipment, GMDSS, first aid, abandoning ship and survival in a life raft, this is the first modern book to tackle the subject from a small craft point of view.

# SUPERYACHT MASTER

## NAVIGATION AND RADAR FOR THE MASTER (YACHTS) CERTIFICATE

Captain Robert Avis
OBE RNVR FRIN

ADLARD COLES NAUTICAL
LONDON

*To my very best friend who now knows far more about superyacht navigation and radar than she ever really wanted to know!*

Published by Adlard Coles Nautical
An imprint of A & C Black Ltd
38 Soho Square, London W1D 3HB
www.adlardcoles.com



First edition 2006

ISBN-10: 0 7136 64452
ISBN-13: 978 0 7136 64454



A CIP catalogue record for this book is available from the British Library.

This book is produced using paper that is made from wood grown in managed, sustainable forests. It is natural, renewable and recyclable. The logging and manufacturing processes conform to the environmental regulations of the country of origin.

Designed by Susan McIntyre
Typeset in Rotis Semi Sans 10/12pt

Printed and bound in Spain by GraphyCems

**Note**: while all reasonable care has been taken in the publication of this edition, the publisher takes no responsibility for the use of the methods or products described in the book.

# Contents

# Foreword

One of the most important task of an Officer of the Watch is to keep a good lookout on the bridge. Having assessed if a risk of collision exists, the OOW and Master must then correctly interpret the 'rules of the road' and take the right avoidance action. He needs to have a clear understanding of all the tools that he has to hand – one of the most important being radar.

In writing this book Robert Avis has not only given clear revision of navigation techniques for students on the OOW, Master's Navigation and Radar courses but has provided extensive explanatory notes for the collision rules and exceptionally clear guidance for radar interpretation. To quote the Director of Lairdside Maritime Centre, John Moores University, Liverpool:

> 'Supported by good examples and advice, this book provides invaluable reference material for those attending the Navigation and Radar Course'.

The author, Robert Avis, served a long apprenticeship at sea. He commanded 12 ships and completed some 50,000 sea miles with the Royal Naval Reserve. He rose to the very highest levels in that organisation, commanding *HMS President* in London. During the last ten years he successfully guided numerous students through their MCA Class 4 courses, and oral preparation. A very charming, witty man with a wealth of knowledge, Robert's brisk and dynamic teaching style held his classes spellbound.

Sadly Robert died from a long illness before the final publication of this book, but it is a lasting tribute to his knowledge, enthusiasm and professionalism. He will be very sadly missed by all who knew him.

Martin Pound MRIN

---


## Acknowledgements

Tim Bartlett
Blue Water Yachting
Harry Cook, MBE
Paul Deeth
Freedom Yachting
Furono Ltd
Phillip Holden
International Maritime Organisation
James Stevens
Kelvin Hughes Ltd
Maritime & Coastguard Agency
Jason Trueman
John Wyborn
Royal Yachting Association (charts on pages 160, 161)
United Kingdom Hydrographic Office

Finally, special thanks to Martin Pound, a true and knowledgeable friend

# 1 The Earth

**THE EARTH IS THE FIFTH-LARGEST PLANET** in our solar system (after Jupiter, Saturn, Uranus, and Neptune). Its mass is about 5.98 x $10^{24}$kg and with an average density of 5520kg/$m^3$ (water has a density of 1027kg/$m^3$). It is the densest planet in our solar system.

The Earth's axis is tilted from the perpendicular to the plane of the ecliptic by an angle of around 23.5°. (It was 23° 26′ 20″ in 2000. This amount reduces by 0.47 of a second each year!) Since the axis is tilted, different parts of the globe are orientated towards the sun at different times of the year. This tilting creates the four seasons of the year: spring, summer, autumn and winter.

More importantly to the navigator, the Earth itself is not a perfect sphere. It is often described as an oblate spheroid, but to be strictly correct it isn't even that. However in order to create a basis upon which navigational calculations can be made, it is generally accepted to be an oblate spheroid, that is to say a football that has been sat upon. If you are a bit of an anorak, the polar radius is 3432.4 nautical miles (nm) (6356.8km) and the equatorial radius is 3443.9nm (6378.1km), the difference being 11.5nm (21.3km) in radius or 23.0nm (42.6km) in diameter.

Until the end of the 15th century, sailors navigated with continuous reference to land. In the Mediterranean it was easy to stay in touch with land masses, and in western and north-west Europe, navigation was entirely coastal. Ships followed the shore from Gibraltar to Norway and the Baltic. The rare exception to this rule was the trade that developed between Scandinavia, Iceland, and Greenland following the discovery of these routes by the Vikings around 1000AD.

When the Portuguese set off on voyages of discovery in the 15th century, navigation became more complex. Portuguese sailors followed the coast of Africa, as they carefully explored southwards. The only reference points available apart from land were heavenly bodies. Locations and courses had to be spatial: navigators needed to be able to locate themselves on a grid of imaginary lines that they developed and later became known as *latitude* and *longitude*.

## Latitude and longitude

Latitude, which gives the location of a position north or south of the Equator, is expressed by angular measurements ranging from 0° at the Equator to 90°N or 90°S at the Poles.

Midway between the North and South Poles, the Equator – the only east/west great circle – divides the Earth into northern and southern hemispheres. Running parallel to the Equator, to the north and to the south of it, are a succession of imaginary circles that become smaller and smaller the closer they get to the Poles. This series of east-west-running circles, known as the *parallels of latitude*, are crossed at right angles by a series of half-circles extending north and south from one Pole to the other, called *meridians of longitude*.

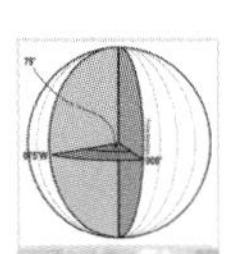



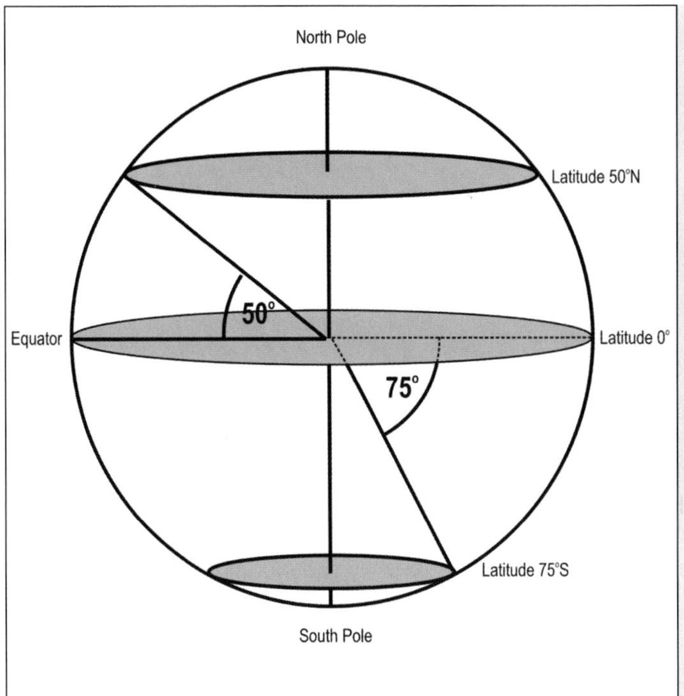


**Fig 1.1** Latitude.

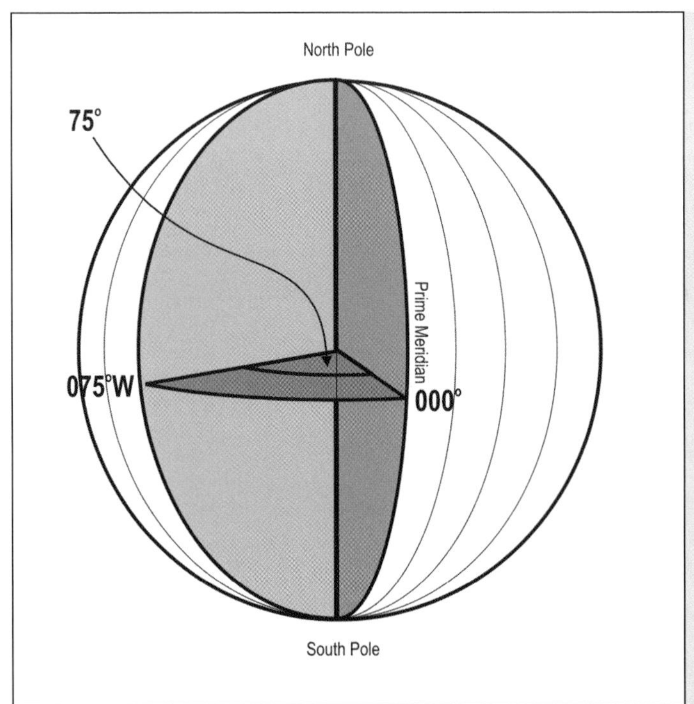


**Fig 1.2** Longitude.

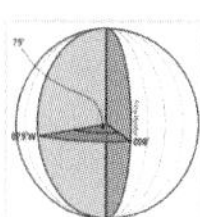

Degrees of latitude are equally spaced, but the slight flattening of the Earth's shape at the two Poles causes the length of a degree of latitude on the Earth's surface to vary from 59.7nm (110.57km) at the Equator to 60.3nm (111.70km) at the Poles. One minute of latitude (1/60 of a degree) is taken to equal a nautical mile (nm), but because of the differences between the measured distance at the Equator and at the Poles, this distance of a nautical mile is taken as one minute of latitude at that latitude.

**TOP TIP**

*When measuring distance on a chart, always measure from the position on the latitude scale that is level with your position.*

Longitude is the measurement of a position east or west of a single north/south line, now known as the *prime meridian*. Because for many years, different countries designated their own 'prime meridians', it was difficult to specify positions on an international basis and so, in 1884, an internationally accepted prime meridian was established through Greenwich in Greater London in the United Kingdom, thus giving an internationally accepted basis against which longitude could be measured. Longitude is therefore measured in degrees ranging from 0° at the prime (Greenwich) meridian up to 180° east or 180° west. The meridian opposite to the prime meridian is the basis for the International Date Line. It is this point which determines the change of the date when travelling from west to east. The International Date Line itself is actually not a meridian in the true sense as it has been set up by International agreement and varies in longitude to include and exclude various countries on each side of itself.

You cannot measure distance using the longitude scale as, although meridians of longitude 1° apart at the Equator are in fact separated by a distance of 60.1nm (111.32km), as they converge towards the North and South Poles, the distance between each degree decreases down to zero at each Pole.

**TOP TIP**

*It is vitally important NOT to measure distance off the longitude scales as the measured distance of one minute of longitude decreases as you move north in the northern hemisphere or south in the southern hemisphere.*

Each degree of latitude and of longitude is subdivided into 60 minutes, and each minute is either divided into tenths and hundreds of a minute or alternatively, it can be divided into 60 seconds. This allows the precise assessment of any location on the Earth's surface. Generally, marine navigators work in degrees, minutes and tenths and hundredths of a minute.

In order to avoid the confusion between latitude and longitude, latitude is written first and it can only ever be two digits (maximum latitude is 90° north or south) whereas longitude can be up to 180° east or west and is written as three digits. When longitude is less than 100°, it is written with zeros in front to make up the three digits ie 015°W.

## Plotting a position in latitude and longitude

Marine charts are marked with latitude scales on the left and right hand sides (and sometimes in the centre also) and longitude scales across the top and bottom. Plotting a position in latitude and longitude on a chart or recording a position in latitude and longitude is not difficult so long as you remember the basics:

1 Latitude is measured from the sides of the chart.
2 Longitude is measured from the top and bottom of the chart.
3 In the northern hemisphere, latitude increases as you go up the chart and vice versa.
4 If you are east of the prime (Greenwich) meridian, longitude increases as you move right.
5 If you are west of the prime (Greenwich) meridian, longitude increases as you move left.

## Example

*Plot a position using latitude and longitude co-ordinates from a GPS:*

Time: 12:50 local time
50° 13′.4N
004° 36′.9E

Minutes of latitude on this scale of chart are divided into tenths. Individual latitude minutes (nautical miles at that latitude) are shown alternately with an extra line as in the diagram. In this example (Figure 1.3), the latitude is in the northern hemisphere so it increases as you move up the chart. There is a latitude line at 50° 15′ so the required latitude is less than that, so move down by 1.6′ to 50° 13′. 4 and draw a horizontal line in the vicinity of the position of the fix.

Similarly, look at the longitude scale and as the longitude is to the east of the prime meridian, it increases as you move to the right. Therefore the correct longitude will be to the right of the 4° 35′ line by 1.9′ and thus gives the second position line. The position is where they cross and is annotated with a circle and time (and possibly a log reading). A fix on the chart with no time is completely useless. The position would be written in the deck log as **50° 13′.4N 004° 36′.9E.**

### TOP TIP

*When writing lat and long, the normal convention is for latitude to be written first and longitude second. Longitude is displayed as three figures to avoid any confusion, as latitude can never be more than 90°.*

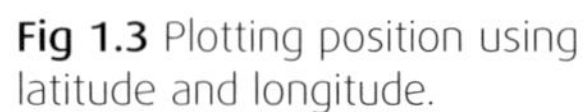
**Fig 1.3** Plotting position using latitude and longitude.

# 2 Compasses

## The magnetic compass

We all played with magnets in the physics lab at school and it didn't take a graduate to get to grips with the fact that 'like' poles repelled one another, and 'unlike' poles attracted. School experiments also showed that by suspending a magnet on a length of cotton, it always seemed to point in the same direction. This is caused by its reaction to the magnetic field generated by the Earth itself.

The magnetic field of the Earth is known to a high degree and the history of its variation against time is no black art. The earliest recorded observations of terrestrial magnetism date back to the 6th century BC and the magnetic compass, in the form of the lodestone, is believed to have been discovered as early as the 2nd century BC.

Some of the earliest declination measurements were made by the Chinese astronomer Yi-Xing in 720AD, and observations recorded in the following centuries permitted an English astronomer, Henry Gellibrand, to discover the variation of declination with time.

It is believed that the concept of using a compass for navigation was first used in the west some time after 1200AD when important investigations using magnets were made by the French scholar, Petrus Peregrinus, in his work *Epistole de Magnete* in 1269. Peregrinus defined the magnetic pole (and thus the dipolar nature of the magnet), the concept of polarity, and the magnetic meridian. Although Peregrinus observed the inclination of the field lines around a typical magnetic pole, he did not apply this concept to the Earth, and thus it was not until 1544 that the first measurements of the terrestrial field inclination were recorded.

It was around 1600 that a better explanation for magnetic variation was put forward. Sir William Gilbert, physician to Queen Elizabeth I, suggested in his book *Of Magnets, Magnetic Bodies, and the Great Magnet of the Earth* that the Earth itself was a giant magnet and that the force that directed the compass originated inside the Earth. Using a model of the Earth made from lodestone, a naturally occurring magnetic rock, he showed that there should be two points on the Earth where a magnetised needle would stand vertically: at the North and South Magnetic Poles. Magnetic charts drawn up in the following two hundred years laid the way for Carl Friedrich Gauss to undertake the very first spherical harmonic expansion of the potential of the Earth's magnetic field in 1838. Using three charts compiled between 1833 and 1837, Gauss calculated the values of the coefficients in the expansion to the fourth degree, and predicted the locations of the geomagnetic pole positions.

This is basically the same definition used today. At the magnetic Poles, the Earth's magnetic field is perpendicular to its surface. Consequently, the magnetic dip, or inclination is 90° or vertical. Therefore, the magnetic declination (the angle between true geographic north and magnetic north) cannot be determined at, or close to the magnetic Poles.

## Magnetic north

The direction in which a compass needle points is known as *magnetic north*, and the difference between magnetic north and the true north direction is known by purists as *magnetic declination*. However mariners tend to use the terms *variation*, *magnetic variation*, or *compass variation* in place of *magnetic declination*.

This variation does not, however, remain constant. The complex motion of fluids in the outer core of the Earth that lies from 2,800 – 5,000km below the surface causes the magnetic field to change slowly with time. Because of this variation of the difference between magnetic north and true north, values shown on charts need to be updated regularly if they are to be used with minimised errors.

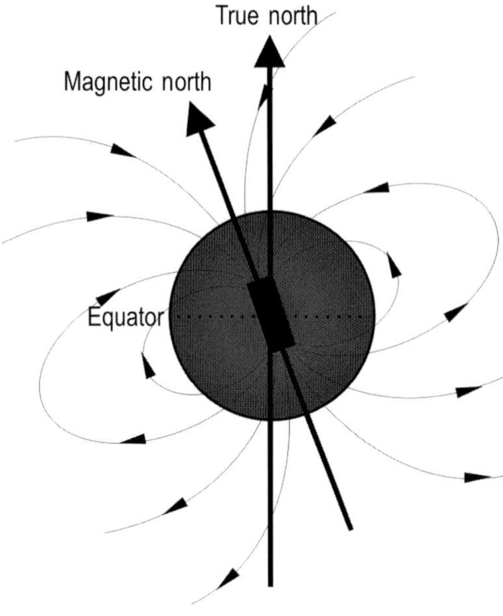


**Fig 2.1** Earth's magnetic field.

## So where is magnetic north?

Sir William Gilbert believed that the magnetic North Pole coincided with the North Geographic Pole. Observations, however, made by explorers in subsequent decades showed that this was not true, and by the early 19th century, the accumulated observations proved that the magnetic North Pole must be somewhere in the north of Canada.

In 1829, Sir John Ross set out on a voyage to discover the Northwest Passage. His ship became trapped in ice off the north-west coast of the Boothia Peninsula, where it remained for the next four years. Sir John's nephew, James Clark Ross, used the time to take magnetic observations along the Boothia coast. These convinced him that the magnetic North Pole was close, and in 1831, he set out to find it. On 1 June 1831 at Cape Adelaide on the west coast of the Boothia Peninsula, he measured a dip of 89° 59′. For all practical purposes, he had reached the magnetic North Pole. The next attempt to establish it was made some 70 years later by the Norwegian explorer Roald Amundsen. In 1903 he left Norway on his famous voyage through the Northwest Passage and although his primary goal was to set up a temporary magnetic observatory in the Arctic, his secondary objective was to try to establish the location of the magnetic North Pole.

Shortly after World War II, Canadian government scientists found a dip of 89° 56′ at Allen Lake on Prince of Wales Island and, in conjunction with other observations made in the vicinity, showed that the Pole had moved some 250km north-west since the time of Amundsen's observations. Later observations in 1962, 1973 and 1984 showed that the general north-westerly movement of the Pole is continuing, and that during the last century, it moved an average 10km per year.

In April and May of 1994, a survey was conducted to determine the average position of the magnetic North Pole at that time. It was predicted that the annual movement of the Pole in the 21st century would be around 15km per year continuing in a north-westerly direction.

## Diurnal movement of the magnetic North Pole

Having established that the magnetic North Pole moves its position over time, it has also been established that it moves according to the time of day; the Sun's position relative to the Earth and the Sun's own magnetic influence also have a bearing on the magnetic North Pole's position. It is important to realise that when we talk about the location of the Pole, we are referring to an 'average' position. The magnetic North Pole will wander daily in a roughly elliptical path around this average position, and could be as much as 75km away from the 'average position' predicted on a chart. All of these movements make it difficult for the navigator to take a magnetic bearing with any sort of fine accuracy.

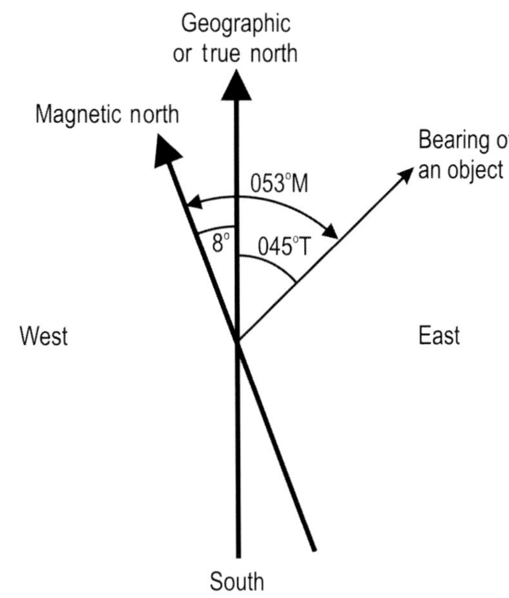


**Fig 2.2** 8° westerly variation.

## Why does it move?

We now know that the cause of the Earth's magnetic field is very complex. It is believed that electrical currents originating in the hot, liquid, outer core of the Earth create a magnetic field. As a simple analogy: consider an electromagnet, in which we can produce a strong magnetic field by passing an electric current through a coil of wire. In nature, processes are seldom as simple as that. The flow of electric currents in the core is continually changing, so the magnetic field produced by those currents also changes. This means that on the surface of the Earth, both the strength and direction of the magnetic field varies over time. This gradual change is called *secular variation.*

In 1995, two American scientists, Gary Glatzmaier and Paul Roberts, created a model that sought to explain some of these mysteries. The Glatzmaier-Roberts model of the geodynamo is essentially a complex set of equations describing the physics of the Earth's core. Scientists had long speculated that the mechanism behind the geomagnetic field involved the motion of the Earth's fluid outer core, which surrounds a solid inner core. Both are composed mainly of iron. The solid inner core is about the size of the Moon and as hot as the surface of the Sun. The flow of heat from the core ultimately drives the geodynamo. The cooling process results in fluid motions in the outer core that produce an electric current, which, like any electric current, generates a magnetic field. The fluidity of the Earth's core and varying strengths of electrical energy being produced account for the gradual change in the apparent position of 'magnetic' north.

## Magnetic and geographic North Pole

The difference between the position of the geographic (true north) Pole and the magnetic North Pole is measured in degrees from any geographic position on the Earth's surface as an offset west or east from the prime meridian running through that position. Bearings taken from that position can then be adjusted by the variation given for that position to change magnetic bearings to true bearings or true bearings into magnetic bearings. In this example (Figure 2.2) a magnetic bearing of an object is 053°(M) and if the variation is 8°W then the true bearing is 045°(T).

## Magnetic meridian

A magnetic meridian is any vertical plane on the Earth's surface that aggregates all the Earth's magnetic influences at that point into one single force. It is the line along which a magnetic compass needle will point if it is not subjected to any exterior magnetic forces (*deviation*).

## True meridian

A true meridian is any vertical plane on the Earth's surface joining the geographic North Pole with the geographic South Pole. The difference in degrees between the direction of the true meridian and the direction of the magnetic meridian at any point on the Earth's surface is known as *magnetic variation.*

## Magnetic variation

So much for the theory, but what is much more important to the mariner, is how to calculate and make allowances for magnetic variation, the difference between what we call true north and what we call magnetic north. Variation varies not only from year to year but also from geographical position to geographical position. Details of variation for each geographical area are printed on navigational charts. On a small-scale chart it is likely that variation is different on one side of the chart to the other. Take a look at the compass rose closest to your position and within it you will find a second rose slightly offset to the west (left) or to the east (right).

In this example (Figure 2.3) the magnetic north compass rose is offset to the west or left of true north. The description along the magnetic north line reads:

7°25′W 1997 (6′E)

This indicates that the magnetic variation which should be allowed in this area was 7° 25′W in 1997, but it is changing 6′ east every year (ie moving back towards true north). So in 2006 when this book was first published, the calculation was as follows:

| 1997 | 7° 25′W |
|---|---|
| 1998 | -6′E |
| 1999 | -6′E |
| 2000 | -6′E |
| 2001 | -6′E |
| 2002 | -6′E |
| 2003 | -6′E |
| 2004 | -6′E |
| 2005 | -6°E |
| 2006 | -6°E |
| Leaving | 6° 31′W |

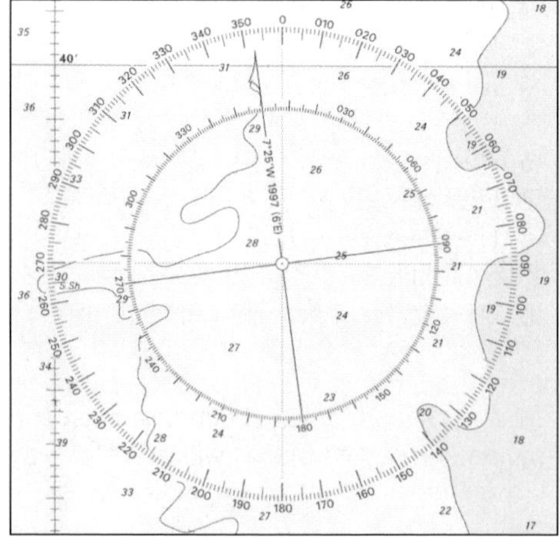


**Fig 2.3** A compass rose.

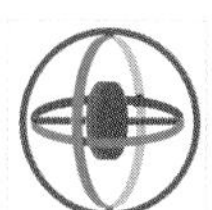

In realistic terms the narrowest that a 2B pencil line can be drawn is to a single degree so 7° west is used.

This means that any true course plotted on the chart would need to be adjusted by 7° to obtain the equivalent magnetic course. The greatest potential problem facing most navigators is assessing whether to add or to subtract the 7°. (See Converting compass bearings to true bearings, later in this chapter.)

The really important thing to remember about variation, in practical terms, is that it is a fixed adjustment to be made for a particular geographical area at a particular time (year) and its value can be found from the compass rose which is nearest to your position on large scale charts or it may be indicated by lines of similar variation on very small-scale charts such as those covering the North Atlantic.

**TOP TIP**

*Variation is based on geographical position and time.*

# Compass deviation

Compass deviation is the second correctable compass error. The deviation error is caused by two types of magnetic influence.

## Permanent magnetism

The first is the *permanent magnetism* of the vessel which is the magnetic field created by and within a vessel by ferrous and electrical equipment such as:

1. Electric motors.
2. Magnetic controllers.
3. Gyro repeaters.
4. Non-married conductors.
5. Loudspeakers.
6. Electric indicators.
7. Electric welding.
8. Large power circuits.
9. Searchlights.
10. Electrical control panels or switches.
11. Telephone headsets.
12. Windscreen wipers.
13. Rudder position indicators, solenoid type.
14. Engine telegraphs.
15. Radar equipment.
16. Magnetically controlled switches.
17. Radio transmitters.
18. Radio receivers.
19. Voltage regulators.

The direction in which a ship lies when she is built will also have an effect on the permanent magnetism of a vessel, as will constant voyages on the same course or long periods of lay up without changes in heading direction. The effects of permanent magnetism can be adjusted by adding, moving or removing athwartships and fore-and-aft corrector magnets in the binnacle (Figure 2.4). Adjustments for heeling of the vessel are made by the position and number of magnets in the vertical tube in the centre of the binnacle. These magnets are the only ones that compensate for both permanent and induced magnetism.

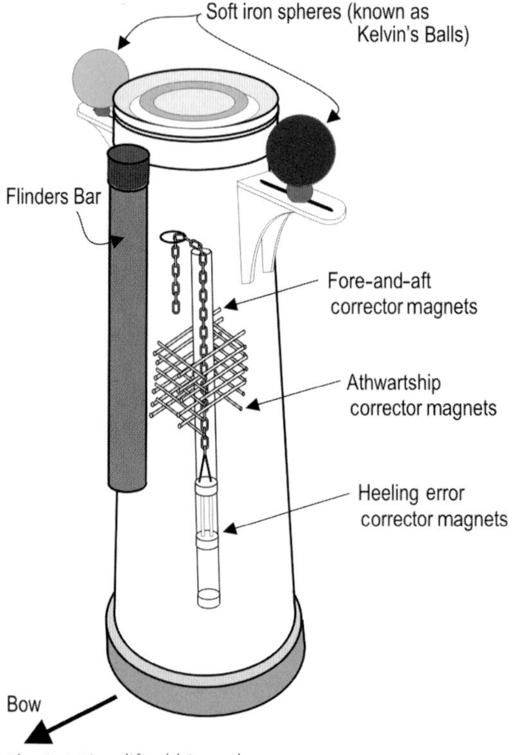


**Fig 2.4** Simplified binnacle.

## Induced magnetism

The second type of magnetism is *induced magnetism* which is the magnetic effect caused by the Earth's magnetic field which varies geographically and according to the angle at which the fore-and-aft line of the vessel cuts the Earth's magnetic field. The effect of induced magnetism can be reduced by the correct size and position of two soft iron spheres either side of the compass card, known as 'Kelvin's Balls'. These remove or reduce the horizontal effect of the Earth's magnetic field and the 'Flinders Bar', the cylindrical column in front of the binnacle removes or reduces the vertical component of it. Both of these devices, being soft iron, absorb the Earth's magnetic field and they are adjusted by increasing or decreasing the size of the soft iron spheres and moving them towards or away from the compass. The Flinders Bar is a soft iron cylinder of soft iron typically 12in, 18in or 24in long which is held in the vertical tube in front of the binnacle and it is raised to the correct position by placing soft wood cylindrical spacing pieces beneath it in the tube.

Adjusting a magnetic compass requires a deep understanding of it and should only be done by an experienced compass adjuster who should be able to reduce deviation to 10° or less on any heading.

Unlike variation, which is position and time dependent, deviation varies according to the ship's heading. So if you change your heading, you will change the deviation that is affecting your compass. The amount of adjustment that needs to be made is given on a deviation card.

The magnetic compass deviation should be checked annually, and after:

- Refit or replacement.
- Addition or removal of any electrical equipment or wiring.
- Dry docking.
- Collision, fire or explosion.
- Lightening strike.
- Heavy power short-circuit.
- Large change in the ship's magnetic latitude.
- Remaining alongside in the same berth for long periods.
- Any major change in deviation noted by routine checks.

**TOP TIP**

*Whilst you may be able to swing your own magnetic compass, unless you have experience, leave any adjustment to the professionals!*

On completion, a deviation card (see Figure 2.5) is issued, from which the deviation on any compass heading can be predicted.

Having established that ships' compasses suffer from variation and deviation, it is important for the mariner to be able to convert from *true* to *magnetic* to *compass* and back again.

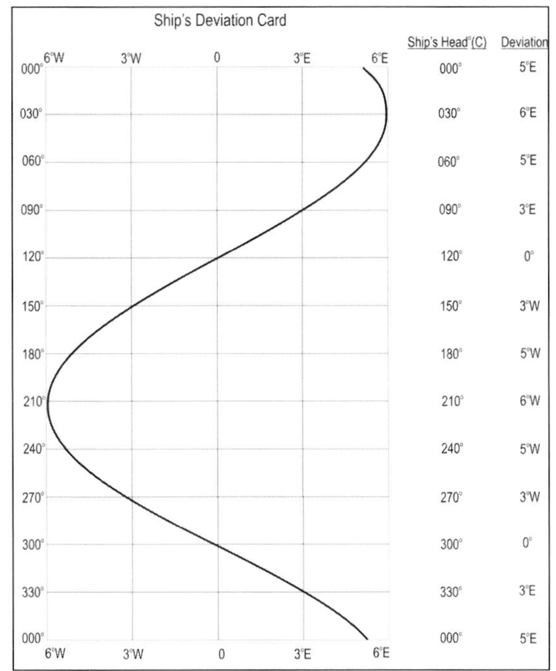


**Fig 2.5** Deviation card.

## Converting true bearings to compass bearings

Firstly you convert a true bearing to a magnetic bearing by taking variation into account. The second stage is to convert the magnetic bearing to a compass bearing by taking deviation into account.

There are many mnemonics around to help mariners remember which is which, but my favourite to adjust a ***true (T)*** course to a ***magnetic (M)*** course to a ***compass (C)*** course is to remember:

**WEST IS BEST – EAST IS LEAST**
So if the magnetic variation/compass deviation is west, you add – and if it is east, you subtract.

As both of these adjustments need to be done to convert each true course through a magnetic course to a compass course, they can be done together in a tabular format as follows:

Changing a **TRUE (T)** course to a **COMPASS (C)** course

| True Course (T) | Variation Course (M) | Magnetic | Deviation | Compass Course (C) |
|---|---|---|---|---|
| 180°(T) | + 5° W | 185°(M) | + 9° W | 194°(C) |
| 325°(T) | –16° E | 309°(M) | –12° E | 297°(C) |
| 159°(T) | +27° W | 186°(M) | + 4° W | 190°(C) |
| 008°(T) | – 1° E | 007°(M) | +18° W | 025°(C) |
| 358°(T) | + 9° W | 007°(M) | –12° E | 355°(C) |
| 100°(T) | –14° E | 086°(M) | – 3° W | 083°(C) |

TOP TIP

*TRUE ± VARIATION = MAGNETIC ± DEVIATION = COMPASS*

## Converting compass bearings to true bearings

When taking compass bearings, for example to provide a position fix, it is necessary to be able to convert these compass bearings back from compass (C) to true (T) so that they can be plotted on the chart. This works in exactly the opposite way to the above example.

COMPASS ADD EAST for TRUE

This works from compass to magnetic and from magnetic to true – add East, subtract West.

Changing a **COMPASS (C)** course to a **TRUE (T)** course

| Compass course (C) | Deviation | Magnetic course (M) | Variation | True course (T) |
|---|---|---|---|---|
| 194°(C) | – 9° W | 185°(M) | – 5° W | 180°(T) |
| 297°(C) | +12° E | 309°(M) | +16° E | 325°(T) |
| 190°(C) | – 4° W | 186°(M) | –27° W | 159°(T) |
| 025°(C) | –18° W | 007°(M) | + 1° E | 008°(T) |
| 355°(C) | +12° E | 007°(M) | – 9° W | 358°(T) |
| 083°(C) | + 3° E | 086°(M) | –14° E | 072°(T) |

If you cannot remember whether deviation comes before variation try my good friend Harry Cook's favourite:

CADETS DON'T MEET VIRGINS TWICE

Whereas if you head up North, Phil Russ from John Moores University, Liverpool, will tell you:

TWO VIRGINS MAKE DELIGHTFUL COMPANY

Isn't it wonderful to have such a wide and varied culture!

TOP TIP

*The really important thing to remember about deviation is that it changes according to the heading of the vessel. So every time you change course, you will need to adjust your deviation calculation accordingly, but variation remains the same in the same area and only changes very slightly from year to year.*

If you take bearings using a magnetic steering compass, then the *deviation* you take into account is that relating to the vessel's *heading* and **NOT** the direction of the *bearing*.

Figure 2.6 shows a vessel heading on a compass course of 147°(C). It observes a distant object on a compass bearing of 217°(C). When converting this bearing to true, the deviation used in the calculation is that for the vessel's heading ie 147°(C) and NOT the deviation for the bearing itself.

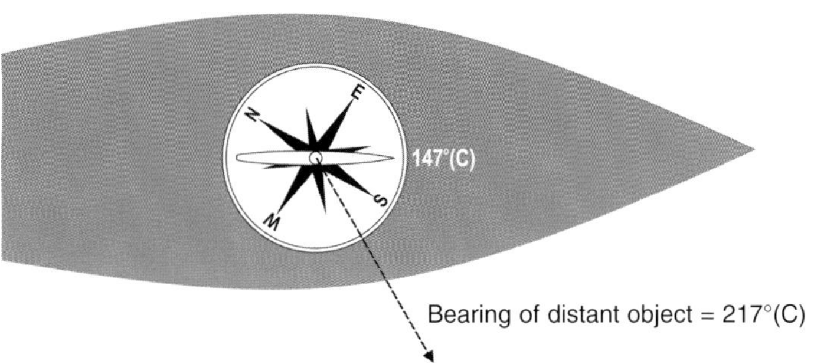


Fig 2.6

**TOP TIP**

*It is essential to understand the principle of converting compass bearings to true, as many aspiring superyacht masters have foundered in written MCA navigation examinations because they failed to remember this extremely important principle.*

# The fluxgate compass

The magnetic compass has serious limitations for the navigator and not every vessel's budget will stretch to a gyrocompass. The fluxgate compass is an electronic magnetic compass that can be set to read in magnetic or true. This is a great help to the mariner who is generally most interested in true north. Most of the work involved with adjusting and compensating a traditional magnetic compass involves removing the effects of magnetic influences other than those from the Earth itself, a complicated and inexact process often involving more art than science. By definition, there will always be errors present in a magnetic compass, even after adjustment and compensation.

The electronic fluxgate magnetic compass has the following advantages over a traditional magnetic one:

1. It is solid state electronics and has no moving parts.
2. It operates using very low power.
3. It has a standardised digital output.
4. It is compact, lightweight and inexpensive.
5. It has a rapid start-up and self-alignment.
6. It has a low sensitivity to vibration, shock and temperature changes.
7. It can self-correct.

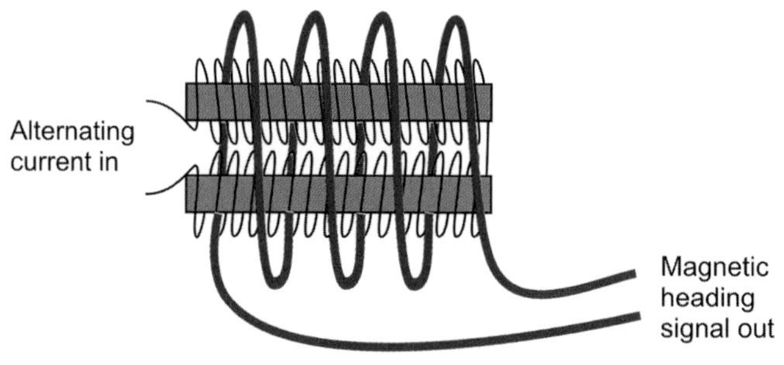


**Fig 2.7** Simplified magnetic fluxgate compass.

The 'fluxgate magnetometer' was developed in 1928. Initially it was used for detecting submarines and for airborne mapping of Earth's magnetic fields. The most common type, called the second harmonic device, incorporates two coils, a primary coil and a secondary coil, both wrapped around soft ferromagnetic cores. When an external magnetic field is present, the soft core's magnetic induction changes. An alternating current applied to the primary winding causes the cores to oscillate. The secondary winding, or sensing coil, receives an induced current from the cores. This induced current is affected by changes in the magnetic field around the device and appears as an amplitude variation in the output of the secondary winding or sensing coil. The signal is then demodulated and filtered to produce a magnetic heading signal (Figure 2.7). After being converted to a digital format, the data can be fed to numerous remote devices, including steering compass repeaters, bearing compasses, emergency steering stations and autopilots.

Since the influence of a ship's own magnetism is inversely proportional to the square of its distance from the position of the compass, if the fluxgate device can be located at some distance from the main magnetic influences of the ship, the influence of the ship's magnetic field can be greatly reduced. Another advantage is that a digital signal can be processed and automatically corrected for deviation. Further, a deviation table, in digital format, can be calculated automatically by merely steering the vessel very slowly in a number of full circles. Algorithms then determine and apply corrections that effectively flatten the pattern of deviation. The theoretical result is zero compass deviation. An index error to provide a northerly direction can be set and applied to all the readings.

Similarly, a correction for variation can be applied manually or with a GPS input so the system knows where it is with respect to the isogonic chart and the variation correction can be applied automatically, thus rendering the output in true degrees, corrected for both deviation and variation. It is important to remember that a fluxgate compass is still a magnetic compass and that it will still be influenced by large changes to the ship's magnetic field. A swing should be instigated after every such change but this is a task that does not generally require a specialist compass adjuster. The fluxgate is also susceptible to large errors when the vessel is heeled unless it can somehow be stabilised in the horizontal.

**TOP TIP**

*Don't forget that a fluxgate compass is still a magnetic compass and is therefore affected by variation and deviation.*

# The gyrocompass

Having looked closely at the use of the magnetic compass in navigation and the relatively complicated and time consuming way that navigators have to establish and then apply corrections for variation and deviation, we now move on to look at the gyrocompass and its solution to continuously pointing in one direction, ie north. If you remember playing with a spinning top as a child and watching in amazement as it seemed to be able to balance on virtually anything and still remain stable, that spinning top was really a very simple gyroscope set in gimbals (Figure 2.8).

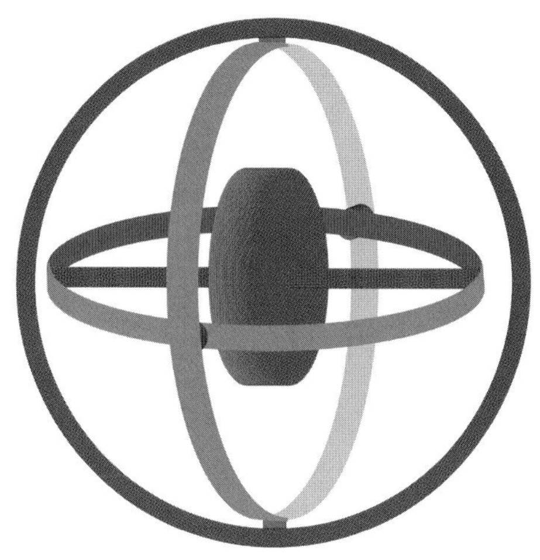

**Fig 2.8** Simple gyroscope set in gimbals.

By spinning a wheel at high speed, it is possible to direct its axis in a particular direction and, no matter where you move its pivot point, the axis continues to point in that direction. This is the principle upon which the gyrocompass is based.

Once set spinning, a gyroscope will exhibit a quality known as *gyroscopic inertia* or *rigidity in space*. That is to say that it will remain pointing in the same *absolute direction* in space. A gyro needs be gimballed with a series of three concentric rings that allow free movement in all directions. If it were to be set up in outer space it would make the perfect direction pointer.

## Horizontal Earth rate

Unfortunately, if the gyro is to be used to give a sense of direction on our spinning Earth, it is necessary to be able to make allowances for the Earth's rotation before the gyro can be set up and used with any confidence. Consider the gyroscope set spinning at the Equator with its axis aligned east/west. As the Earth rotates, the gyroscope maintains its rigidity in space, but to an observer standing on the Earth, the gyro will appear to turn slowly round its horizontal axis. This is known as the *horizontal Earth rate*. It appears to turn to the right at a rate of 15° per hour as the surface of the Earth rotates 15° in the same period of time. (The Earth rotates 360° in 24 hours, ie 15° per hour). So although it appears on Earth to be changing direction, in 'absolute' terms it remains pointing in the same direction.

## Vertical Earth rate

Now if we were to move the free spinning gyroscope to the North Pole and still keep the spin axis in the horizontal plane as the Earth rotates, the gyroscope will remain fixed in space and appears to rotate about its vertical axis at 15° per hour. This effect is known as the *vertical Earth* rate.

Let us now move it in-between the Equator and the North Pole, to a latitude of, say 45°N, with its spin axis lying north/south and appearing to be horizontal. As the Earth rotates, the free gyroscope will tend to swing to the east about its vertical axis and the north-pointing end of the spin axis will tend to rise from the horizontal. These two movements are caused by the direct effect of the rotation of the Earth at this 'in-between' position.

To make the gyroscope behave on the Earth's surface as if it were in space, it is necessary to be able to compensate for the easterly swing and the rise of the north-pointing end of the axis caused by the rotation of the Earth. Both of these adjustments must be applied continuously and at a rate proportional to the speed of the rotation of the Earth and the latitude of the gyrocompass.

## Precession

If, say, a force is applied to the spinning gyroscope to try and rotate the gyro wheel about its horizontal axis or push one side of the spin axis down, then the gyroscope reacts by rotating itself about the vertical axis moving its spin axis toward the direction of tilt. This behaviour is known as *precession.*

Motorcyclists use the effect of precession to go around corners by leaning the bike into the turn. The resultant vector is a combination of the forward speed of the bike and the angle of lean applied. In a simple rotating wheel it causes a rotation around the vertical axis. If the gyro is tilted around the horizontal axis it will cause the spin axis to tip upwards or downwards in the same way. By applying force in these two directions we can cause the gyro to move in such a way as to stop it pointing at the same spot in space and point towards true north instead.

Returning to the free gyroscope at latitude 45° north, we can now see that if we were to apply a small continuous torque about the horizontal axis, the gyro would slowly 'precess' to the west. If the torque is the correct amount, the gyro will remain pointing north, taking into account the rotation of the Earth. The criterion for north-pointing is that the gyro must remain in the local horizontal. Some gyros use gravity to provide this effect. By having a reservoir of liquid mercury suspended from the wheel, the upward tilt of the gyro caused by the rotation of the Earth makes more mercury move to one side which in turn provides a torque causing the gyro to 'precess' to the west and back towards north.

## Latitude adjustment

We have seen that a marine gyrocompass has to apply torque in two planes in order to make the gyro continuously seek north. The amount of torque required in each direction varies with latitude. A gyro on the Equator with the spin axis facing east/west will appear to rotate around the horizontal axis. A gyro pointing in the same direction at the North Pole will appear to rotate around its vertical axis. The amounts of torque required in each direction have an inverse relationship to each other. The gyro must therefore 'know' what the latitude is so that it can apply the corrections in the correct amounts. For this purpose all marine gyrocompasses have a 'latitude rider' that must be correctly set. If it is incorrectly set, there will be an unnecessary gyro error. If the gyrocompass is connected to an electronic position fixing system, it can automatically establish its latitude from that. Alternatively there may be a manually adjustable 'latitude rider' which will need to be monitored as the vessel moves north or south.

## Speed input

When a gyrocompass is mounted in a vessel on the Equator steaming west at 30 knots, the absolute speed of the vessel, taking into account the speed of rotation of the Earth (about 900 knots at the Equator) minus the speed of the vessel is hardly significant. However when the vessel is at, say 60°N, its absolute speed is about 450 knots so 30 knots of ship speed is a little more significant. If the vessel were close to the North Pole, the absolute speed of the vessel would be very small so the vessel's speed would become very significant.

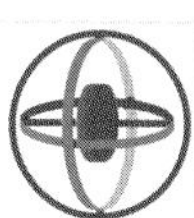

The speed of the vessel in a north/south direction will also influence the gyro as the amount of tilt of the spin axis increases or decreases. Most modern gyros obtain the vessel's speed from the log input so this is generally not an important issue to the navigator unless of course the log is inaccurate or it fails completely. In this case, unless the navigator enters the vessel's speed manually, there will be a correctable gyro error. If the speed input is taken from an electronic fixing system, care needs to be taken to understand the difference between speed through the water (log speed) and speed over the ground (SOG). In areas with strong tidal streams, the differences can be significant.

## Speed error charts

Gyros used in smaller vessels often do not have any facility for speed input. It is therefore necessary to use a speed error correction chart that is supplied with the equipment. Failure to use this could result in substantial errors. For example a yacht at 60°N on a heading of 010° could have a 3° gyro error if the speed correction is not correctly applied. So in this example, after a 1,000 mile voyage, the yacht which didn't allow for speed error would be more than 50 miles off her planned landfall position!

**TOP TIP**

*It is vitally important to ensure that the latitude rider and log input are set correctly.*

## Gyro error

No matter how much care maintainers and navigators take, gyrocompasses are susceptible to error. This error can be adjusted out but this is only possible if a correct bearing can be established unless you are a navigator extraordinaire!

Prudent navigators will check their gyro for accuracy at every opportunity. A charted transit is likely to be the most accurate. Charts are annotated with many transits in the form: *Leading lights 051°* or abbreviated to *Ldg Lts 070°* as in Figure 2.9. If the two leading lights referred to are in line, the gyrocompass should read 051° or 070° respectively.

Making up one's own transits using headlands and other landmarks is an equally satisfactory way of checking the gyro and the prudent navigator will always keep one eye open for every opportunity of a gyro check.

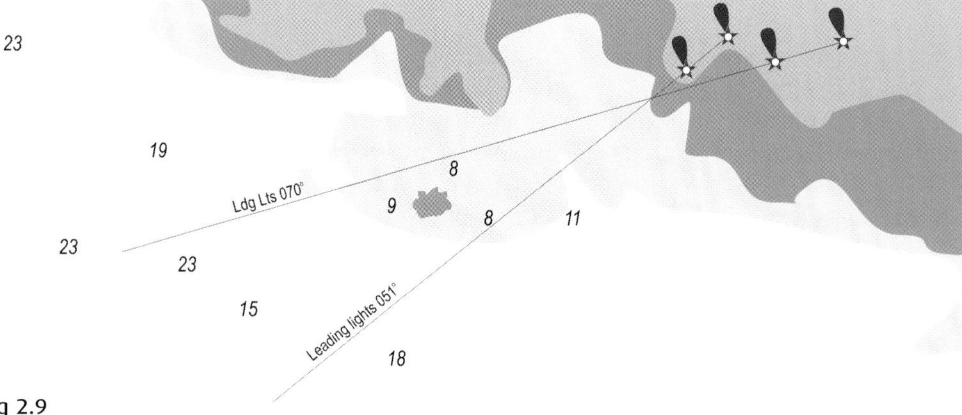


Fig 2.9

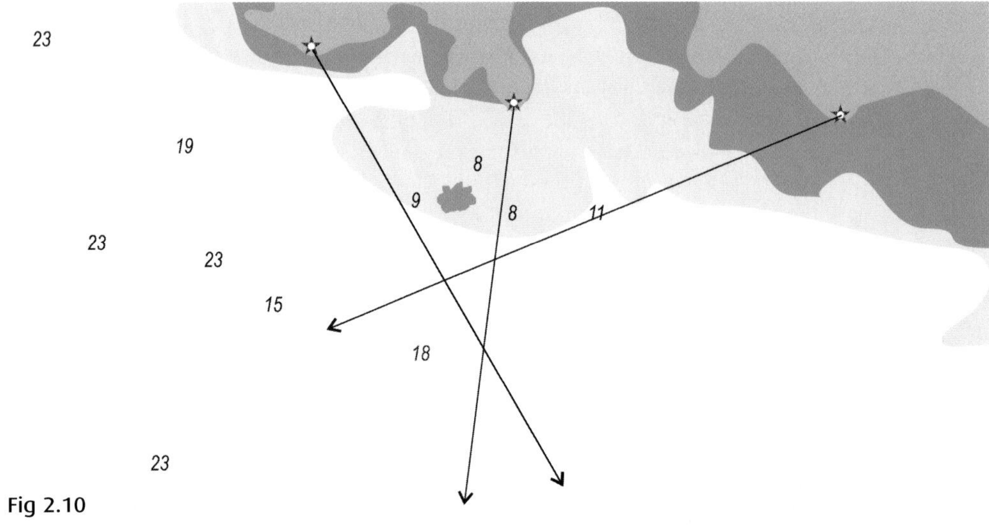


Fig 2.10

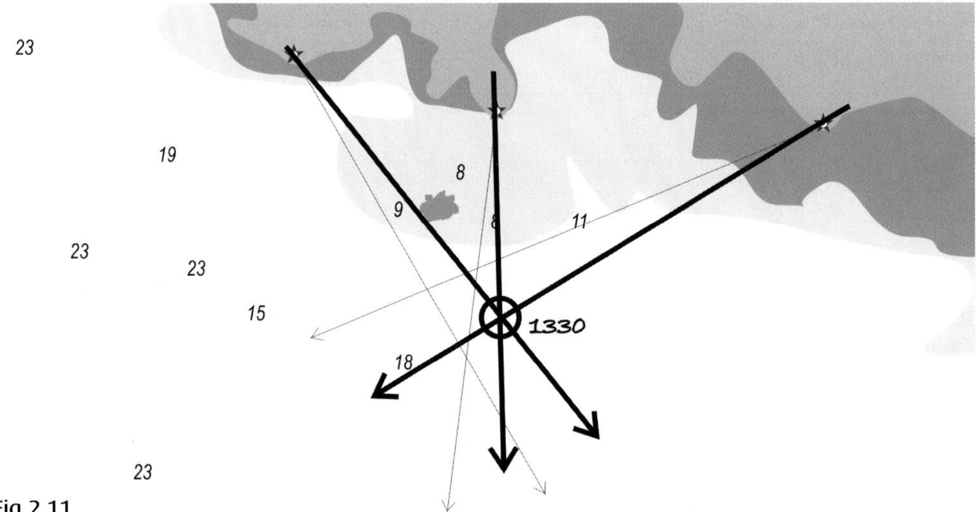


Fig 2.11

Early indications of a gyro error could be a succession of poor visual fixes or large 'cocked hats' when taking visual fixes. If you feel you have lost your touch and each visual fix you take is far from perfect, note down each of the bearings and calculate the difference between each. Then using a station pointer, if you are lucky enough to have one, or more simply draw the three position lines relative to each other on a piece of tracing or greaseproof paper (speak to the chef), and slide the station pointer or tracing paper over the chart until the lines coincide with the fixing points (Figure 2.10). There will only be one position on the chart where all three position lines pass through each of the fixing points. The true position of the fix is given where these lines cross.

To establish the gyro error, measure the bearings from each point to this true position and each one will differ from the original bearings by the same difference. This is known as *gyro error*. The

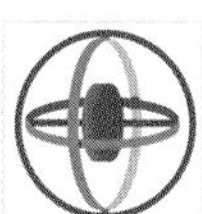

Steering position with magnetic compass and gyro repeater (centre).

gyro error is reported as 'high' or 'low'. So if the gyro reading should read 067° and it actually reads 077° it will be said to be reading 10° high. Gyro error should be adjusted out at the first opportunity and if a ship carries a gyro error, a record of it should be made in the deck log to inform all bridge watch keepers.

In Figure 2.11 a gyro error of 10° high gives a large cocked hat but by reducing each bearing by 10° the correct position is established. Note in this case that the correct position is actually *outside* the area of the cocked hat.

It is generally prudent, when faced with a cocked hat, to assume that the ship's position is closest to the nearest point of danger but you should be aware that this can only be an approximation and the example given demonstrates that there is no guarantee that you will be within the cocked hat. Another, more accurate fix needs to be established at the first opportunity.

# 3 Charts and Publications

## Chart projections

It is impossible to accurately project a curved surface such as the Earth on to a flat piece of paper and many different methods of projection have been developed; each has its own advantages and its own problems. From the mariner's perspective, the priorities are to be able to show the correct shape of land masses and to be able to plot an accurate position, to draw courses and lay off speed vectors which, as closely as possible, demonstrate what will happen in real life. It is not possible to meet all criteria in any one type of projection and therefore marine cartographers have established three primary means of projection of the Earth's surface.

### Mercator projection

Gerardus Mercator (1512–1594) was the Latin name of the Flemish cartographer, Gerhard Kremer. He was best known for his mapping work, especially the way he used straight lines rather than curved ones to indicate lines of longitude. He produced his first map in 1537 and his first map of Europe was published in 1554. This was generally thought to be the best of its kind for many decades. He later went on to produce a map of the British Isles in 1564 and in 1568 he devised and produced a method of map projection, now known as 'Mercator' projection. This system represents the meridians of longitude by parallel lines and the parallels of latitude by straight lines intersecting the meridians of longitude at right angles.

The insight, which is key to the Mercator projection, is that if you want to avoid distorting angles (like courses and bearings), you have to maintain the same scale in latitude and longitude on the chart. Whatever the horizontal scale is at a point on the map, the vertical scale should be the same. Mercator figured out how to construct such a map using only a compass and a protractor.

Edward Wright explained the theory of Mercator projection in 1599 as follows:

> *'Make a globe out of a spherical balloon. Place it in a larger glass cylinder. Blow it up slowly so that it first touches at the equator. Continue blowing it up slowly. Each point on the balloon globe is blown up until it is pressed against the wall of the glass cylinder. Higher latitudes are blown up more. The final result is a Mercator projection.'*

***Rhumb lines*** on a Mercator projection chart are straight. A rhumb line is described as a constant compass orientation between any two-point locations. Therefore, a rhumb line crosses all meridians at a constant angle.

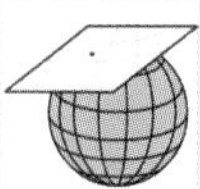

**TOP TIP**

*A Mercator projection exaggerates the size of regions furthest from the Equator relative to those areas adjacent to the Equator. For example Greenland will appear to be the same width as Africa on a Mercator projection chart even though, in fact, Africa is three times wider.*

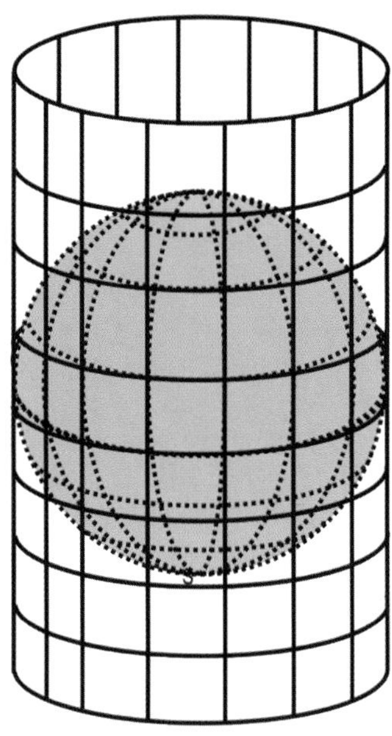

**Fig 3.1** Mercator projection.

*Parallels of latitude* on a Mercator projection chart are straight lines, each of which is parallel to the Equator.

*Meridians of longitude* on a Mercator projection chart appear as straight lines at right angles to the parallels of latitude.

Distances are measured by taking one minute of latitude *at that latitude* as one nautical mile. Because of the method of projection, a nautical mile at the top of a chart will vary in length from a nautical mile at the bottom. This is why it is important to measure distance *at the latitude of the distance to be measured.*

The majority of navigation charts other than those covering the North and South Poles and large scale harbour charts are of Mercator projection.

## Transverse Mercator (or Gauss Conformal Projection)

This projection is a Mercator projection turned through 90° (Figure 3.2). The effect is to standardise distances on the latitude scale (unlike the standard Mercator projection) so that one nautical mile will measure the same length at any point on the latitude scale. This method of projection has been used on British Admiralty charts, mainly for large-scale harbour charts, since the 1970s.

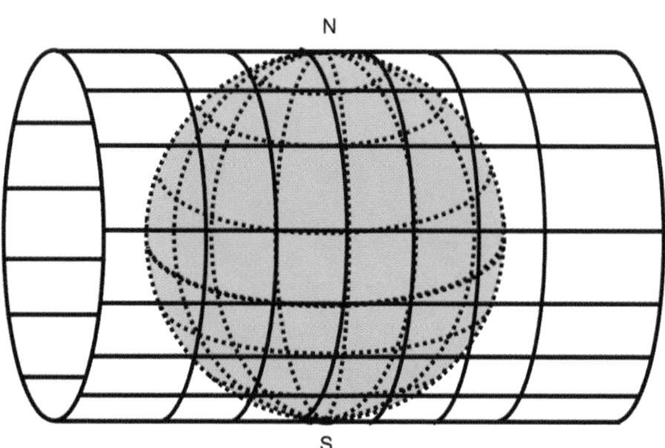


**Fig 3.2** Transverse Mercator projection.

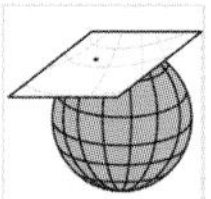



## Gnomonic projection

The gnomonic projection is an *azimuthal* (or zenithal) projection. It is represented as a plane tangent to the globe (Figure 3.3). At this point of tangency, also known as the *standard point* (which can be anywhere on the Earth's surface), all major characteristics are retained. As you move away from the standard point it ceases to be conformal, is not equal-area and distances are no longer true to scale. Only areas of less than a hemisphere can ever be shown and distortion becomes radially pronounced with increasing distance from the standard point. All aspects (polar, oblique and equatorial) can be shown.

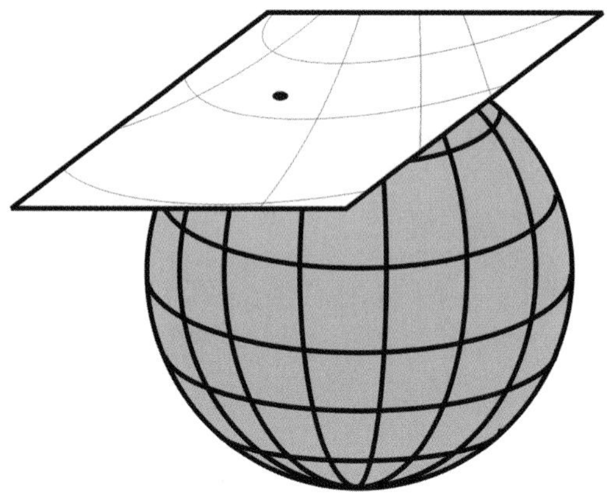

**Fig 3.3** Gnomonic projection.

Every complete line of longitude is a *Great Circle*. The Equator is also a Great Circle but all other parallels of latitude are known as Small Circles.

The gnomonic projection has a unique characteristic that any straight line drawn on a gnomonic chart represents part of a Great Circle, whereas a rhumb line between the same points plotted on a gnomonic chart will be a curve. Gnomonic charts are used when it is convenient to be able to draw Great Circles as straight lines. A Great Circle is the shortest distance between two points and, on a long passage, this should be recognised at the planning stage.

To give a comparison, a Great Circle track drawn on a gnomonic chart as a straight line would be plotted as a curve on a Mercator chart (Figure 3.4).

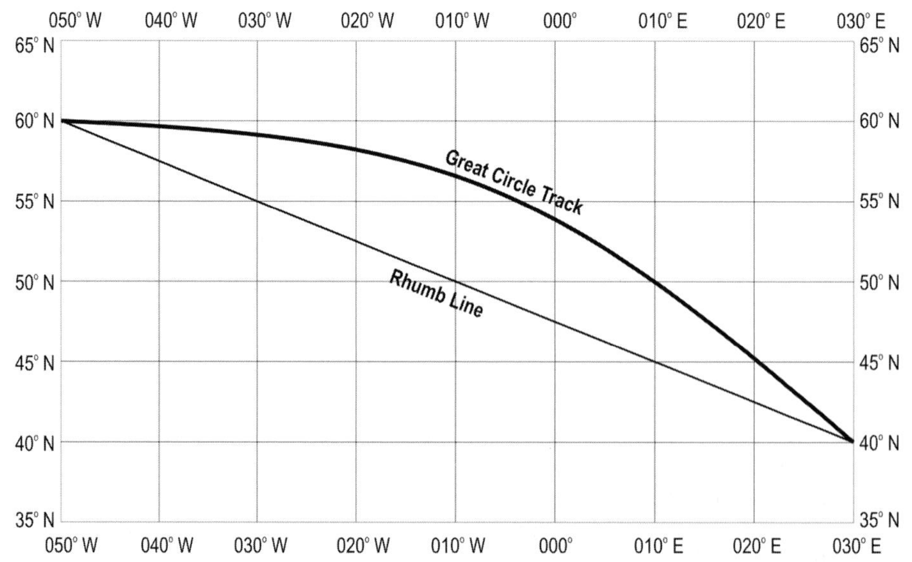


**Fig 3.4** Plotting a Great Circle track onto a Mercator projection chart.

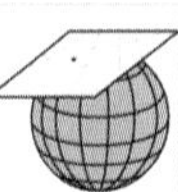

**TOP TIP**

*A Great Circle track on a Mercator Projection chart is always a curve whereas on a Gnomonic Chart it will be a straight line.*

## Cartographers' datums

This is not the same as chart datum (see Tides).

Cartographers draw every chart to a predetermined navigational datum. In simple terms, this establishes a relationship between the positions of all the data on a chart and a fixed datum point. In earlier times, this was calculated by *triangulation*. The first triangulation in Great Britain was started in 1784, and was adjusted by least squares using logarithmic tables. The origin of the datum was defined at the old Greenwich Observatory in London. In the early 1900s as navigational techniques improved, the lack of consistency of previous charting became apparent and it was decided that a new triangulation was required. The Re-triangulation of Great Britain was carried out between 1935 and 1951, and formed the Ordnance Survey of Great Britain 1936 (OSGB36) Datum.

**Satellite-derived positions**

Positions obtained from satellite navigation systems are normally referred to WGS84 Datum; such positions should be moved 0.13 minutes NORTHWARD and 0.09 minutes EASTWARD to agree with this chart.

At the same time throughout the world, cartographers were all using individual datums to create their own national charts. This presented no real problems until the advent of accurate positioning systems when it was discovered that there could be substantial anomalies between the datums being used by satellite systems and those being used by the cartographers. Charts in many different datums started to be appended with notes in the chart title detailing adjustments that should be made to positions taken from satellite positioning systems to bring them into line with the positions indicated on the chart. This has sensibly led to a move to standardise datums in an effort to remove the inaccuracies of which we were previously oblivious.

The World Geodetic Datum 1984 (WGS84) was set up by the United States Department of Defense and is now becoming an internationally adopted standard datum for marine navigation positioning. It is this datum that is now used by the principal satellite navigation systems and it is viewed as the best global datum available for worldwide positioning and navigation. It is also becoming the standard to which cartographers are drawing new charts and re-drawing existing ones.

Just because a chart is 'up to date' with small corrections, do not assume it has been surveyed recently. Take a look at the Source Data diagram on the chart and you may be surprised to find that many common charts have not actually been subject to a survey for a considerable time.

To give you some idea of the different datums in use around the world, my hand-held GPS with 1998 software has a choice of 107 different international datums from which to choose.

In 1999 I found myself working aboard a 12,500 ton cruise ship looking for an anchorage on a tiny charted shallow patch in a huge Norwegian Fjord. The ship's GPS was set to WGS84 datum.

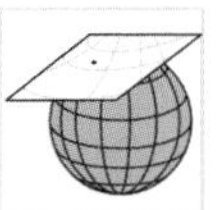



We searched for about 40 minutes without success until I realised that the chart from which we had established the anchorage position was constructed using the ED50 datum. A quick dive into my bag revealed my small, inexpensive hand-held GPS and by changing the datum in use from WGS84 to ED50 we were able to find the anchorage within minutes. The Captain of the ship was really impressed with my 'magic' little hand-held as he called it! Problems of this kind will cease to exist once a standardised international datum becomes the norm.

# Publications to be carried aboard UK ships

*Source: The Merchant Shipping (Carriage of Nautical Publications) Regulations 1998, Statutory Instrument No. 2647 of 1998, MSN 1719(M) and Chapter 18 of Annual Notices to Mariners*

There are regulations that specify the publications to be carried on certain UK ships. The regulations apply to ships and hovercraft registered in the United Kingdom wherever they may be and to other ships or hovercraft within United Kingdom waters. They do not apply to ships or hovercraft that are less than 12m in length or to pleasure vessels.

*The expression 'pleasure vessel' means any vessel which at the time it is being used, is used only for the sport or pleasure of the owner or the immediate family or friends of the owner; or in the case of a vessel owned by a body corporate, the persons on the vessel are employees or officers of the body corporate, or their immediate family or friends and on a voyage or excursion which is one for which the owner does not receive money for or in connection with operating the vessel or carrying any person, other than as a contribution to the direct expenses of the operation of the vessel incurred during the voyage or excursion.*

*It also includes any vessel wholly owned by or on behalf of a members' club formed for the purpose of sport or pleasure which, at the time it is being used, is used only for the sport or pleasure of members of that club or their immediate family; and for the use of which any charges levied are paid into club funds and applied for the general use of the club.*

Having said that, it is good seamanship for the appropriate publications to be carried by those vessels not legally obliged to do so.

## Additional publications

These publications must be carried by UK sea-going ships and hovercraft over 13.7m:

| Publication | Publisher |
|---|---|
| *International Code of Signals (INTERCO)* | International Maritime Organisation |
| *Mariners' Handbook* | Hydrographer of the Navy |

## Other publications

Publications of which only those parts relevant to a ship's voyage and operation must be carried:

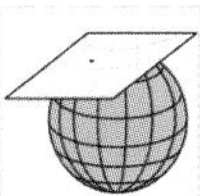

- Charts as necessary for the intended voyage.

  *Charts should be of such a scale and contain sufficient detail to show all navigational marks that may be used by a ship when navigating the waters comprised by the chart. They must be of the latest obtainable edition and be corrected up to date from the latest relevant obtainable Notices to Mariners or Radio Navigational Warnings.*

| Publication | Publisher |
|---|---|
| *Merchant Shipping Notices* | Maritime and Coastguard Agency |
| *Marine Guidance Notes* | Maritime and Coastguard Agency |
| *Marine Information Notes* | Maritime and Coastguard Agency |
| *Notices to Mariners* (weekly, cumulative and annual) | Hydrographer of the Navy |
| *Lists of Radio Signals* | Hydrographer of the Navy |
| *Lists of Lights* | Hydrographer of the Navy |
| *Sailing Directions* | Hydrographer of the Navy |
| *Nautical Almanac* | Hydrographer of the Navy |
| *Navigational Tables* | Hydrographer of the Navy |
| *Tide Tables* | Hydrographer of the Navy |
| *Tidal Stream Atlases* | Hydrographer of the Navy |

- Operating and maintenance instructions for navigational aids carried by the ship.

  In accordance with SOLAS V, all UK registered ships over 150 GT on international voyages and on all UK registered ships over 500 GT on domestic voyages shall also carry:

| Publication | Publisher |
|---|---|
| *International Aeronautical and Maritime Search and Rescue Manual Volume III (Mobile Stations)* | IMO |

An increasing number of these publications are now available and approved to be carried in electronic form.

### Penalties

The owner and master shall be guilty of an offence if these regulations should not be complied with and a ship may be detained if it is seen not to comply with these regulations.

## Notices to Mariners

### Weekly Notices to Mariners

British Admiralty Charts, of which there are over 3,300 currently published, are corrected by the issue of weekly *Notices to Mariners* published by the United Kingdom Hydrographic Office (UKHO) at Taunton. Each weekly edition is divided into six sections:

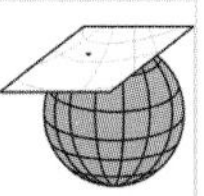



I Explanatory Notes. Indexes to Section II
II Admiralty Notices to Mariners. Updates to Standard Navigational Charts
III Reprints of Navigational Warnings
IV Amendments to Admiralty Sailing Directions
V Amendments to Admiralty Lists of Lights and Fog Signals
VI Amendments to Admiralty List of Radio Signals

**TOP TIP**

Notices to Mariners *are now available free from the Internet:* www.ukho.gov.uk/weekly_nms.cfm

In addition to *Weekly Notices to Mariners*, the UKHO also produces supplementary publications:

- Notices to Mariners Block Corrections – to adhere to charts where a large or detailed alteration is required.
- Notices to Mariners Tracings – to assist in the correction of charts.

## Cumulative Notices to Mariners

These are published twice yearly in January and July and contain the corrections by chart for the past two and a half/three years. This enables the navigator to be able to check on any missed corrections for this period. These are also downloadable from the internet: www.ukho.gov.uk/cumulative_nm_list.html

## Annual Notices to Mariners

This is a substantial book that includes considerable useful information to the mariner but its main contents are a list of all the Temporary and Preliminary Notices (Ts and Ps) in force on 1st January and corrections to Sailing Directions (Pilot Books) that were issued in the preceding 12 months.

Guidance on how to apply the corrections in *Weekly Notices to Mariners* can be found in Admiralty Publication NP294, *How to Correct your Charts the Admiralty Way*. This enables a standardised, neat and formal record of corrections. It is recommended that a formal chart correction log be used to record details of corrections applied.

## Chart corrections

Chart corrections take the following format:

**1893 NORTH AMERICA, East Coast – Florida - Florida Keys – American Shoal Northeastwards - Wreck**

Insert (+++) 23° 33′.06N., 081° 47′.89W.

**Chart** [*Last correction*] - **1086** [*2765/05*] – **1315** [*2765/05*] – **2975** [*3224/05*]
US Notice 50/1264/05 *(HH. 912/638/05).*

The correction reference 1893 refers to North America adjacent to Florida Keys where the symbol for a wreck should be appended in position 23° 33′.06N., 081° 47′.89W. In order to check that no corrections have been missed, the three charts required for this amendment are

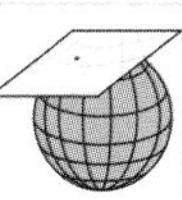

chart numbers 1086, 1315 and 2975 and the last correction on each chart should be correction number 2765 of year 2005 for chart number 1086, chart correction 2765 of year 2005 for chart number 1315 and correction number 3224 of year 2005 for chart number 2975. The source of the information was from the US authorities with their reference 50/1264/05 and the Hydrographic Office reference is 912/638/05.

If a large or complicated alteration to a chart is required then a complete block is supplied in the *Notices to Mariners* that can be cut out and stuck to the revised area on the chart.

It is important to remember to annotate the list of small corrections with the number of the correction on the bottom left hand corner of the chart to indicate that a correction has been completed. This is the only way to ensure that corrections are made in the correct order. Each correction can be checked that is the next sequential one because the correction indicates the last correction on each chart.

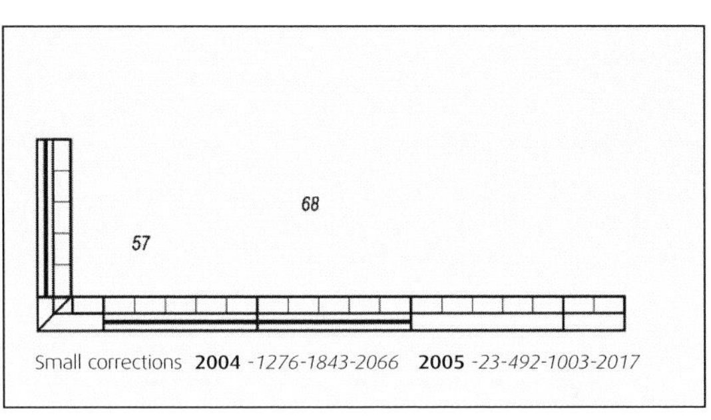


**TOP TIP**

*You must remember that even though you have all your corrections up to date, there is an inevitable time lag between information becoming available and the* Notices to Mariners *being published, so a chart folio can never be completely up to date.*

## Official Status of Admiralty Notices to Mariners

The *Admiralty Notices to Mariners Bulletin* (ANMB) is published by the UKHO. The UK Maritime & Coastguard Agency (MCA) accepts that both the paper and digital forms of the ANMB comply with carriage requirement for *Notices to Mariners* within Regulation 19.2.1.4 of the revised Chapter V of the Safety of Life at Sea (SOLAS) Convention, and the Merchant Shipping (Safety of Navigation) Regulations, both of which came into force 1 July 2002.

## Hydrographic notes

If it is found that a chart is not accurate then it is incumbent on every seafarer to keep the Hydrographic Office informed at the first opportunity. Form H102, known as a Hydrographic Note (and H102a for amendments to port information) is printed at the back of every copy of *Notices to Mariners* and this should be completed and forwarded to: UK Hydrographic Office, Admiralty Way, Taunton, Somerset, TA1 2DN, UK. If you cannot get hold of the correct form it is not a hanging offence. The Hydrographic Office would rather hear by non-conventional means than not at all!

Form H102 asks for the following information:

- Sender's name, address, telephone, fax, e-mail.
- General locality.
- Subject.
- Position in latitude and longitude.
- British Admiralty charts affected.

- Position fixing system used (including the Datum in use).
- Latest *Notices to Mariners* held on board.
- Other publications affected.
- Details of the observation.
- A tracing of the largest scale chart held on board with the alteration detailed in red if possible with black tracings of adequate details to enable its easy recognition.

Additionally Form H102a is used for changes to port information and asks for information on the following:

- General remarks.
- Anchorages.
- Cargo handling.
- Communications.
- Cranes.
- Directions.
- Pilotage.
- Port authority.
- Repairs.
- Rescue and distress.
- Services.
- Small craft facilities.
- Supplies.
- Tugs.
- Views.
- Wharves.

Other publications which are corrected using *Notices to Mariners* are as follows:

**TOP TIP**

*Always do your best to keep the Hydrographer of the Navy and his team as up to date as possible. He relies upon your updates to keep his publications up to date!*

## Navigational warnings

Navarea warnings broadcast by radio are printed weekly showing all those messages in force at the time of issue. They are divided geographically as follows:

| | |
|---|---|
| Navarea I | NE Atlantic |
| Navarea II | E Atlantic |
| Navarea III | Mediterranean |
| Navarea IV | NW Atlantic |
| Navarea V | W Atlantic |
| Navarea VI | SW Atlantic |
| Navarea VII | SE Atlantic |
| Navarea VIII | Indian Ocean |
| Navarea IX | Persian Gulf, Red Sea, NW Arabian Sea |
| Navarea X | Australia, New Guinea |
| Navarea XI | Malacca Strait, China Sea, N Pacific |
| Navarea XII | NE Pacific |
| Navarea XIII | NW Pacific |
| Navarea XIV | SW Pacific |
| Navarea XV | SE Pacific |
| Navarea XVI | E Pacific |
| Hydropacs | Pacific, Indian Ocean |

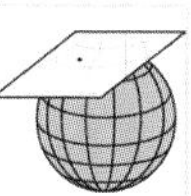

## Sailing Directions

*Admiralty Sailing Directions* which are published in 74 volumes are often referred to as 'pilot books'. They are designed to assist all types of sea-going vessel to safely navigate around the globe, and provide essential information on all aspects of navigation.

*Sailing Directions* are used to supplement Admiralty charts and worldwide coverage is provided. They are published every three years and contain high quality colour photography and views. They include:

- Information on hazards and buoyage.
- Meteorological data.
- Details of pilotage, regulations and port facilities.
- Guides to major port entry.

## Admiralty List of Lights and Fog Signals (All)

There are 11 volumes that make up the *Admiralty List of Lights and Fog Signals* (NP74–NP84). They provide a complete and comprehensive listing of all lighthouses, lightships, lit floating marks (over 8m in height), fog signals and lights of navigational significance.

The 11 volumes of the *Admiralty List of Lights and Fog Signals* (A–L) are divided up as follows:

| | | |
|---|---|---|
| A | (NP74) | British Isles and North Coast of France |
| B | (NP75) | Southern and Eastern Sides of the North Sea |
| C | (NP76) | Baltic Sea |
| D | (NP77) | Eastern Atlantic Ocean, Western Indian Ocean and Arabian Sea |
| E | (NP78) | Mediterranean, Black Sea and Red Sea |
| F | (NP79) | Bay of Bengal and Pacific Ocean |
| G | (NP80) | Western Side of South Atlantic Ocean and East Pacific Ocean |
| H | (NP81) | Northern and Eastern Coasts of Canada |
| J | (NP82) | Western Side of North Atlantic Ocean |
| K | (NP83) | Indian Ocean and Pacific Ocean |
| L | (NP84) | Northern Seas |

New Editions of the *Admiralty List of Lights and Fog Signals* are published annually, with important changes to lights (including temporary ones) listed in Section V of *Weekly Admiralty Notices to Mariners.*

Information contained within each publication focuses primarily on the characteristics of lights and fog signals, together with a detailed and comprehensive listing of equivalent foreign language light descriptions. Tables for the calculation of the geographical and luminous ranges of lights are also included.

Details for all lights listed within each publication are tabulated to include:

- Identifying number.
- Location and/or name.
- Geographical co-ordinates.
- Characteristics and intensity.
- Elevation above MHWS in metres.
- Range in sea miles.
- Description of structure.

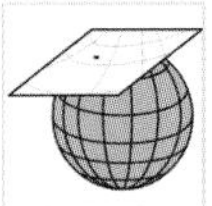



**Example**

| | | | | | | |
|---|---|---|---|---|---|---|
| 0030 Wolf Rock (T) | 49 56.7<br>5 48.5 | Fl W 15s | 34 | **23** | Grey round granite tower. black lantern<br>41 | Racon. Shown 24 hours. Helicopter landing platform above lantern |
| | | Horn 30s | | | | bl 2.5 |

## Admiralty List of Radio Signals (ALRS)

The series of *Admiralty List of Radio Signals* (ALRS) are a comprehensive source of information covering all aspects of maritime communications.

Contents range from listings of stations handling maritime public correspondence to a full range of products and services essential for compliance with the Global Maritime Distress and Safety System (GMDSS).

ALRS volumes also feature details of those radio stations broadcasting weather services, forecasts and a detailed explanation of the complexities of global satellite position fixing systems.

| | |
|---|---|
| Volume 1 | Maritime Radio Stations NP281 (Parts 1 & 2) |
| Volume 2 | Radio Aids to Navigation, Satellite Navigation Systems, Legal Time, Radio Time Signals and Electronic Position Fixing Systems NP282 |
| Volume 3 | Maritime Safety Information Services NP283 (Parts 1 & 2) |
| Volume 4 | Meteorological Observation Stations NP284 |
| Volume 5 | Global Maritime Distress and Safety System (GMDSS) NP285 |
| Volume 6 | Pilot Services, Vessel Traffic Services and Port Operations NP286 |

New Editions of the *Admiralty List of Radio Signals* are published annually with important changes to lights (including temporary ones) listed in Section VI of *Weekly Admiralty Notices to Mariners.*

Chart table with Weatherfax, GPS readout display and Navtex.

# 4 Tides and Tidal Streams

**THE RISE AND FALL IN SEA LEVEL** in tidal regions is caused by a combination of the effects of the gravitational pull from the Moon and Sun and the rotation of the Earth on its axis.

Although the Moon is subjected to the gravitational pull of the Earth, the Moon itself also exerts a gravitational force on the Earth, the two forces acting together lock the Moon in orbit around the Earth. Water on the surface of the Earth reacts to the attraction of the Moon's gravity by being pulled towards it. This results in a build up in the water level on the side of the Earth closest to the Moon, where the gravitational pull is strongest. On the opposite side of the Earth where the Moon's gravity has minimal effect, a second, slightly lesser, build up occurs. In between these two bulges, the water level is lower.

The Moon orbits the Earth approximately every 28 days. In actual fact it goes round Earth in 27½ days, but because Earth has gone 1/12 of the way around the orbit of the Sun in the same period, it actually takes 29½ days before the *apparent* lunar orbit is completed. Consequently the higher levels of water, one on each side, pass around the Earth, following the Moon, apparently on a 29½ day cycle. As the Earth spins on its axis every 24 hours, virtually any point on the Earth's surface will pass through two high water and two low water phases. The Earth spins in the same direction as the Moon's orbit, so it takes approximately 12 hours and an extra 25 minutes from the time of high water at a particular place to the time of the next high water. This is known as a *semidiurnal* tidal cycle that means it happens every 'half-day'.

**Fig 4.1** Gravitational pull of the Sun and Moon at spring tides.

The Moon's orbit does not follow a path at right angles to the axis on which the Earth spins; if it did it would follow an orbit around the Equator. Its orbit is offset so that it passes over the northern and southern hemispheres. This factor, together with landmasses which divide up the oceans, results in some areas experiencing a single high water every 25 hours, called a *diurnal tide*, meaning once per day.

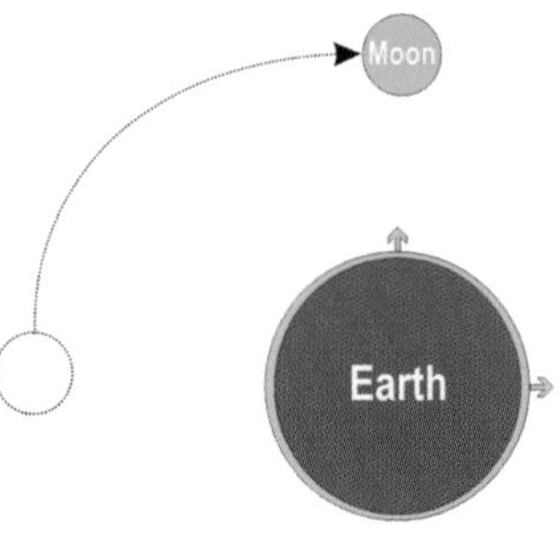

**Fig 4.2** Gravitational pull of the Sun and Moon at neap tides.

In addition to being subjected to the Moon's gravity, water on the surface of the Earth is also affected by the gravity of the Sun. The gravitational pull of the Sun is not as strong as that of the Moon, but if the Sun, Moon and Earth are in line, their combined gravity raises the height of sea level even higher. This occurs at (or just after) the time of the new Moon and full Moon, when the Earth, Moon and Sun are in close alignment. When the Sun and Moon are out of alignment, the gravitational forces are no longer pulling together so the gravitational effect is reduced and the sea level is lower. This makes a cycle of higher high tides, with lower low tides, every 14 days, and lower high tides and higher low tides, a week later. The higher high tides are known as *spring tides* or *springs* and the lower high tides are called *neap tides* or *neaps*.

The closest alignment of the Earth, Moon and Sun occurs twice each year when the Sun passes over the Equator in March and September. This gives the highest high tides and the lowest low tides, which are known as *equinoctial springs*. When this equinoctial alignment coincides, with the Earth, Moon and Sun closest to each other, the highest and lowest tides will occur.

The timing of these events is known in advance and consequently the times and levels of high and low water can be predicted in the form of tide tables.

The geography of an area will affect the rise and fall of tide. The Atlantic Ocean for example, is a basin between two continents, with the rise and fall building into a regular semi-diurnal rhythm backwards and forwards within that basin, whereas the Mediterranean Sea being almost completely land-locked, experiences a very small rise and fall of sea level.

Atmospheric and meteorological conditions can also affect tidal heights. High pressure can suppress the rise of tide and low pressure can increase it, while strong onshore winds can maintain a high tidal level for longer than predicted and strong offshore winds can delay and reduce the rise of a high tide. These changes can be significant. They can exceed 1m and may not be evident in the tide tables but comments may feature in Sailing Directions.

# Tidal terms and definitions

**Chart Datum** (CD) is the lowest sea level expected (excluding meteorological conditions) and is closely related to the lowest astronomical tide (LAT). It is possible for tidal heights to fall below CD or LAT and, in these cases, the tidal height is shown in tide tables as a negative figure.

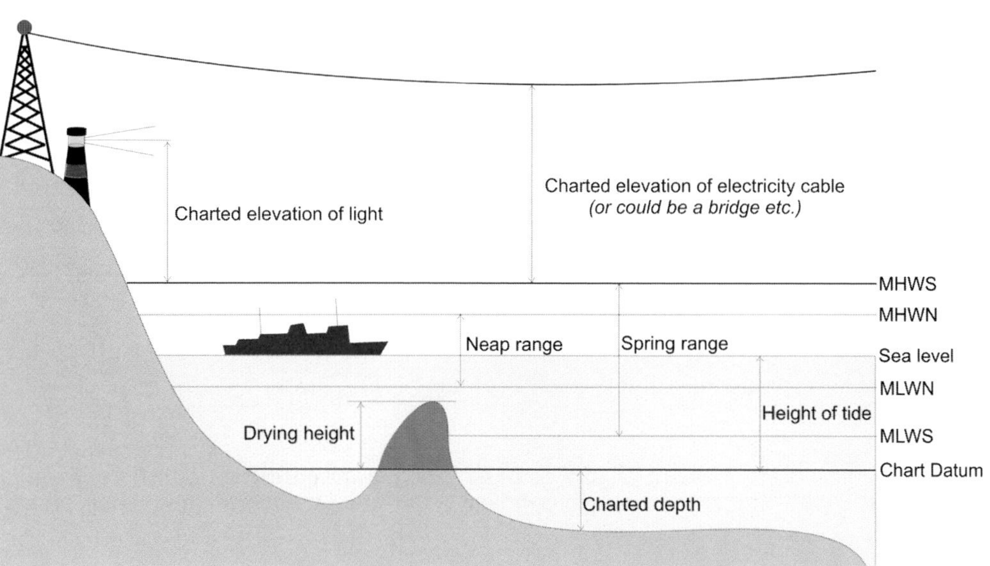


Fig 4.3

**Charted depth** is the depth of water shown as a sounding on the chart. This depth can be expected if the height of tide given in tide tables is zero. The height of tide should be added to the charted depth in order to find the actual depth at a particular position.

**Charted elevation** is the height of an object, which is permanently above water. It is measured from the level of mean high water springs (MHWS), *not* from Chart Datum.

**Drying height** shows the height above Chart Datum of an object, such as a rock or shoreline, which is exposed as the tide falls and covers as the tide rises.

**Ebb tide** is a falling tide. A falling tide is said to be *ebbing* or *on the ebb.*

**Equinoctial springs** are exceptionally high and low tides that occur at the times of the spring and autumn equinoxes in the third week of March and the third week of September each year.

**Fall of tide** is the reduction in the sea level since the last high tide.

**Flood tide** is a rising tide. A rising tide is said to be *flooding* or *on the flood.*

**Height of tide** is the actual sea level at any moment, measured from the level of Chart Datum.

**High water** (HW) is the highest sea level reached during the current tidal cycle.

**Low water** (LW) is the lowest sea level reached during the current tidal cycle.

**Lowest astronomical tide** (LAT) is the lowest level of water predicted due to the influence of planetary bodies and often indistinguishable from Chart Datum.

**Mean high water neaps** (MHWN) is the average height of high water at neap tides and can be found on charts and in tide tables.

**Mean high water springs** (MHWS) is the average height of high water at spring tides and can be found on charts and in tide tables.

**Mean low water neaps** (MLWN) is the average height of low water at neap tides and can be found on charts and in tide tables.

**Mean low water springs** (MLWS) is the average height of low water at spring tides and can be found on charts and in tide tables.

**Neaps** are the tides, which occur when the planetary bodies are out of alignment, giving a small tidal range, with a lower high water and a higher low water.

**Neap range** is the difference between mean high water neaps ands mean low water neaps.

**Range of tide** is the difference between the levels of high and low water on a particular day.

**Rise of tide** is the increase in sea level since the last low water.

**Soundings** are the depths of water shown on a chart, which are the depths when the water level is at its lowest astronomical tide or Chart Datum.

**Springs** are the tides, which occur when the planetary bodies are closely aligned, giving a large tidal range, with a higher high water and a lower low water.

**Spring range** is the difference between mean high water springs and mean low water springs.

## Tide tables

The times and heights of high and low water are predictable and are published in tide tables or as computer programmes. The United Kingdom Hydrographic Office (UKHO) in Taunton, publish tidal predictions in four volumes covering the whole of the Earth's surface. They also offer 'Total Tide' a computer prediction programme which is acceptable to the Maritime and Coastguard Agency (MCA) as an alternative to paper publication predictions. The computer predictions are divided into seven different areas. Further information can be obtained from their website: www.ukho.gov.uk

The times are stated in the standard time of the relevant country. In the UK for example the published times are in Universal Time (UT) which equates to Greenwich Mean Time (GMT), whilst across the English Channel in France, the published times refer to European Standard Time, which is one hour ahead of UT.

If the time zone in the area of operation changes for summer time, an adjustment has to be made to tide table times. Be aware that there are some tide table suppliers whose tidal predictions already have the summer time adjustment taken into account. British Admiralty Tide Tables do not.

Tide tables give not only the time but also the predicted height of high and low water for *standard ports*. Because of the huge number of ports around the world, only major ports have their own tidal predictions. Smaller ports, known as *secondary ports*, are supplied with time and height adjustments to add or subtract from the tidal information supplied for their standard port. This is to reduce the size of tide tables. Computer prediction software does not differentiate between standard and secondary ports and therefore secondary port calculations do not have to be made if using computer software.

## Tide Table extract

*Information in tide tables includes:*

Standard Port name
Time Zone
Month
Date
Day
High Water time and height (m)
Low Water time and height (m)
The day and date of a New Moon ●
The day and date of a Full Moon ○

**TIME ZONE (UT)**
**For Summer Time add ONE hour in non-shaded areas**

**MAY**

| | Time | m | | Time | m |
|---|---|---|---|---|---|
| **1** | 0402 | 5.0 | **16** | 0445 | 5.3 |
| | 1014 | 1.1 | | 1014 | 0.8 |
| W | 1630 | 5.1 | TH | 1630 | 5.4 |
| | 2236 | 1.2 | | 2236 | 0.7 |
| **2** | 0447 | 5.2 | **17** | 0528 | 5.4 |
| | 1014 | 0.9 | | 1149 | 0.8 |
| TH | 1713 | 5.2 | F | 1749 | 5.3 |
| | 2321 | 0.7 | ● | | |
| **3** | 0447 | 5.2 | **18** | 0047 | 0.8 |
| | 1014 | 0.9 | | 0608 | 5.2 |
| F | 1713 | 5.2 | SA | 1229 | 0.8 |
| ○ | 2321 | 0.7 | | 1827 | 5.3 |

The height of water at any time between high water and low water is not specified in the Admiralty Tide Tables (other than for Plymouth [Devonport], Poole Harbour, Southampton, Portsmouth, Rosyth, Liverpool, Avonmouth and St Helier in Part 1a) but it can be calculated using the tidal curve that is printed in the tide tables adjacent to the tidal information for each standard port. If it is necessary to calculate tidal information for a secondary port, the tidal curve for the standard port to which it relates should be used.

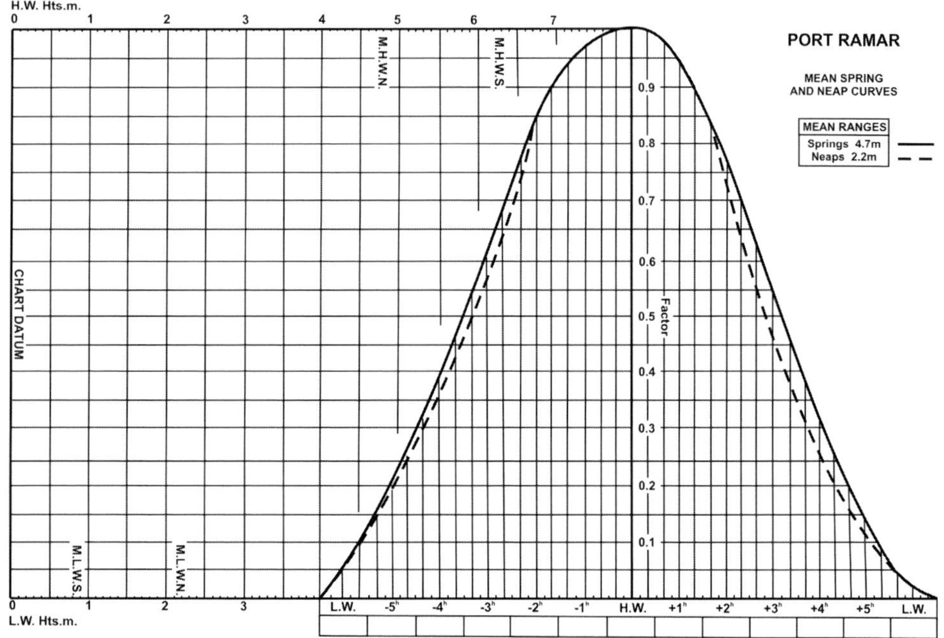


**Fig 4.4** Tidal curve example.

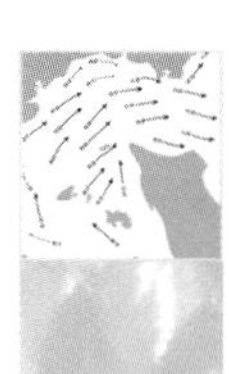

## Standard port calculation

As an example, let's say that on the morning of Friday 17 May on a falling tide, we need to know the duration of a height of tide in excess of 3m.

Using the extract from the tide tables given above on Friday 17 May, we see that the first high water (HW) is at 0528UT with a predicted tidal height above Chart Datum of 5.4m and the second HW is at 1749UT with a predicted height of 5.3m. Low water (LW) is predicted at 1149UT with a height above Chart Datum of 0.8m.

High water and low water times in UK ports are given in Universal Time (UT). Times in other parts of the world are related to UT by telling you what to do to get to UT. In France, for example, times are described as -0100 which indicates that to get to UT you subtract one hour. However, Port Ramar is in the UK and because we are looking at May, British Summer Time (BST) is in force so an hour needs to be added to convert the tidal predictions into local time. My advice is *always* to make all tidal calculations in the same time zone as is given in the tide tables, otherwise confusion can easily occur particularly when making secondary port calculations, of which more later. Once the final answer is calculated, then convert the answer to local time.

Choose the high and low water times that are either side of the time of interest, remembering that sometimes the previous or next high water may be on the day before or the day after. Write down the information in a tabular format and there is much less chance of making a mistake:

| **PORT RAMAR** | | | | |
|---|---|---|---|---|
| Friday 17 May | *HW time* | *HW Ht* | *LW time* | *LW Ht* |
| | 0528UT | 5.4m | 1149UT | 0.8m |

Take the high water time 0528UT and enter it in the centre time box labelled HW beneath the tidal curve as shown in Figure 4.5. Then add other appropriate times to the adjacent boxes. Every time you write a time down ensure you suffix it with the time zone (eg UT). It is very easy to forget to designate the time zone and then invariably the time of the final answer will be incorrect.

Take the high water height, 5.4m, and mark this along the top line to the left of the top of the curve and mark the low water height, 0.7m, on the bottom line to left of the bottom of the curve. Join these two marks together with a solid diagonal pencil line.

Establish the tidal range (subtract the low water height from the high water height), 5.4m - 0.7m = 4.7m, and compare this against the mean ranges shown in the box to the right of the tidal curve. This will indicate whether to use the solid curve or the hatched curve. In this case the range, 4.7m, is exactly a spring tidal range and the solid curve should be used.

In order to establish for how long on the morning of 17 May there will be in excess of 3m of tidal height, start on the top line at 3m mark and draw a vertical line down to cross the diagonal line. At this point draw a horizontal line across to the right until it crosses the downward slope of the tidal curve (we are interested in the falling tide) and then drop a vertical line from this point down to the time scale at the bottom. It hits the time scale between +3h and +4h. Each of the smallest divisions indicates 10 minutes. So if +3h was at 0828UT then the point where the line crosses is 0828UT + 10 minutes = 0838UT = 0938BST.

Some tidal curves have a solid and a hatched line. The solid line should be used for spring tides and the hatched one for neap tides. If the tidal range is in between, a certain amount of dexterity needs to be used to determine where between the two curves you use.

To calculate the height of tide at a given time it is simply a matter of reversing the process.

**TOP TIP**

*Make up your own tabular format including vessel draught and safety margin to ensure consistency of calculation.*

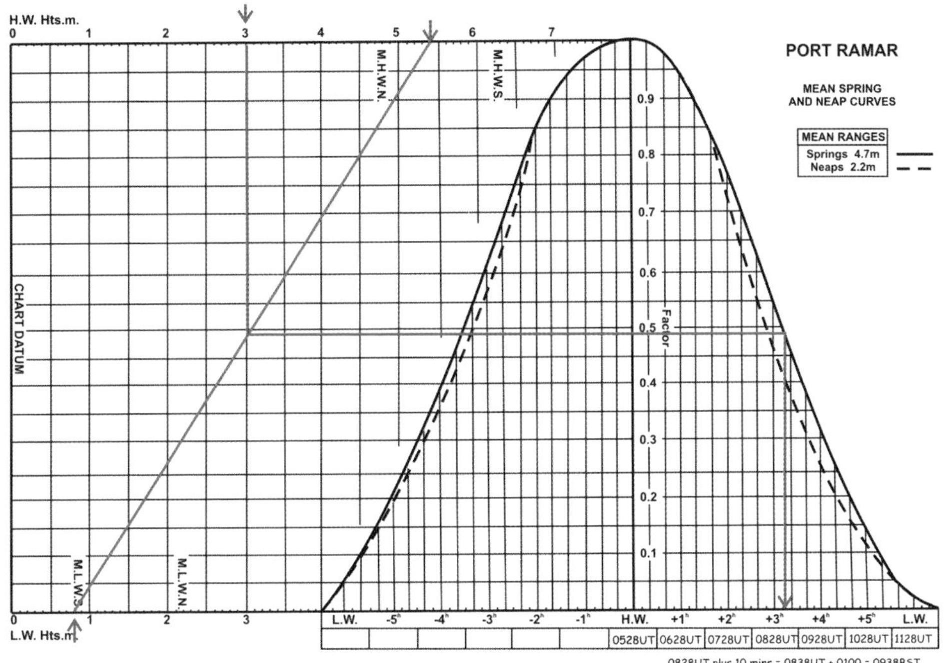


**Fig 4.5** Tidal calculation example (on a falling tide). Up until what time will there be in excess of 3m of tidal height?

# Secondary port calculation

For secondary ports there is a set of differences to apply to the information from the standard port, as is shown in the extract below. In order to calculate the time or height of high water at nearby Blueport we follow the procedure below:

Enter the time of high water and the heights of HW and LW for the standard port (Port Ramar) in tabular format for 17 May, as shown:

| PORT RAMAR | | | |
|---|---|---|---|
| Friday 17 May | *HW time* | *HW Ht* | *LW Ht* |
| | 0528UT | 5.4m | 0.8m |

Now look at the differences between the standard port: Port Ramar and its secondary port: Blueport.

It can be seen from the secondary port extract for Blueport (right) that if the time of HW is at 0100 or 1300 then there is no adjustment to make (0000), but if the time of HW is at 0600 or 1800 then it is necessary to add 10 minutes (+0010). The reason that different adjustments are made for different times of HW and LW relate to the different HW and LW times and heights during spring and neap tides.

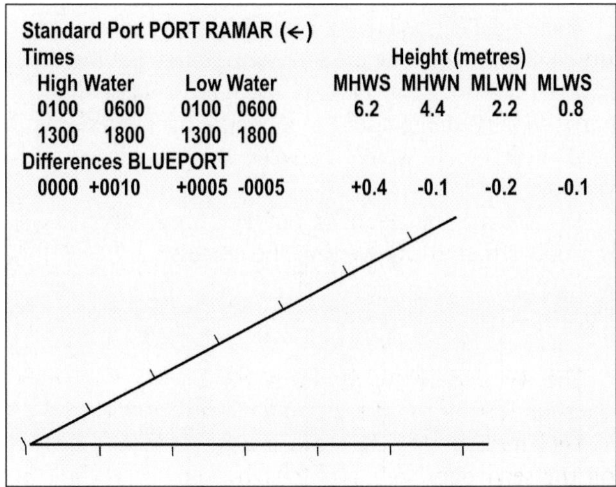

**Standard Port PORT RAMAR (←)**

| Times | | | | Height (metres) | | | |
|---|---|---|---|---|---|---|---|
| High Water | | Low Water | | MHWS | MHWN | MLWN | MLWS |
| 0100 | 0600 | 0100 | 0600 | 6.2 | 4.4 | 2.2 | 0.8 |
| 1300 | 1800 | 1300 | 1800 | | | | |
| **Differences BLUEPORT** | | | | | | | |
| 0000 | +0010 | +0005 | -0005 | +0.4 | -0.1 | -0.2 | -0.1 |

Fig 4.6

The greatest problem facing most navigators is what to do if the HW time is somewhere between the two! In this example HW is at 0528. That is somewhere between 0100 and 0600. There are many different ways of calculating the adjustment but one of the simplest is to draw two straight lines on a piece of paper at about 20° apart and mark them with six or seven equally spaced dashes starting from the point where the two lines intersect (Figure 4.6).

Then, using the information from the secondary port data in the tide tables, enter the HW times either side of the time of interest (0528UT) ie 0100 and 0600, along the bottom axis and the time adjustment along the upper axis. Make sure that the time relating to the 0000 (+0000) is written adjacent to it and then fill in the other time adjustment figures appropriately spaced to the number of dashes on the upper axis (Figure 4.7). Don't worry if the number of dashes is too many. The important thing is to get the minutes sufficiently far apart so that the answer can be read off. Having completed this, join the two right hand entries (0600 and +0010) with a straight line. The time which is of interest to us is 0528UT so a line through 0528UT on the bottom axis and parallel to the RH line just drawn will cut the upper axis at the number of minutes that have to be adjusted.

Care needs to be taken if the time of interest is between 0600 and 1300 – let's say 1030UT – as the minute adjustments need to be reversed so that the +0010 and the 0600 are together and the 0000 and the 1300 are together. See Figure 4.8.

This takes care of the HW time for a secondary port but in order to use the tidal curve, we also need the HW time and the heights of HW and LW.

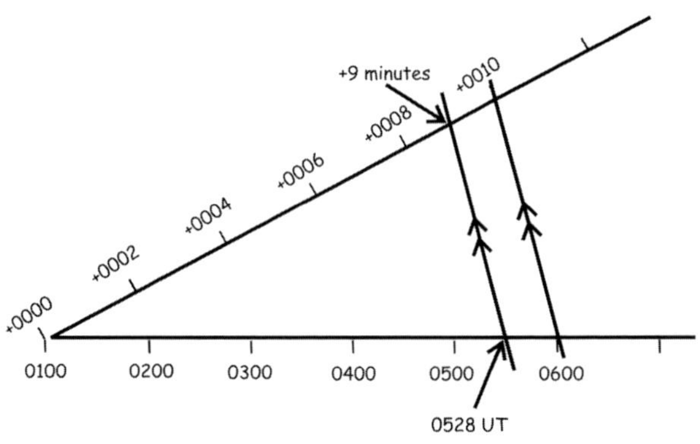


Fig 4.7

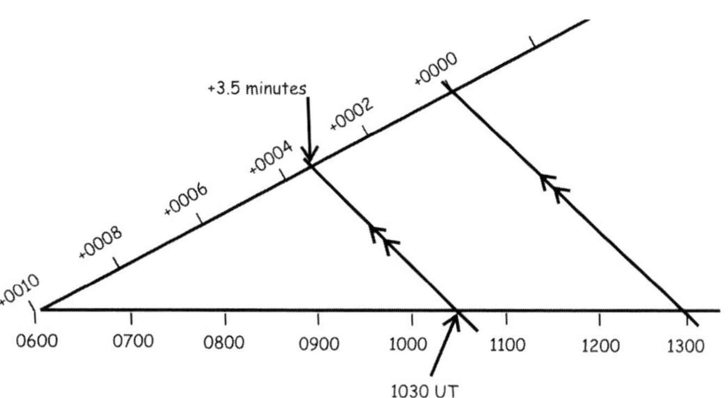


Fig 4.8

The HW and LW height adjustments can be made in exactly the same way. On the day in question HW height at Port Ramar is 5.4m and LW height is 0.8m.

Looking first at the HW adjustment, our HW height is 5.4m, which is between 6.2m and 4.4m on the secondary port data for HW and the adjustment needs to be adjusted by somewhere between +0.4m and –0.1m. A similar drawing to Figure 4.8 can be made to calculate the adjustment for 5.4m ensuring that the 6.2m and corresponding +0.4m are at the LH end of the scale and the 4.4m and –0.1m are at the RH end of the scale (Figure 4.9).

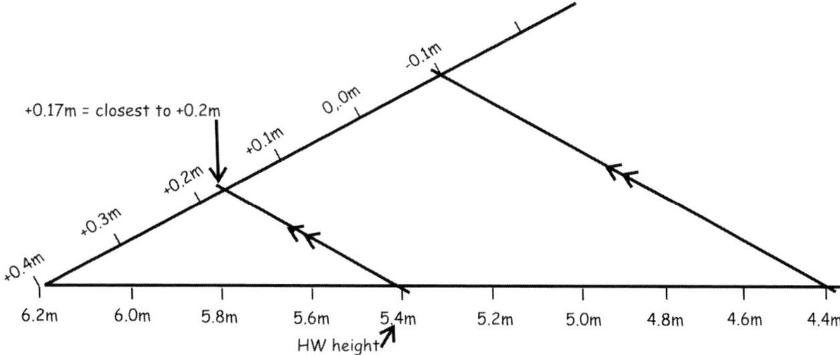


Fig 4.9

The LW height is 0.8m and that happens to coincide with one of the two figures given in the secondary port data. Therefore the LW adjustment does not need to be calculated as it is –0.1m. So tabulating the results:

**PORT RAMAR**

| | HW time | HW Ht | LW Ht |
|---|---|---|---|
| Friday 17 May | | | |
| Adjustment for | 0528UT | 5.4m | 0.8m |
| **BLUEPORT** | +0009 | +0.2m | -0.1m |
| | 0537UT | 5.6m | 0.7m |

**TOP TIP**

*There is generally no requirement to calculate the adjustment to LW time as this is only required on special tidal curves such as those for the Solent (UK) area which are based upon LW time and not HW time.*

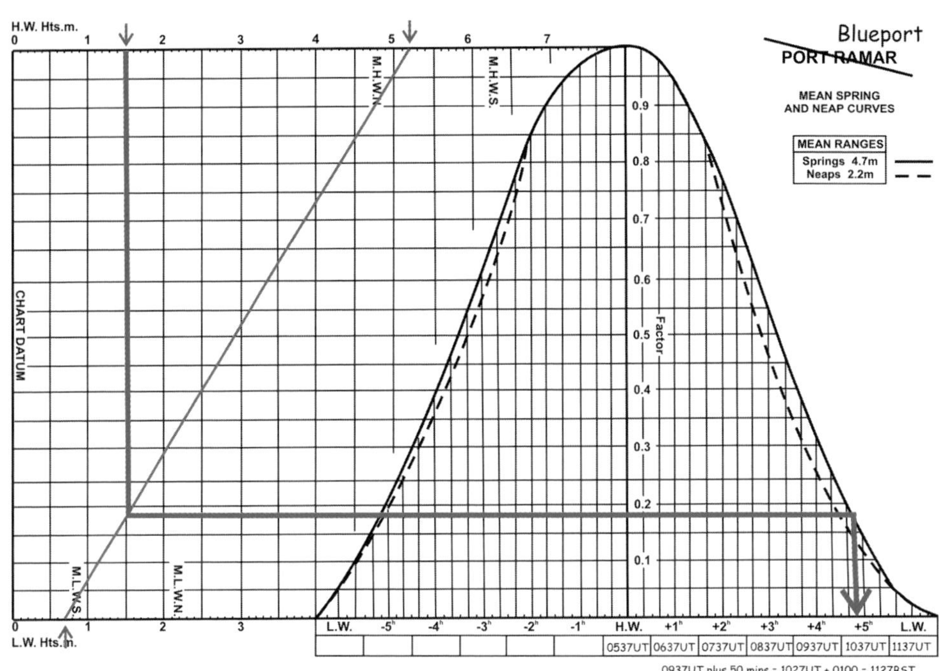


**Fig 4.10** Tidal calculations example – on a falling tide up until what time will there be at least 1.5m of tidal height?

These adjusted figures can then be used on the standard port tidal curve enabling any height or time to be calculated for the corresponding time or height. To change the example, lets look to see when there will be 1.5m of tidal height on a falling tide on 17 May at Blueport (Figure 4.10).

In exactly the same way as the standard port example, enter the secondary port HW height, 5.6m on the top scale and the low water height, 0.7m on the bottom scale and join the two marks with a pencil line. Enter the time of HW in the centre box under the curve and fill in each subsequent hour as we are interested in a falling tide, ie after high water. The height of tide of interest is 1.5m on a falling tide so draw a vertical line on the LH side through the 1.5m mark until it crosses the slanting line, then horizontally across until it meets the falling side of the tidal curve and read off the time. In this example: HW plus 4 hours and 50 minutes. HW was at 0537UT, therefore our answer is 1027UT or more correctly 1127BST which puts the answer into the correct local time zone for 17 May.

**TOP TIP**

*You have now worked out how to calculate information to a high degree of accuracy. Do not forget that these are predictions which can be radically altered by changes in wind conditions and pressure systems.*

# Tidal streams

As the tide rises and falls, the huge volumes of water flow to and fro creating currents or tidal streams. These tidal streams generally follow the direction of the flood and ebb of the tide but they are commonly distorted by the geography of the seabed and the irregular shape of coastlines. In the same way that tidal heights can be predicted, the direction of flow and speed of tidal streams can be predicted. There are two main sources of tidal stream information:

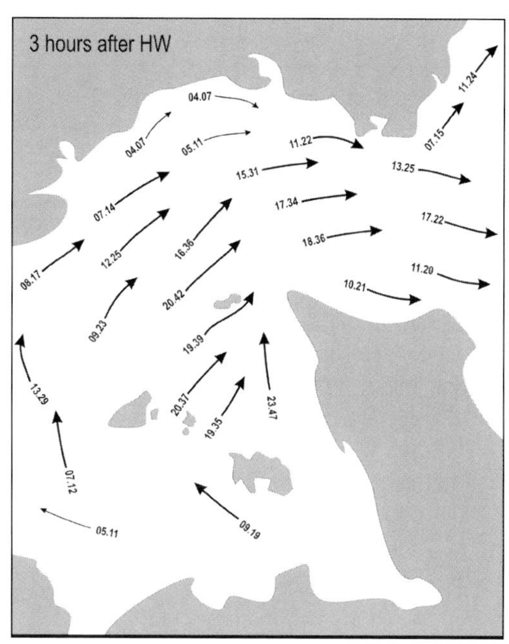


Fig 4.11

## Tidal stream atlas

A tidal stream atlas gives, in simple chart format, the tidal streams expected for each hour before, and each hour after HW for a specified port. A separate chart indicates the direction and rate for each hour. The speeds referred to are given in the form: 05.11 meaning 0.5 knot at neap tides and 1.1 knots at spring tides (Figure 4.11).

Generally if tidal information is taken from tidal stream atlases, adjustments between spring rates and neap rates are done by a rule of thumb and the bearing of the tidal stream is difficult to measure with much accuracy. If you are anxious to predict tidal streams with as much accuracy as possible, then the alternative is to use the tidal diamonds printed on charts.

## Tidal diamonds

Apart from very small scale ones, Admiralty charts are appended with magenta coloured tidal diamonds at strategic navigational points to indicate the direction and speed of a tidal stream or current based upon the time of HW at a nearby standard port. Each diamond on the chart is designated a letter of the alphabet starting with A and the geographical position of each diamond is given in a table on the chart (upper part of Figure 4.12) in latitude and longitude. The information relating to direction and speed is given for every hour from 6 hours before HW through HW and on to 6 hours after HW. Two columns are given for the speed in knots and these refer to spring tides and neap tides respectively. In order to calculate a more accurate speed for tides in between springs and neaps, nautical almanacs have a Computation of Rates Table that allows the correct speed for a given tidal range to be calculated.

*When applying tidal streams to navigational problems, the generally accepted method of calculation is to say that if a tidal stream is running say, 010° at 1.2 knots at 0938UT, then it is actually having the same effect from half an hour before 0938UT to half an hour after. Therefore the 1.2 knots of tidal stream would be applied from 0908UT – 1008UT.*

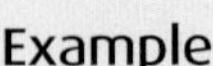



## Example

*Find the tidal stream at diamond ◇D at 1449BST on Friday 17 May using tidal information for Port Ramar.*

- HW at Port Ramar is at 1749UT and the range is 5.3m – 0.8m = 4.5m.
- The spring range for Port Ramar is 4.7m and the neap range is 2.2m (from the tidal curve). Therefore the tidal range on 17 May at 4.5m is just falling off springs.
- 1449BST equates to 1349UT and is four hours before HW at 1749UT. The tidal diamond ◇D indicates that the tide will be running in the direction 214° at somewhere between 2.4 and 1.2 knots.

Tidal Streams referred to HW at Port RAMAR

| Hours | | ◇ Geographical Position | ◇D 50° 15.2'N 001° 19.2'W | |
|---|---|---|---|---|
| | | Direction of streams (degrees) | Rates at spring tides (knots) | Rates at neap tides (knots) |
| Before High Water | 6 | 208 | 1.1 | 0.1 |
| | 5 | 220 | 2.3 | 1.1 |
| | 4 | 214 | 2.4 | 1.2 |
| | 3 | 211 | 1.6 | 0.9 |
| | 2 | 280 | 0.9 | 0.4 |
| | 1 | 011 | 0.3 | 0.2 |
| High Water | | 025 | 1.1 | 0.1 |
| After High Water | 1 | 035 | 1.9 | 0.9 |
| | 2 | 043 | 2.1 | 1.0 |
| | 3 | 060 | 1.9 | 0.8 |
| | 4 | 100 | 1.4 | 0.7 |
| | 5 | 125 | 0.5 | 0.2 |
| | 6 | 210 | 0.3 | 0.1 |

**TIME ZONE (UT)**
**For Summer Time add ONE hour in non-shaded areas**

**MAY**

| Day | Time | m | Day | Time | m |
|---|---|---|---|---|---|
| **1** W | 0402 | 5.0 | **16** TH | 0445 | 5.3 |
| | 1014 | 1.1 | | 1014 | 0.8 |
| | 1630 | 5.1 | | 1630 | 5.4 |
| | 2236 | 1.2 | | 2236 | 0.7 |
| **2** TH | 0447 | 5.2 | **17** F ● | 0528 | 5.4 |
| | 1014 | 0.9 | | 1149 | 0.8 |
| | 1713 | 5.2 | | 1749 | 5.3 |
| | 2321 | 0.7 | | | |
| **3** F ○ | 0447 | 5.2 | **18** SA | 0047 | 0.8 |
| | 1014 | 0.9 | | 0608 | 5.2 |
| | 1713 | 5.2 | | 1229 | 0.8 |
| | 2321 | 0.7 | | 1827 | 5.3 |

Fig 4.12

Entering this data into the computation of rates table (Figure 4.13), the spring rate is 2.4 knots and this is circled on the springs hatched line. The neap rate is 1.2 knots so this is circled on the neaps hatched line. A diagonal line through the two circles is drawn. The tidal range on 17 May is 4.5m, so finding the 4.5m reading on the LH column, a horizontal line is extended to the right until it meets the diagonal line and then it is dropped vertically to meet the speed scale at the top or bottom. This indicates a tidal rate of 23 tenths of a knot or 2.3 knots for the period from half hour before 1449BST to half an hour after, ie from 1419BST to 1519BST.

**TOP TIP**

*It is important to remember that tides run in the direction of the bearing but winds come from the direction indicated.*

## Types of tides

So far we have looked only at the type of tides found in and around the British Isles. These are semidiurnal tide patterns where there are two high waters and two low waters per tidal day.

Tides are classified one of three types, semidiurnal, diurnal, or mixed, according to the characteristics of the tidal pattern. In the semidiurnal tide, there are two high and two low waters each tidal day, with relatively small differences in the respective highs and lows. Tides in Northern Europe and on the Atlantic coast of the United States are of the semidiurnal type.

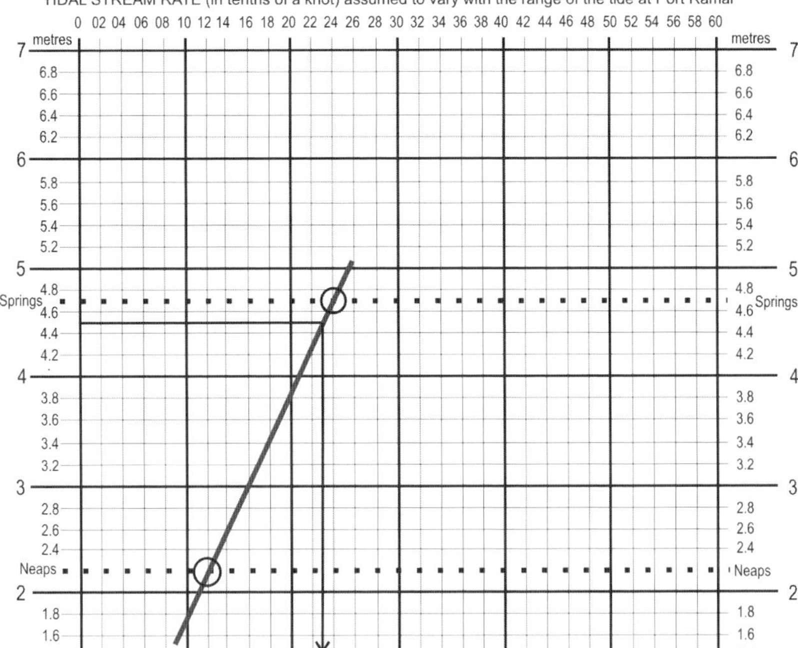


Fig 4.13

Diurnal tides, as the name suggests, occur only once with a single high and single low water occurring each tidal day. Diurnal tides occur along the northern shore of the Gulf of Mexico, in the Java Sea and the Gulf of Tonkin.

In areas with mixed tides, the diurnal and semidiurnal oscillations are both important factors and the tide is characterised by large differences in high water heights or low water heights, or both. There are usually two high and two low waters each day, but occasionally the tide may become diurnal. Such tides are common in the Pacific Ocean.

## Currents and surface drift

Having looked at tidal streams, it is important to mention currents and surface drift which are not created by the gravitational pull of the Sun and Moon. Currents flow in the major oceans of the world at all depths but from a marine navigator's perspective, it is those on the surface that are of greatest interest. The world climatic charts in *Ocean Passages for the World* (NP136) give details of the general direction of these currents. They are caused mainly by the effect of the direct action of the wind and there is a close relationship between prevailing winds and ocean currents. The north-east trade winds in the northern hemisphere and south-east trade winds in the southern hemisphere are the power behind the mid-latitude surface currents. Surface currents are generally in the region of 2–4 knots but higher speeds can be encountered of up to 5 knots.

# 5 Chartwork

## Chartwork symbols

There are a series of internationally accepted symbols used in chartwork, so that in the unlikely event that the person responsible for navigation becomes incapacitated, anyone else who has been trained can easily pick up the reins and continue the passage safely (Figure 5.1).

## Plotting a course

If you know where you are starting from and you know where you wish to end up, you could mark those two positions on the chart, join them with a line, establish the direction of the line in degrees, steer it and arrive safely and without difficulty. That is if your compass reads in true° (°T) *and* you could guarantee to steer a perfect course *and* there was no tide, current or wind (leeway) to worry about! In real life that is an unlikely scenario.

In earlier chapters, we looked at calculating true courses (°T) and directions from compass (°C) or magnetic (°M) ones and how to estimate a tidal stream for an area. In chartwork, we can now combine all that information together to either predict where we shall be in the future if we were to follow a particular course by *dead reckoning* (DR), fine tune it to *estimated position* (EP) by taking into account the tide or current and wind or, better still, calculate a *course to steer* (CTS) to arrive where we want to, taking into account the tide or current and wind.

### Dead reckoning (DR)

Dead reckoning is simply a prediction of a future position based upon a course steered and a speed achieved. It is written on the chart as follows in Figure 5.2.

### Estimated position (EP)

The difference between a 'DR' and an 'EP' is taking into account the known or predicted tidal stream or current and the effect of the wind (known as *leeway*). After plotting a DR position using the distance travelled in the direction of the vessel's heading and the speed, it is important to account for the leeway first before the tide or current is added. In examination questions, you will be given an amount for leeway in degrees and the wind direction. It will be up to you to calculate whether leeway should be added or subtracted from the water track.

So if you are heading towards the north and the wind is from the east, you will be 'blown' from east to west, in this case to the left and your actual course through the water will be reduced by the number of degrees of leeway (Figure 5.3).

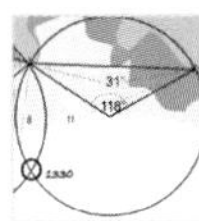

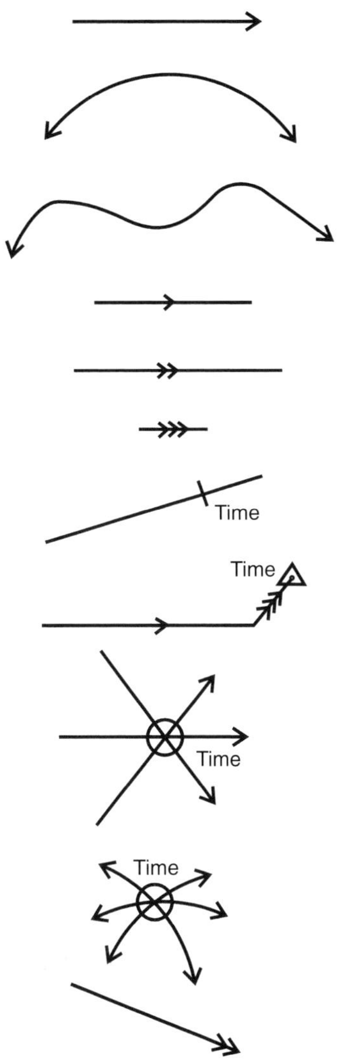

Visual position line (arrow points away from the mark from which the bearing was taken)

Range position line (as given by radar or a vertical sextant angle)

Depth of sounding position line (following a depth contour on the chart)

Water track – direction through the water

Ground track – distance and course over ground

Tidal stream

Time

Dead reckoning – DR (used to predict a future position without taking tide, current or wind into account)

Time

Estimated position – EP (used to predict a future position when tide, current and wind are taken into account)

Time

Three-point visual fix

Time

Three-range fix as produced by taking radar ranges

Transferred position line (used in fixing a position such as a running fix)

**Fig 5.1** Chart symbols.

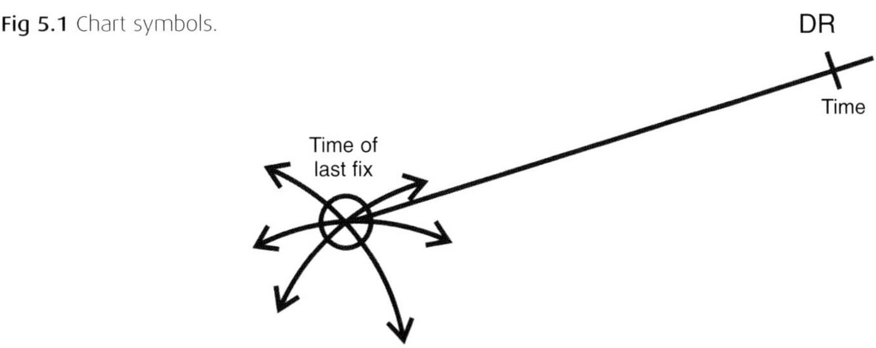


**Fig 5.2** No allowance is made for tide or current and wind.

Similarly if you are heading west and the wind is from the south, your course through the water will be increased by the number of degrees of leeway (Figure 5.4).

There are no tables to estimate leeway; it is a real black art. Old salts will sit on their taffrails and put a finger in the air and make an educated guess of leeway based upon their experience of the vessel. Don't think for one moment that leeway is confined to sailing vessels. It is not. A power-driven vessel will also be affected by leeway based upon the size and outline of its aspect to the wind, its draught and its speed through the water.

Once you know your heading – in this next example: 070° (see Figure 5.5) – and you have been told (or you estimate) that there is 10° leeway in a northerly wind, you can lay off your course steered with a length relating to your speed through the water thus establishing the DR. The wind coming from the north will tend to blow you sideways (towards the south) by 10° so your water track will be increased by 10° to 080°. The length of the water track can be established by drawing a line at 90° to the DR position on the course steered line from which point the tide or current and surface drift can be added. In most cases a time period of one hour is used. However there is no reason why 30 minutes or even 15 minutes couldn't be used on a suitably scaled chart.

If, because of the scale of the chart, you choose to plan over periods of more than one hour, don't forget to add different tidal vectors for each of the hours. The length of the water track will be your speed in knots but plotted in nautical miles. So a speed of 10 knots will result in a water track of 10 miles. The last part of the EP calculation is to account for the tidal stream using its speed and direction over the time period used for the water track. The resultant position is known as an estimated position or EP and is shown as a triangle. The feint line between the original fix and the EP is known as the *ground track*. This is the line over which your vessel would pass if the effects of wind and tide or current were constant

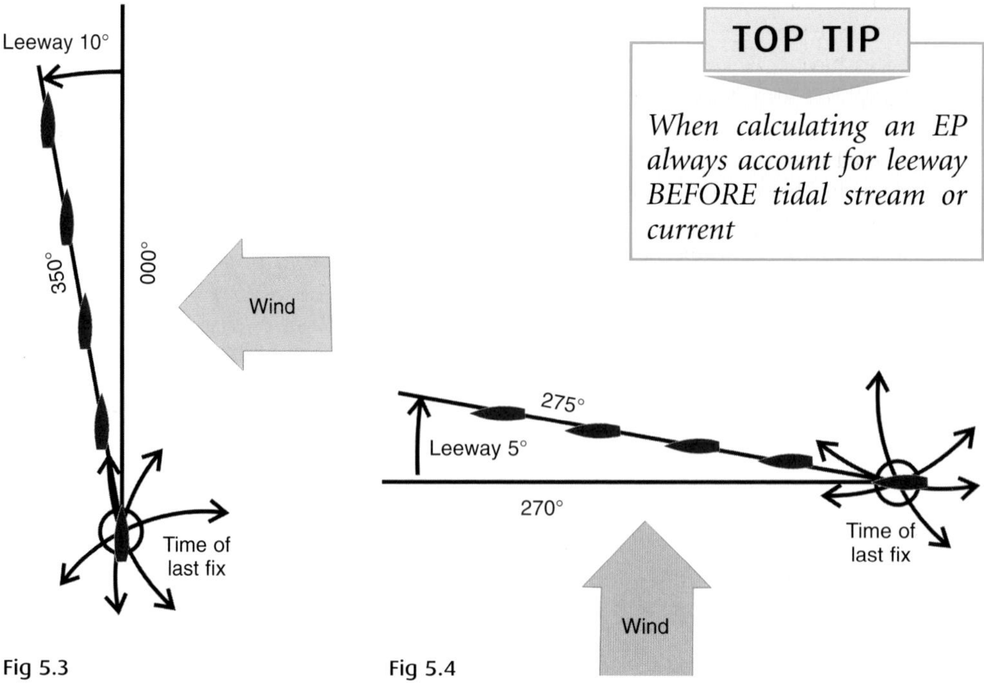


Fig 5.3

Fig 5.4

**TOP TIP**

*When calculating an EP always account for leeway BEFORE tidal stream or current*

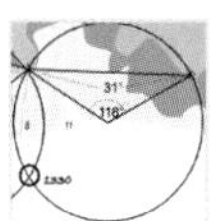

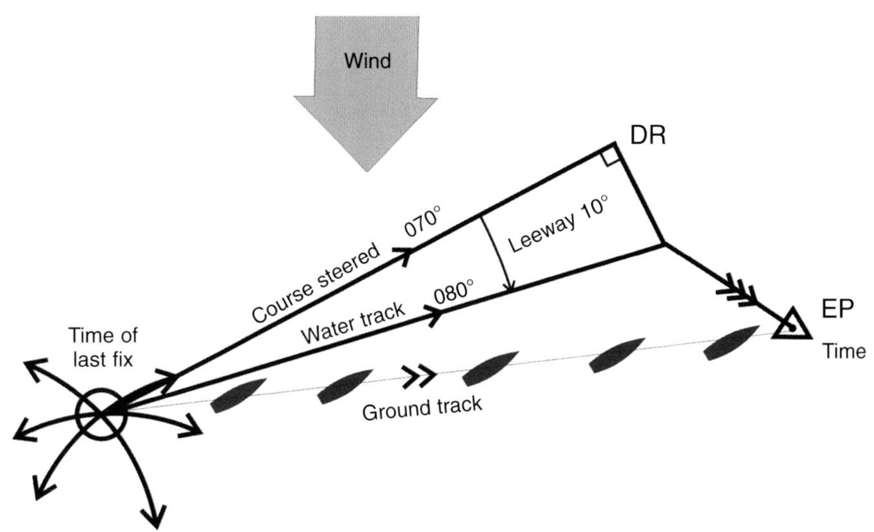


Fig 5.5

throughout the calculation period. In practical terms this is unlikely to be the case, but in examination situations, it is taken as so.

This is all very well but in most cases, you know where you want to end up so it is important to be able to calculate a course to steer to a predetermined point.

## Course to steer (CTS)

In order to reach a destination and avoid being swept off course by tidal stream or current and wind, allowance must be made in advance for the effect that the tide or current and wind are predicted to have. If we look at an example of a man paddling across a tidal river, we know instinctively that setting a course directly towards the destination results in the boat drifting downstream with the current. To reach a point directly opposite in a tidal river requires the boat to be paddled upstream to some extent to compensate for the flow of tide or current or the effects of wind. The combination of the boat's momentum going across the river, and the push of the stream flowing down river or the blowing of the wind, keeps the boat on the desired track towards a point directly opposite. Exactly how far upstream the boat needs to head depends on the speed of the tide or current, the speed of the wind and the speed at which it is being paddled.

When shaping a course to steer at sea, the tidal stream or current flowing on the intended route and the effect of the wind or leeway must be predicted, so that an allowance can be made for its effect. Unlike an EP calculation above, the leeway is not applied to a CTS first. A line is drawn on the chart from the start position to the proposed destination, and extended past it. This represents the desired ground track or course over the ground. By measuring the distance to be travelled and the intended speed, an estimate of the likely time required, can be predicted.

Using tidal information from a tidal diamond or from a tidal stream atlas, the speed of flow of the tidal stream can be calculated for the time period. A line indicating the tidal stream is then drawn on the chart, from the starting position for a distance equal to the distance the current would carry the vessel during the time period estimated for the passage. This may involve more than one hour of tide and more than one direction of tidal stream. At the end of this line or lines, using a pair of compasses set at the distance the vessel would travel in the total calculated time period, scribe an arc on the line joining the start point and the destination. This may be short of or beyond the destination point but it is very, very unlikely that it will pass through the destination point. A line drawn between the end of the tide vector line and the point where the arc cuts the ground track shows the heading required to get from the initial starting point to the destination along the intended ground track, taking into account the tidal stream.

This heading, worked out on the chart, will be in 'true' therefore it should be adjusted for variation and deviation before being given to the helmsman as a course to steer. Also, if it is anticipated that the yacht might suffer leeway, as a result of being blown sideways by the wind, the course to steer should be further adjusted to steer up into the wind so that the yacht is then blown back onto the required course. See the following example.

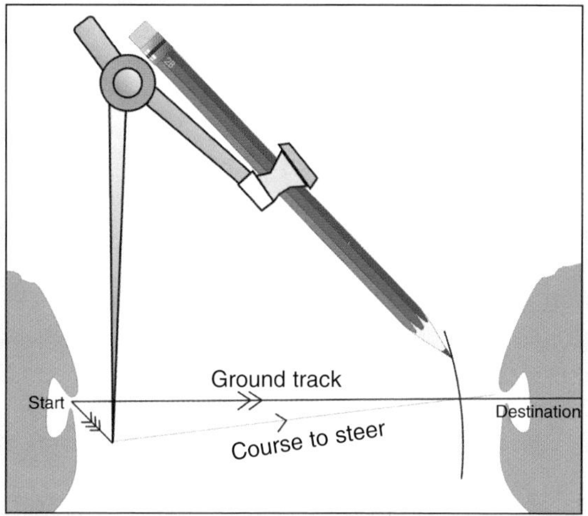


1 Join the start position to the destination, and continue this line just in case. This represents the desired ground track. Mark it with two arrows.
2 Measure the distance from start to destination, and work out the approximate time that the passage will take at the chosen cruising speed. Calculate the tidal stream(s) for this period of time and lay off a tidal vector or vectors if the time period extends to more than one hour. Mark it with three arrows.
3 Open a pair of compasses to the distance you will travel in the chosen time period at the predicted cruising speed. Place the point at the end of the tidal stream vector and scribe an arc to cross the ground track line. This will not cut the destination point.
4 Draw a line from the end of the tidal stream vector to the point where the arc crosses the ground track. Mark it with one arrow. The direction of this line is the course to steer.
5 If there is any leeway to apply, add or subtract it to/from the course to steer remembering that in a course to steer question you are going to steer into the wind to make good your CTS but in the EP question you let the wind blow you away from your planned track.
6 If the planned passage will take more than one hour, it may be necessary to add a number of tidal stream vectors one after the other. Put the point of the compasses at the end of all the tidal stream vectors opened for the distance travelled in the total time.

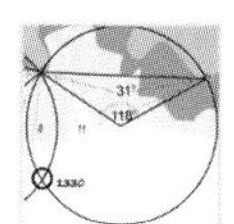

**TOP TIP**

*When calculating a CTS always account for leeway AFTER tidal stream or current but BEFORE you make any allowance for deviation*

## Estimated time of arrival (ETA)

A competent navigator will always have his estimated time of arrival (ETA) in the back of his mind. Whether it is to placate a screaming child or a frustrated owner, it is important to keep a regularly updated ETA available. The speed-time-distance triangle is one way of calculating an ETA. If you know any two of the three Speed – Time – Distance variables, you can easily calculate the third.

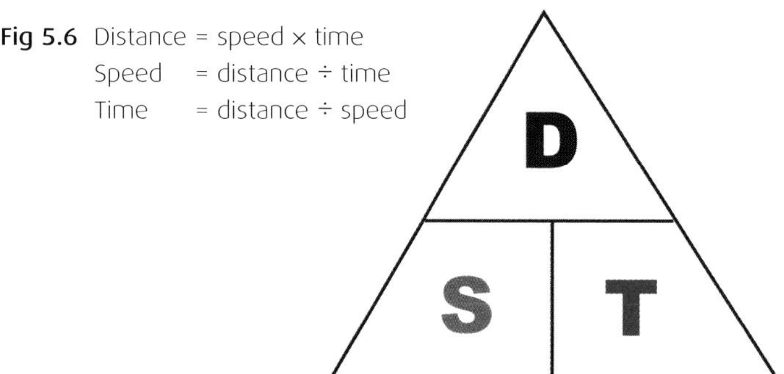


**Fig 5.6** Distance = speed × time
Speed = distance ÷ time
Time = distance ÷ speed

### Example

You have 292.5 miles to run at 15 knots. How long will it be before you arrive?

Time = distance ÷ speed

Time = 292.5 ÷ 15 = 19.5 hours = 19 hours 30 minutes

If it doesn't work out quite so nicely as that and, say, you have 19.78333333 hours to go, just remove the 19 hours leaving 0.78333333 hours to convert into minutes. Multiply the hour fraction by 60 (minutes in an hour)

0.78333333 x 60 = 47 minutes

So the remaining time is 19 hours and 47 minutes.

## Running fix

A running fix is a method of fixing your position when only one known fixing point is available. You need to know the time, your heading, any leeway, the tidal stream and your speed through the water.

First take a bearing of the single point and note the time, say 1530, your heading and your log speed. Convert the compass bearing to a true bearing and plot it on the chart.

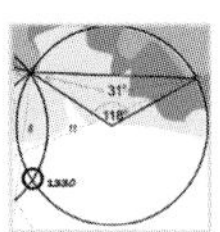

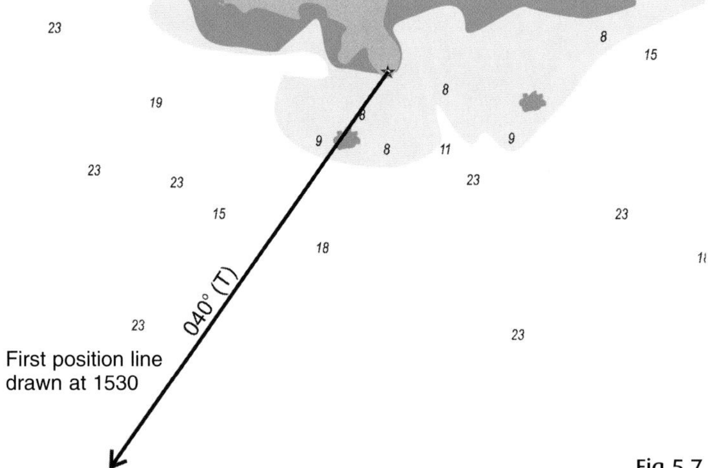


Bearing 040°(T)
Heading 090°(T)
Leeway 10° in a northerly breeze
Log speed 12 knots

Fig 5.7

Then run for a fixed amount of time checking your heading and log speed throughout to make sure they are consistent; let's say one hour. Take a second bearing from the fixing point and plot the bearing on the chart. In this case 325°(T) (Figure 5.8).

Now we come to the bit that requires a bit of imagination! Choose any point along the first position line (040°) and lay off your heading, leeway and tide. I recommend keeping a fair distance off the fixing point to give a bit more room for the chartwork and less opportunities for confusion or error.

The heading should be drawn first then any allowance for leeway made, in this case 10° in a northerly breeze, then the tidal stream, 172° (T) at three knots. This gives an EP or estimated position.

The final stage is to transfer the first position line across to run through the EP position and extend it so that it crosses the second position line. The resultant position is the fix at 1630 (Figure 5.9).

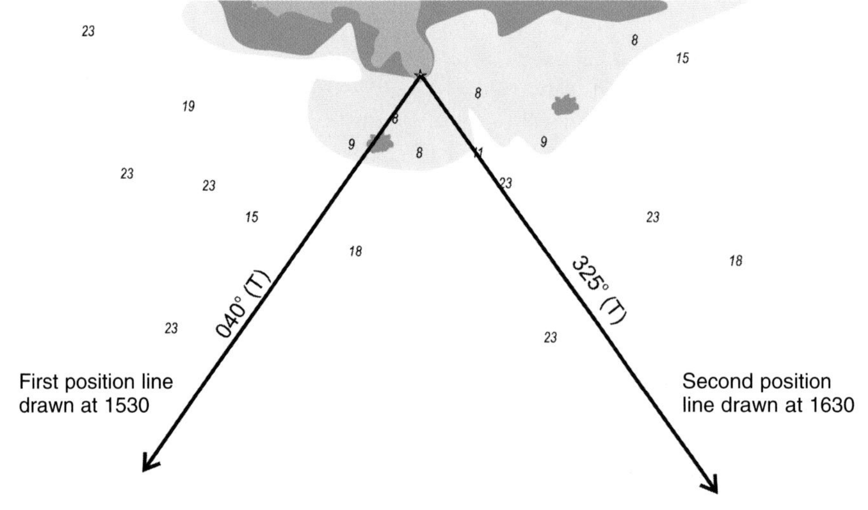


Fig 5.8

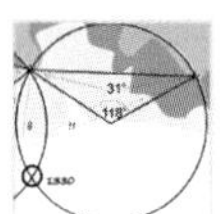

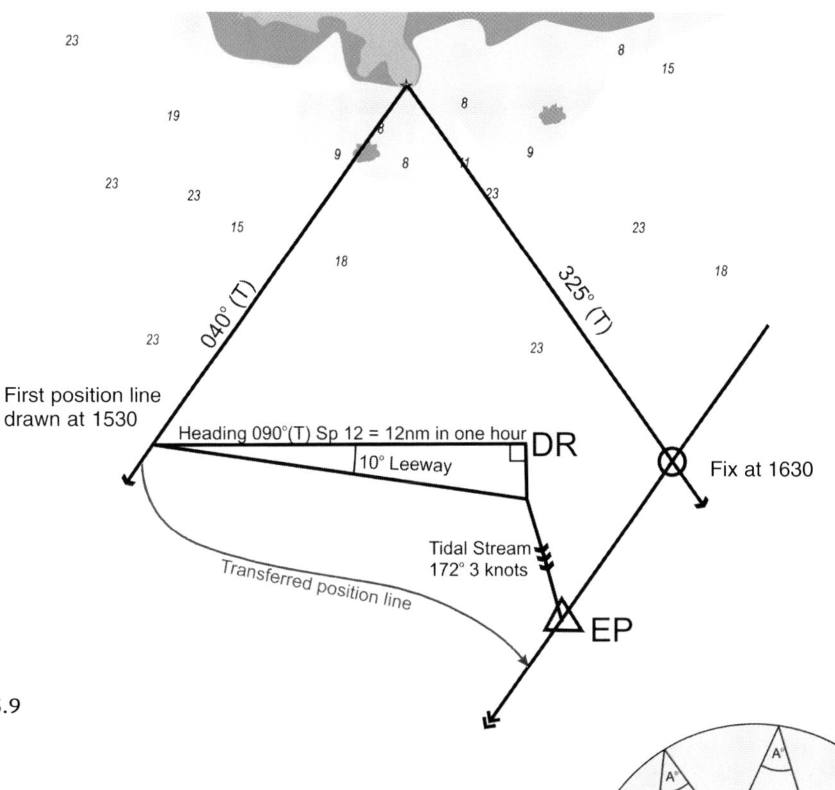


Fig 5.9

## Plotting a fix using two horizontal sextant angles

This method can also be used to establish a gyro error.

If you remember any basic geometry, you will recall that any circle with any two points marked on the circumference, will subtend the same angle from those two points to any point on same side of the circumference. Also the angle subtended from the same two points through the centre of the circle will subtend an angle that is twice any angle subtended at the circumference (Figure 5.10).

If we now simplify the drawing and join the two points we originally chose on the circumference with a straight line, we then create two triangles, one to the circumference and one to the centre of the circle. The angles marked 'B' must be the same size because two of the sides of the triangle are the same (the radii of the circle) and because the triangle is said to be *isosceles* (equal sides) (Figure 5.11). The sum of all the angles of a triangle add up to 180°, therefore if:

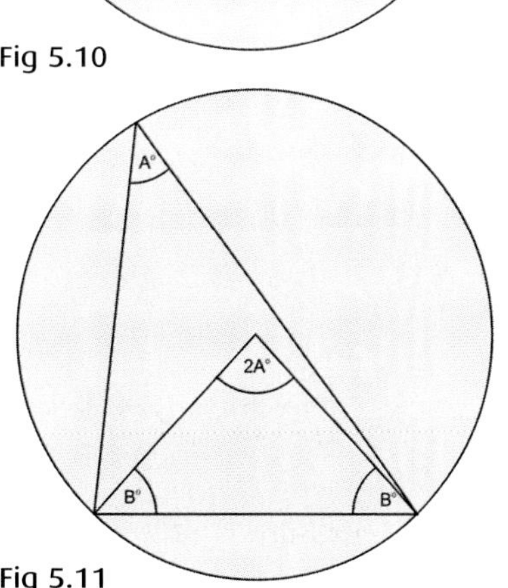


Fig 5.10



Fig 5.11

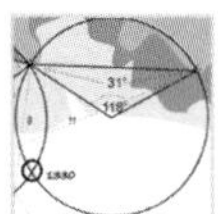

$$2A° + B° + B° = 180°$$

then halving both sides of the equation:

$$A° + B° = 90°$$

It follows that relationship between angle 'B' and angle 'A' must be:

$$B° = 90° - A°$$

Therefore if we know the angle between two bearing lines, A°, and we know the two fixing points, then we can construct a circle running through those points knowing that any point on the circle subtended from those two points would have an angle A°. The centre of that circle will be at the peak of a triangle formed from the two points using two lines angled 90° – A° on each side.

This all sounds rather complicated, but if we take two horizontal sextant angles between three known points, let's say the horizontal sextant angles are 41° and 59° respectively.

Using the mathematical principal outlined above, for the LH pair of fixing points, the isosceles triangle that needs to be constructed to create the centre of the circle will have two angles of 49° (90° – 41°) and a similar triangle can be constructed for the RH circle using angles of 31° (90° – 59°). This enables two circles to be drawn and the point at which they intersect is the correct position for the fix. No one said navigation is easy! It's what keeps some of us in business!

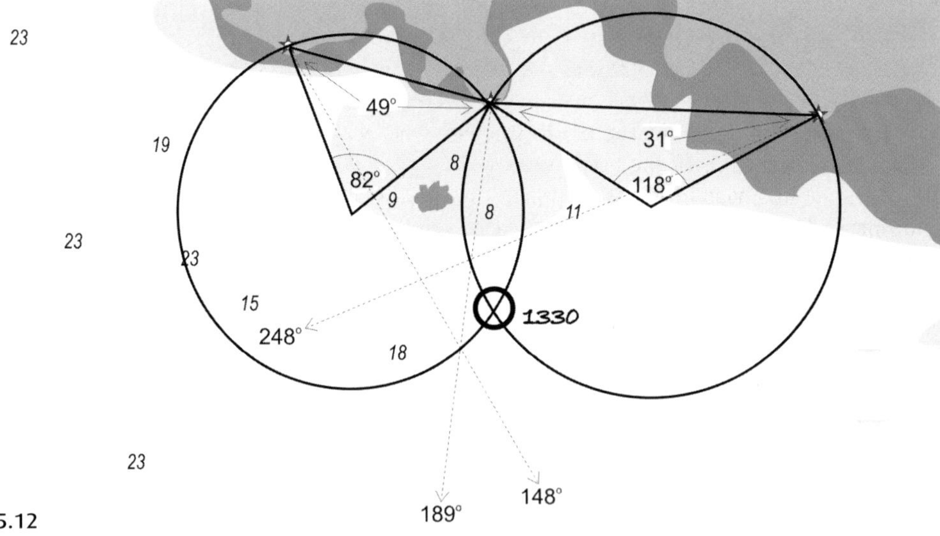


Fig 5.12

The same principle can be used to establish a gyro error by taking the gyro bearings as shown above as hatched lines: 248°, 189° and 148° and measuring the differences between them, namely 41° and 59°, and constructing a similar pair of circles which give the correct fix position where they cross (Figure 5.12). The correct gyro bearings can then be established from this fix and, surprise, surprise, the error will be the same on each bearing.

# 6 Buoyage and Lights

## Buoyage

Mariners have made navigational hazards conspicuous with markers for hundreds of years. Towards the end of the 19th century, lights started to appear on navigational hazards but in all this time there was no unifying system that mariners could rely upon. Inevitably this led to confusion and many shipwrecks. You only have to look at the charts of busy world shipping lanes to see the thousands of vessels lost, many of which would have been because of confusion over buoyage.

Many attempts have been made to unify world buoyage and, in 1936, agreement was almost achieved at Geneva under the leadership of the League of Nations. However the outbreak of war in 1939 precluded its final ratification. The Geneva Agreement proposed that nations should choose between a lateral system where channels were marked by coloured buoys on either side of the channel or alternatively a cardinal system where cardinal buoys were used to indicate a safe direction relative to their own position.

At the end of the war, many of the countries which had been prepared to support the Geneva discussions found their own buoyage systems either destroyed or in a poor state of repair and went ahead and adopted the Geneva rules anyway. But this was very haphazard and totally missed the aims of the originators.

It all came to a head in 1971 when there were a series of disastrous wrecks in the Dover Straits and whilst attempts were made to mark the wrecks in a way that everyone would understand, there was confusion as there was no internationally accepted way of doing so.

As recently as 1976 there were still more than 30 different types of buoyage systems throughout the world, many of which were at odds with each other and unnecessary navigational accidents continued to increase.

This caused the Executive Committee of the International Association of Lighthouse Authorities (IALA) to put both sets of proposed rules together to form the The IALA Maritime Buoyage System. Unfortunately countries had still not agreed on one lateral system so IALA 'A' and IALA 'B' were born. The rules for

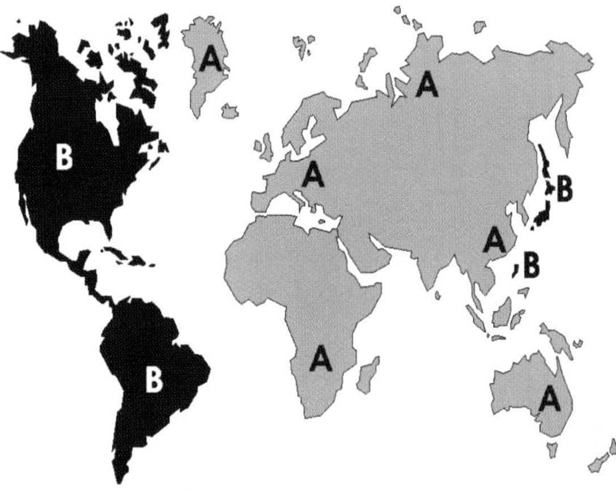


**Fig 6.1** IALA 'A' and IALA 'B' areas.

IALA 'A' were completed in 1976 and began to be introduced in 1977 throughout Europe, Australia, New Zealand, Africa, the Gulf and most Asian Countries. The IALA 'B' rules were completed in 1980 and adopted by Canada, North, Central and South America, Japan, Korea and the Philippines.

The new IALA system of buoyage was formally adopted in November 1980 by more than 50 countries and nine international authorities concerned with the safety of navigation. Within the IALA system of buoyage all but the lateral marks are common to both IALA 'A' and IALA 'B'.

**Cardinal marks** – used to indicate safe water in the direction indicated from the mark; ie there will be safe water to the north of a North Cardinal Buoy. Used in both IALA 'A' and IALA 'B' areas.

| Buoy | Description | Colour | Top mark | Light |
|---|---|---|---|---|
| | *North cardinal:* does not have a distinctive shape but normally pillar or spar shaped | Black over yellow (BY) | Two black arrows pointing upwards | White light Continuous quick flashing Q *or* Very quick flashing VQ |
| | *West cardinal:* does not have a distinctive shape but normally pillar or spar shaped | Yellow over black over yellow (YBY) | Two black arrows pointing together | White light Quick flashing 9 times every 15 seconds Q(9) 15s *or* Very quick flashing 9 times every 10 seconds VQ(9) 10s |
| | *East cardinal:* does not have a distinctive shape but normally pillar or spar shaped | Black over yellow over black (BYB) | Two black arrows pointing apart | White light Quick flashing 3 times every 10 seconds Q(3) 10s *or* Very quick flashing 3 times every 5 seconds VQ(3) 5s |
| | *South cardinal:* does not have a distinctive shape but normally pillar or spar shaped | Yellow over black (YB) | Two black arrows pointing downwards | White light Quick flashing 6 times plus one long flash every 15 seconds Q(6) + LFl 15s *or* Very quick flashing 6 times plus one long flash every 10 seconds VQ(6) + LFl 10s |

## Safe water marks – used in both IALA 'A' and IALA 'B' areas.

| Buoy | Description | Colour | Top mark | Light |
|---|---|---|---|---|
| | *Safe water mark or fairway buoy*: Spherical or pillar or spar shaped and used as mid-channel or landfall marks | Red and white vertical stripes (RW) | Single red sphere | White light<br>Long flash every 10 seconds LFl 10s<br>*or* Morse 'A' (dit dah) Mo A<br>*or* Isophase – Iso<br>*or* Occulting – Oc |

## Isolated danger marks – used in both IALA 'A' and IALA 'B' areas.

| Buoy | Description | Colour | Top mark | Light |
|---|---|---|---|---|
| | *Isolated danger mark*: optional shape but not conflicting with lateral marks. Pillar or spar preferred | Black with one (or more) broad horizontal red bands (BRB) | Two black spheres in a vertical line | White light<br>Group flash of two GpFl(2) |

## Special marks – not primarily intended to assist navigation but which indicate a special area referred to in appropriate nautical documents. These buoys may be used to mark special areas or features marked on navigational documents and include: Ocean Data Acquision Systems (ODAS) marks, traffic separation marks where use of conventional channel marking may cause confusion, spoil grounds, military exercise areas, cables or pipelines, recreation areas. Used in both IALA 'A' and IALA 'B' areas.

| Buoy | Description | Colour | Top mark | Light |
|---|---|---|---|---|
| | *Special mark*: leave to port when making passage in the general direction of buoyage | Yellow (Y) | May have a yellow cross topmark | Yellow light<br>The rhythm will not conflict with any other white navigational light in the near vicinity |

| Buoy | Description | Colour | Top mark | Light |
|---|---|---|---|---|
| | *Special mark*: leave to starboard when making passage in the general direction of buoyage | Yellow (Y) | May have a yellow cross topmark | Yellow light<br>The rhythm will not conflict with any other white navigational light in the near vicinity |
| | *Special mark*: pass either side | Yellow (Y) | May have a yellow cross topmark | Yellow light<br>The rhythm will not conflict with any other white navigational light in the near vicinity |

**Lateral marks used in area IALA 'A'** – everywhere *except* North, Central and South America, Japan, Korea and the Philippines

| Buoy | Description | Colour | Top mark | Light |
|---|---|---|---|---|
| | *Starboard hand*: note 'conical' shape left to starboard when making passage in the general direction of buoyage | Green (G) | May have a green conical topmark | Green light with any combination *except* composite group flashing (2+1) |
| | *Port hand*: note 'can' shape left to port when making passage in the general direction of buoyage | Red (R) | May have a red can topmark | Red light with any combination *except* composite group flashing (2+1) |
| | *Preferred channel to port*: note 'conical' shape left to starboard when making passage in the general direction of buoyage | Green with one broad horizontal red band (GRG) | May have a green conical topmark | Green light with composite group flashing (2+1) (GpFl G (2+1) |

| Buoy | Description | Colour | Top mark | Light |
|---|---|---|---|---|
| | *Preferred channel to starboard*: note 'can' shape left to port when making passage in the general direction of buoyage | Red with one broad horizontal green band (RGR) | May have a red can topmark | Red light with composite group flashing (2+1) GpFl R (2+1) |

**Lateral marks used in area IALA 'B'** – North, Central and South America, Japan, Korea and the Philippines

| Buoy | Description | Colour | Top mark | Light |
|---|---|---|---|---|
| | *Starboard hand*: note 'conical' shape left to starboard when making passage in the general direction of buoyage | Red (R) | May have a red conical topmark | Red light with any combination *except* composite group flashing (2+1) |
| | *Port hand*: note 'can' shape left to port when making passage in the general direction of buoyage | Green (G) | May have a green can topmark | Green light with any combination *except* composite group flashing (2+1) |
| | *Preferred channel to port*: note 'conical' shape left to starboard when making passage in the general direction of buoyage | Red with one broad horizontal green band (RGR) | May have a red conical topmark | Red light with composite group flashing (2+1) (GpFl R (2+1) |
| | *Preferred channel to starboard*: note 'can' shape left to port when making passage in the general direction of buoyage | Green with one broad horizontal red band (GRG) | May have a green can topmark | Green light with composite group flashing (2+1) GpFl G (2+1) |

**New Danger** – a new danger may be marked by at least one duplicated navigational mark. Whilst it is usually the cardinal marks which are used in this way, it can include *any* navigational mark.

| Buoy | Description | Colour | Top mark | Light |
|---|---|---|---|---|
| | New danger: safe water to the east of these marks | Any navigational buoy may be duplicated to mark a new danger | RACON 'D' (dah dit dit) may be used to supplement a new danger | Lights appropriate to the navigational marks in use. It is unlikely that a new danger will be charted |

## Points to note

The fact that buoyage is identifiable by colour, shape, topmark and light is important as in different conditions, only one of these features may be recognised.

- The cardinal marks have top marks pointing up for north, down for south, together for west and apart for east. The lights are always white and follow the numbers on a clock face: north = continuous flashing, east = 3 flashes, west = 9 flashes, south = 6 flashes plus one long flash. They are identical in IALA 'A' and IALA 'B'.
- The safe water mark is the only one with vertical stripes, the isolated danger buoy has two balls on top indicating a 'balls up' if you get too near.
- Special marks are yellow and may have a cross on the top.

Figure 6.2 demonstrates the practical use of IALA 'A' when going into harbour.

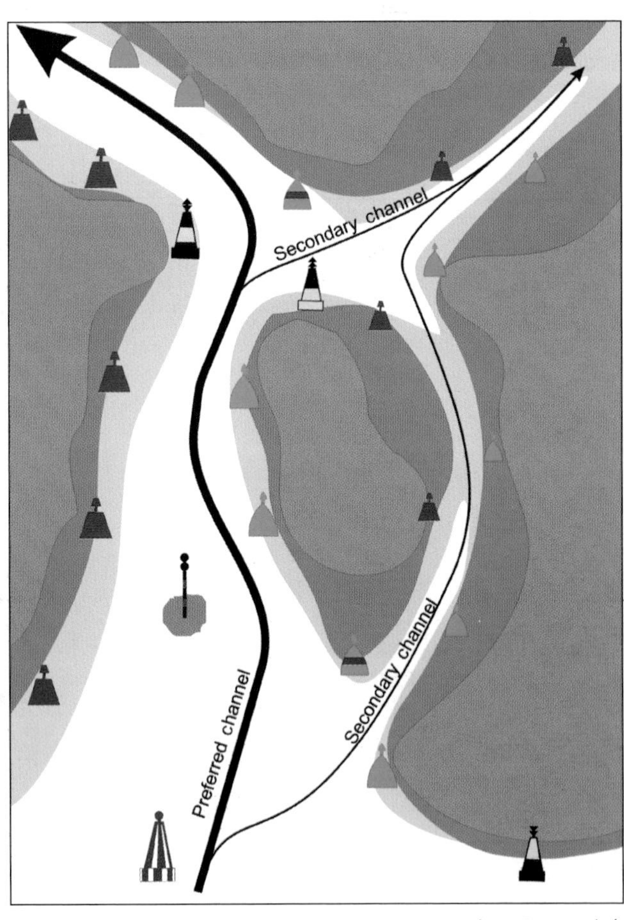


**Fig 6.2** IALA 'A'.

**TOP TIP**

*The lateral marks may cause confusion because of the differences between IALA 'A' and IALA 'B' but although the colours change, the shapes always remain the same in both. So if in doubt look at the shape rather than the colour. Whether IALA 'A' or 'B', when travelling in the general direction of buoyage, leave 'conical' buoys to starboard and 'can' buoys to port.*

# Lights

No book on navigation would be complete without mention of lights and how useful they can be to the navigator.

Lights exhibit a distinctive appearance by which they are recognised, eg fixed (F) – on all the time, flashing (Fl), occulting (Oc) or isophase (Iso). See page 61.

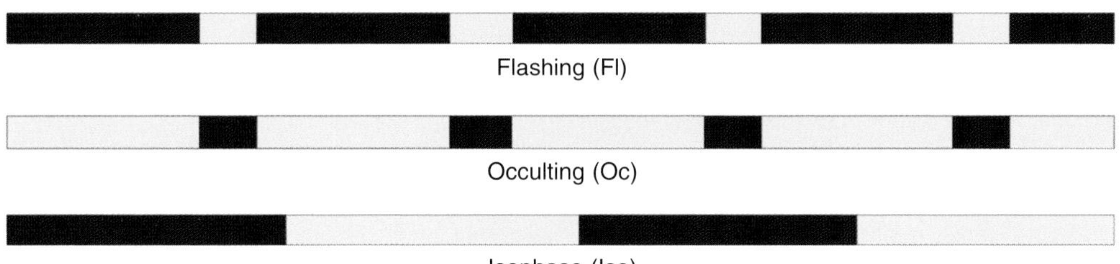


Fig 6.3

The lights are distinguished by their character or characteristic. The principal characteristics are generally the sequence of intervals of light and dark exhibited and, in some cases, combined with the sequence of colours of light exhibited.

Normally, all lights other than fixed lights exhibit a sequence of intervals of light and darkness, the whole sequence being repeated at regular intervals. Such lights are called *rhythmic lights*, and the time taken to complete one sequence is called the 'period' of the light. Each element of the sequence is known as a *phase*.

Rhythmic lights which exhibit different colours during each sequence are called *alternating lights*. The period of an alternating light is the time taken to exhibit the complete sequence, including all changes of colour.

The intensity of lights is measured in *candelas*. Where the intensity of a light is capable of being varied, or where it is different in different sectors, or parts of sectors, two or more range values are given on the chart.

## Elevation

The elevation of a light is the vertical distance between the focal plane of the light and the level of mean high water springs (MHWS) as given in *Admiralty Tide Tables* and on charts. It is measured in metres (m) on a metric chart and feet (ft) on a fathoms chart.

## Luminous range

Luminous range is the maximum distance at which a light can be seen at a given time, as determined by the intensity of the light and the meteorological visibility prevailing at that time. It takes no account of the observer's height of eye or the curvature of the Earth. It is measured in nautical miles (nm). A diagram for estimating the range of a light in various states of visibility is given inside the cover of the *Admiralty Lists of Lights*.

## Nominal range

Nominal range is the luminous range when the meteorological visibility is 10 sea miles. Nominal range is measured in nautical miles (nm).

## Geographical range

Geographical range is the maximum distance at which a light can theoretically be seen by an observer, and is limited only by the curvature of the Earth, the refraction of the atmosphere, the elevation of the light and the height of eye of the observer. It is given in nautical miles (nm). A table of geographical ranges is given inside the front cover of the *Admiralty Lists of Lights*.

## Loom

The diffused glow observed from a light below the horizon or hidden by an obstacle, due to atmospheric scattering is known as the loom. This is the first indication of a light and at the instant a light itself first appears, it gives the navigator a means of constructing a range position line from knowing the height of the light and the observer's height of eye. The range can be calculated by using a table published in almanacs or with a calculator using the following formula:

For a *metric chart* (metres): range of the light = (2.08 × √Height of eye) + (2.08 × √Height of light)

For a *fathoms chart* (feet): range of the light = 1.15 × √Height of eye + √Height of light

## Sector light

A light presenting different appearances, either of colour or character over various parts of the horizon is of interest to maritime navigation.

## Leading lights

Two or more lights associated so as to form a leading line to be followed in pilotage.

## Lts in line

Lights described as 'Lts in line' are intended to mark limits of areas, alignments of cables, alignments for anchoring, etc; they do not generally mark a direction to be followed.

## Direction light

This is a light showing over a very narrow sector, forming a single leading light. This sector may be flanked by sectors of greatly reduced intensity, or by sectors of different colours or characteristics. Direction lights are also used to mark the limits of areas, etc, in the same way as 'Lts in line'.

## Types of light

*Flashing* (Fl) – where the period of darkness is longer than the period of light.
*Occulting* (Oc) – where the period of light is longer than the period of darkness.
*Isophase* (Iso) – where the periods of light and darkness are identical.

### Other descriptions:

| | |
|---|---|
| W | white |
| R | red |
| G | green |
| Y | yellow, amber or orange |
| Bu | blue |
| Vi | violet |
| Fl | flashing |
| Q | quick flashing |
| VQ | very quick flashing |
| UQ | ultra quick flashing |
| Al | alternating |
| Dir Lt | directional light |
| F | fixed light |
| Lanby | large automatic navigational buoy |
| M | nautical mile |
| m | metres |
| Mo | Morse code for a light or fog signal |
| Racon | radar responder beacon |
| Ramark | radar beacon (continuous) |
| RTE | radar target enhancer |
| Whis | whistle |

# 7 The International Regulations for Preventing Collisions at Sea

**STATUTORY REGULATIONS FOR PREVENTING COLLISIONS AT SEA** have only been around for about 150 years or so. Trinity House were originally responsible for the introduction of basic rules and these were eventually incorporated in the Steam Navigation Act of 1846. The 1972 International Convention was introduced because the Collision Regulations of 1960 were seen to be out of date and no longer covered the basic requirements of the seafarer.

One of the most important additions to the 1972 Convention was the recognition given to traffic separation schemes. Rule 10 introduced guidance in determining safe speed, the risk of collision and the conduct of vessels operating in or near traffic separation schemes. The first such traffic separation scheme was established in the Dover Straits in 1967. It was operated on a voluntary basis at first but, in 1971, the IMO Assembly adopted a resolution stating that that the observance of all traffic separation schemes would be made mandatory – and the COLREGS now make this obligation clear.

Traffic density at sea has increased at a phenomenal rate in recent years and, just as one would not expect to take to the road or the air without a good understanding of the appropriate 'Highway Code', it is equally important to have a good understanding of the Collision Regulations, colloquially known as the 'COLREGS'. These include 38 Rules divided into 5 sections: Part A – General; Part B – Steering and Sailing; Part C – Lights and Shapes; Part D – Sound and Light signals; and Part E – Exemptions. There are also four Annexes containing technical requirements concerning lights and shapes and their positioning; sound signalling appliances; additional signals for fishing vessels when operating in close proximity, and international distress signals.

It is important to understand the spirit of the Rules when interpreting their content. Commercial yacht deck officers are expected to have a thorough understanding of the COLREGS and it used to be a common requirement for MCA Deck Oral candidates to learn the Rules by heart before appearing before an examiner. However it was realised that learning the Rules by rote does not necessarily indicate a thorough understanding. The following explanations refer to Part A and Part B of the COLREGS, Rules 1 – 19, and give advice on how to apply them in various situations where a positive command decision is required.

The Rules are written in legalistic terms and imply a one-to-one situation. Most ROR situations are more complex than that and action which is taken by one vessel may be

misunderstood by a vessel which has a number of vessels in close proximity. Similarly, a course correction in accordance with the navigational plan may be seen by another vessel to be an alteration in contravention of the IRPCS.

# Part A: General Rules

## RULE 1

### *Application*

(a) These Rules shall apply to all vessels upon the high seas and in all waters connected therewith navigable by seagoing vessels.

*The Rules apply to all vessels (see Rule 3a for a description of a vessel) and this includes seaplanes, air-cushion craft and warships. Seaplanes, Wing-in-Ground (WIG) and air-cushion craft come under the general description of power driven vessels regarding lights and shapes but with possible modifications.*

(b) Nothing in these Rules shall interfere with the operation of special rules made by an appropriate authority for roadstead, harbours, rivers, lakes or inland waterways connected with the high seas and navigable by seagoing vessels. Such special rules shall conform as closely as possible to these Rules.

*Most harbour authorities make local regulations in order to control traffic within their jurisdiction, especially when commercial shipping and pleasure craft are navigating in close proximity to one another. These local regulations are enforceable by law and contravention of them carries penalties. It is important to read all relevant sailing directions and local notices before arrival (or departure), as ignorance of them is no defence. A port authority's jurisdiction can extend well beyond its natural boundaries and details are given on the appropriate scale chart(s). The actual nature of local regulations varies from port to port but can include restrictions on the navigation of small craft in the form of small craft channels, and areas of concern. It is important to note that locally set rules take precedence over the International Rules but also that local rules should, as far as possible, follow the spirit of the International ones. In the USA and in Europe there are comprehensive sets of rules for inland waters. Knowing these Rules and where they apply is essential when operating in these waters.*

(c) Nothing in these Rules shall interfere with the operation of any special rules made by the Government of any State with respect to additional station or signal lights, shapes or whistle signals for ships of war and vessels proceeding under convoy, or with respect to additional station or signal lights, shapes or whistle signals shall, so far as possible, be such that they cannot be mistaken for any light, shape or signal authorised elsewhere under these Rules.

*Any additional signal lights, shapes and whistle signals should not be confused with the requirements of Rule 1(e). Special local sound signals may also be in force, for example four short blasts followed by one or two short blasts meaning: I am turning short around to starboard or port, ie doing a 180° turn in a narrow channel or river. Details are found in almanacs and sailing directions. Amendments and augmentation of the International Rules must, as far as possible, comply with the intention and spirit of the International Rules.*

**(d)** Traffic separation schemes may be adopted by the Organisation for the purpose of these Rules.

*The International Maritime Organisation (IMO), is the internationally recognised authority responsible for ships routeing.* ***Most*** *Traffic Separation Schemes (TSS) have been adopted by the IMO, and Rule 10 of the COLREGS must be complied with in those adopted schemes. TSS schemes are shown in magenta on charts and, where adopted by the IMO, a note to this effect is included on the chart. British Admiralty charts include traffic routeing schemes established by nations in their own territorial waters, which have not been adopted by the IMO. Additions and amendments to routeing schemes are promulgated in* Weekly Admiralty Notices to Mariners. *Infringement of Rule 10 in a TSS carries heavy penalties, and mariners are advised to ensure their charts and publications are up to date.*

**(e)** Whenever the Government concerned shall have determined that a vessel of any special construction or purpose cannot comply with the provision of any of these Rules with respect to the number, position, range or arc of visibility of lights or shapes, as well as to the disposition and characteristics of sound-signalling appliances, such a vessel shall comply with such other provisions in regard to the number, position, range or arc of visibility of lights or shapes, as well as to the disposition and characteristics of sound-signalling appliances, as her Government shall have determined to be the closest possible compliance with the Rules in respect of that vessel.

*Warships represent the main body of vessels where, because of their special 'construction and purpose', they are unable to comply fully with the Rules concerning lights, shapes and sound signals.*

*Aircraft carriers have their masthead lights placed off the centreline. Their sidelights may either be placed on each side of the hull or on each side of the superstructure, in the latter case the port sidelight may be up to 50m or more from the port side of the vessel and give no real indication of the true width of the ship. Anchor lights may additionally consist of four white lights suitably placed below the corners of the flight deck.*

*The navigation lights of submarines are placed relatively low compared to their length, and are well forward on the hull. The forward masthead light may be lower than the sidelights, and the stern light may be so low as to be seriously obscured by the wake.*

*Some warships of length well in excess of 50m may carry only one masthead light, or carry the second light in a position which does not strictly comply with the provisions of Annex 1 of the COLREGS.*

## RULE 2

### *Responsibility*

(a) Nothing in these Rules shall exonerate any vessel, or the owner, master or crew thereof, from the consequences of any neglect to comply with these Rules or the neglect of any precaution which may be required by the ordinary practice of seamen, or by the special circumstances of the case.

*The implications of this Rule place the onus of responsibility not only on the Master and Officer of the Watch of the vessel and her crew but also on the owner and possibly the owner's agent for the consequences of any neglect in complying with the Rules. It is, for example, the responsibility of the Master to ensure that a person delegated to take a watch is competent and capable. It is also the responsibility of the owner or the owner's agent to ensure that the vessel is competently manned in accordance with the minimum requirements laid down by the MCA for a British flagged vessel.*

*The 'ordinary practice of seaman' might well be defined as nautical common sense.*

(b) In construing and complying with these Rules due regard shall be had to all dangers of navigation and collision and to any special circumstances, including the limitations of the vessels involved which may make a departure from these Rules necessary to avoid immediate danger.

*In simple language, no matter what the circumstances are, you must take whatever action is appropriate to avoid a collision or, if collision is imminent, do whatever is possible to minimise damage. A departure from the Rules is allowed, in exceptional circumstances, to avoid immediate danger.*

*Consideration must be given to the 'limitations of the vessels involved'. A yacht crossing a busy shipping lane might be well advised to take very early avoiding action to ensure that a risk of collision does not develop. The skipper of a small vessel will have a very different perception of when a risk of collision exists to that of the Master of a large ship. There is always the chance that a small vessel may not be easily seen from the bridge of a large ship in a moderate or rough sea.*

*When a collision is deemed to be imminent, this Rule allows any action to be taken to avoid or lessen the damage of a collision. The best course of action may be to alter course towards the other vessel so as to meet her close to head on, rather than to expose the side of one's own vessel. This action might appear to break the Rule but, if the circumstances are 'exceptional', this could be the best option to avoid or minimise immediate danger and damage.*

## RULE 3

### *General definitions*

For the purpose of these Rules, except where the context otherwise requires:

(a) The word 'vessel' includes every description of water-craft, including non-displacement craft, WIG craft and seaplanes, used or capable of being used as a means of transportation on water.

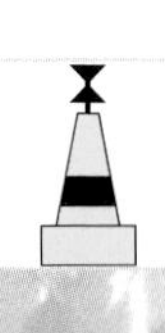



*This definitive description of a vessel is very broad. Basically if it floats and is capable of transportation – it's a vessel.*

*Chain ferries and floating bridges are not specifically mentioned in the Rules, as they do not come under the category of vessels at anchor. Local regulations apply to these types of vessel and mariners should navigate with particular caution as they have very limited manoeuvring ability; they generally can only either move in one of two directions or stop!*

**(b)** The term 'power-driven vessel' means any vessel propelled by machinery.

*An auxiliary sailing vessel is treated as a power-driven vessel when she is motor sailing, and is required to show the navigation lights for a power-driven vessel at night and display a black cone (point down) by day. Many sailing vessels proceeding under power fail to observe this Rule. Cynically, one might say that downward pointing black cones are only guaranteed on vessels whose skippers are undertaking RYA Yachtmaster examinations!*

*Vessels that are hampered, for example vessels restricted in their ability to manoeuvre (RAM [or RIATM]), vessels not under command (NUC) and fishing vessels, are not categorised as 'power-driven' vessels under the Rules. It is however very important to remember that a vessel constrained by her draught (CBD) is still regarded as a power-driven vessel even though she is given certain advantages not to be impeded. However at no stage does she cease to be a power-driven vessel within the meaning of the Rules.*

**(c)** The term 'sailing vessel' means any vessel under sail provided that propelling machinery, if fitted, is not being used.

**(d)** The term 'vessel engaged in fishing' means any vessel fishing with nets, lines, trawls or the fishing apparatus which restrict manoeuvrability, but does not include a vessel fishing with trolling lines or other fishing apparatus which do not restrict manoeuvrability.

*In order to be classed as a 'vessel engaged in fishing' within the meaning of the COLREGS, a vessel must be actively engaged in fishing with gear which restricts her manoeuvrability. This does not make a fishing vessel restricted in her ability to manoeuvre. In many encounters with 'fishing vessels' it is often quite obvious that they are not actively engaged in fishing but are nevertheless displaying fishing shapes or lights. When not engaged in fishing they are power-driven vessels and should carry the lights appropriate for a power-driven vessel of their size.*

The Mariner's Handbook, *Chapter 3, Sections 55 – 66 has a wealth of information on the various types of fishing vessels and how their gear is used.*

**(e)** The word 'seaplane' includes any aircraft designed to manoeuvre on the water.

**(f)** The term 'vessel not under command' means a vessel which through some exceptional circumstances is unable to manoeuvre as required by these Rules and is therefore unable to keep out of the way of another vessel.

*In order to qualify as being 'not under command' (NUC) a vessel must be suffering from exceptional circumstances that have caused an inability to be able to comply with the COLREGS. NUC is nothing whatsoever to do with the mental state of the Captain, as I have been told on several occasions by Yachtmaster Exam candidates! A sailing vessel becalmed and without an operational engine would constitute being 'not under command' and a vessel riding out a storm under exceptional circumstances or deploying a sea anchor or drogue might also be NUC. Generally it is a steering or propulsion problem that renders a vessel NUC but a twin-screw vessel without steering might still be able to manoeuvre in accordance with the Rules even though she has lost her steering.*

*A confused watchkeeper switching on the NUC lights in the hope that vessels in his vicinity will disappear is most certainly not an acceptable reason! There have been many reports of vessels of exhibiting NUC signals when drifting off a port awaiting permission to enter presumably so that the watch keeper can relax his watch. If vessels are underway (not aground, made fast to the shore or at anchor) and able to manoeuvre as required by the Rules, such vessels cannot be possibly classed as NUC and are certainly not justified in displaying NUC signals.*

**(g)** The term 'vessel restricted in her ability to manoeuvre' means a vessel which from the nature of the work is restricted in her ability to manoeuvre as required by these Rules and is therefore unable to keep out of the way of another vessel. The term 'vessels restricted in their ability to manoeuvre' shall include but not be limited to:

(i) a vessel engaged in laying, servicing or picking up a navigation mark, submarine cable or pipeline;

(ii) a vessel engaged in dredging, surveying or underwater operations;

(iii) a vessel engaged in replenishment or transferring persons, provisions or cargo while underway;

(iv) a vessel engaged in the launching or recovery of aircraft;

(v) a vessel engaged in mine clearance operations;

(vi) a vessel engaged in towing operation such as severely restricts the towing vessel and her tow in their ability to deviate from their course.

*In order for a vessel to come under the heading 'restricted in her ability to manoeuvre' (RAM [or RIATM]), she must be restricted due to the nature of her work, not to any navigational constraints. It is important to remember the expression* ***'nature of her work'*** *when considering which vessels may be considered as RAM (or RIATM) vessels and equally remember that fishing vessels have their own category. The Rule also states that she 'is unable to get out of the way of another vessel'. Overtaking would appear to present an anomaly in this respect, as an overtaking RAM (or RIATM) vessel is expected to 'keep out of the way of the vessel being overtaken' (Rule 13). Should such a situation arise in practice, the vessel being overtaken should navigate with extreme caution.*

*Vessels involved in mine clearance operations are also said to be restricted in their ability to manoeuvre but carry their own distinctive signals (Rule 27). The reason for their differentiation is that they are given an exclusion zone of 1,000m – just in case their operations go wrong!*

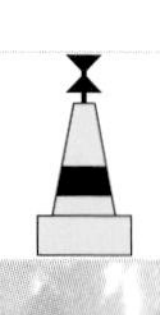



**(h)** The term 'vessel constrained by her draught' means a power-driven vessel which, because of her draught in relation to the available depth and width of navigable water, is severely restricted in her ability to deviate from the course she is following.

*Vessels 'constrained by their draught' (CBD) can only ever be power-driven vessels within the meaning of the COLREGS. This Rule does not apply to any other type of vessel and certainly not to vessels under sail. To be classed as 'constrained by draught' a vessel must be navigating in such a manner that she could not 'deviate' from her course due to the depth of water in relationship to her draught and also the width of the navigable channel. Although she may be given an advantage by not being impeded, at no time does she lose her status as a power-driven vessel and if she is impeded, she will revert to the Rules for a power-driven vessel in the same position.*

**(i)** The word 'underway' means that a vessel is not at anchor, or made fast to the shore, or aground.

*A vessel that is stopped in the water is still 'under way' within the meaning of the Rules.*

**(j)** The words 'length' and 'breadth' of a vessel mean her length overall and greater breadth.

**(k)** Vessels shall be deemed to be in sight of one another only when one can be observed visually from the other.

*'In sight of one another' includes seeing by eye only – not by radar.*

**(l)** The term 'restricted visibility' means any condition in which visibility is restricted by fog, mist, falling snow, heavy rainstorms, sandstorms or any other similar causes.

*If you are in doubt about the visibility, assume the worst.*

**(m)** The term 'Wing-in-Ground (WIG)' craft means a multimodal craft which, in its main operational mode, flies in close proximity to the surface by utilizing surface-effect action.

*WIG craft (Wing-in-Ground) is a new means of high-speed transport, flying close to, but above the water surface. It makes use of the ground (water surface) effect, which greatly enhances the lift/drag ratio and aerodynamic efficiency. WIG craft have many advantages compared to high-speed ships and conventional aircraft. It flies like an aeroplane, but with a greatly reduced risk of crashing. It is very safe and comfortable like a ship but without the continuous motion. It is cheaper to manufacture and operate than an aeroplane. It can take off from and land on water or level ground without the need for a runway. WIG craft are likely to become more common in the future.*

# Part B: Steering and Sailing Rules

## Section I – Conduct of vessels in any condition of visibility

### RULE 4

#### *Application*

Rules in this section apply in any condition of visibility.

*This is important to note as the three sections refer to different states of visibility. Section 1 is any state of visibility; ie rules to be followed regardless of the visibility.*

### RULE 5

#### *Look-out*

Every vessel shall at all times maintain a proper look-out by sight and hearing as well as by all available means appropriate in the prevailing circumstances and condition so as to make a full appraisal of the situation and of the risk of collision.

*This is one of the most important Rules in the COLREGS. Failure to keep a proper look-out may, sooner or later, result in a collision or a grounding. It is important to keep an all round look-out by all available means. This includes not only just the Mark I eyeball, but also ears, nose, radar, echo sounder, radio etc. Don't forget to keep a eye open astern even though you may expect an overtaking vessel to keep clear and before attempting any manoeuvre:* ***LOOK ASTERN BEFORE YOU TURN!***

*Proper use must be made of radar even in clear weather. It is an excellent means of determining a risk of collision at an early stage if the radar is correctly set in 'sea stabilised' mode. If your radar is set in 'ground stabilised' mode, it is not recommended that ARPA (or MARPA) is relied upon for collision avoidance information as it may generate an incorrect aspect.*

*All vessels should monitor their VHF but the MCA strongly advise against using VHF to contact other vessels where a risk of collision is developing. Calls of* ***'ship on my port bow, this is ship on your port bow'*** *should be treated with extreme caution. Collisions have occurred where the inappropriate use of VHF has been a contributing cause. This is colloquially known as a 'VHF assisted collision'. Never discuss a manoeuvre with another vessel unless you can absolutely, definitely, positively identify her and you can be equally sure that she knows which ship you are.*

*A look-out can be regarded as performing the most important job on the vessel at any given time and it is important the he is not distracted from his duties. The importance of keeping a proper look-out cannot be overstated. It is often under good conditions that look-outs become too relaxed with potentially dire consequences. Look-out duties are by their very nature very tiring and boring. Ensure that look-outs are rotated on a regular basis. In restricted visibility, 15 minutes may well be long enough!*

*It is equally important to keep a proper look-out even when the vessel is not under way, particularly if she is anchored in an exposed area.*

## RULE 6

### *Safe speed*

Every vessel shall at all times proceed at a safe speed so that she can take proper and effective action to avoid collision and be stopped within a distance appropriate to the prevailing circumstances and conditions.

In determining a safe speed the following factors shall be among those taken into account:

(a) By all vessels:
(i) the state of visibility;

*The **visibility** is at times very difficult to estimate, especially at night and or in hazy conditions. At night a semi-displacement or planing vessel becomes vulnerable at speed. She is at risk from hitting unlit objects. It is advisable to proceed at displacement speed in the dark.*

(ii) the traffic density including concentrations of fishing vessels or any other vessels;

*The concentration of **traffic density**, such as fishing fleets, naval exercises and popular yachting areas on a summer weekend.*

(iii) the manoeuvrability of the vessel with special reference to stopping distance and turning ability in the prevailing conditions;

*The **manoeuvrability** of the vessel is vital to the formulation of a safe speed. Stopping distance and turning circles are important to take into account and don't forget to appreciate the thought process of the watchkeepers on other vessels. Their perspective of a situation may be very different from your own.*

*Stopping distances of vessels vary tremendously from a couple of boat lengths for a small vessel to several miles for a VLCC. When a large ship is navigating in pilotage waters she may not be able to make a quick reduction in speed to avoid a collision; smaller craft must bear this in mind if they are required to 'avoid impeding the passage' of another vessel.*

*A large vessel passing a small craft in a narrow channel can cause the small craft to sheer violently off course due to the 'interaction' caused by pressure waves created by the larger vessel. A large vessel can suck away so much water from the side of a narrow channel through shallow water effect that a small boat might end up left high and dry for a few moments until the large vessel has passed when equilibrium will be restored. In order to avoid this, large vessels should reduce their speed when passing small craft in shallow channels.*

(iv) at night the presence of background light such as from shore lights or from back scatter of her own lights;

*The **background lighting** of a port or coastline can easily mask the lights of small craft and large vessels that may only be recognised by the moving shadow they cast against the background.*

*Backscatter from a vessel's own lights is often the first sign that the visibility is deteriorating.*

(v) the state of wind, sea and current, and the proximity of navigational hazards;

*A strong current may require a power-driven vessel to use more power to generate sufficient speed to overcome or lessen the effects of a current. A sailing boat (because of her relatively slow speed) will generally be more susceptible to* ***wind, sea and current*** *than faster craft. A power-driven vessel should take account of the problems that may be encountered by a sailing boat when proceeding at what he considers to be a safe speed as his 'safe' speed may cause excessive wash.*

(vi) the draught in relation to the available depth of water.

*Even shallow* ***draught*** *vessels can suffer from a phenomenon known as 'squat' when navigating too fast in shallow water. This causes the stern to settle lower in the water than usual, increasing the draught and the possibility of grounding. This effect is amplified by higher speed and a vessel will become very difficult to manoeuvre if she is required to take avoiding action. Power-driven vessels also create a greater wash in shallow water that may endanger small craft.*

**(b)** Additionally, by vessels with operational radar:
(i) the characteristics, efficiency and limitations of the radar equipment;

*Radar technology has developed hugely in recent years but there are still* ***efficiency limitations.*** *Contacts, which show at ten miles range in clear weather, might not show in dense fog at much more than six miles due to attenuation (power loss) of the radar pulse. This imposes a considerable limitation on detection range at a time when it is most needed and speed should be adjusted to allow for this.*

*The comparatively wide beamwidth of many small craft radars (anything up to 6°), combined with reluctance of the inexperienced to adopt a North-Up display, precludes the keeping of an accurate radar plot. It should be noted that the placing of a bearing cursor (EBL) on a contact and observing its relative motion does not constitute a proper radar plot and any action based on such a procedure is classed as 'scanty radar information' and should be used with extreme caution.*

(ii) any constraints imposed by the radar range scale in use;

*It is important to use an effective range scale and this includes increasing and decreasing range on a regular basis to ensure that close and distant contacts are not missed. If only one range scale is used, there will be* ***range constraints*** *in your ability to detect all contacts. Do not forget that unless the radar is automatically tuned, it will be necessary to manually retune after each change of range scale.*

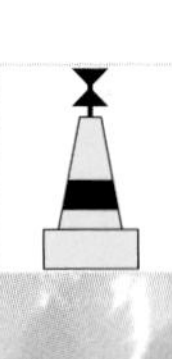



(iii) the effect on radar detection of the sea state, weather and other sources of interference;

*Radar scanners, antennas or aerials are mounted as high as possible, frequently in excess of 30 metres above sea level on large ships. Whilst this has a beneficial effect in the detection of contacts at long range by increasing the radar horizon, it also extends the close-in range and increases the effects of sea clutter making it more difficult to detect small targets at close range. It is not uncommon for sea clutter to extend out to a range in excess of six miles in heavy weather. The worst scenario for the detection of small contacts is strong wind and a heavy sea together with heavy rain or drizzle when* ***small objects are difficult to determine at adequate range.***

*Rain clutter and attenuation of the radar pulse can be major problems. It can be difficult to detect all but the largest targets in heavy rain even with sophisticated anti-rain clutter controls.*

(iv) the possibility that small vessels, ice and other floating objects may not be detected by radar at an adequate range;

*If you have to rely totally on radar, it is quite possible that* ***small objects*** *will not be recognised at an adequate range. Safe speed needs to take this into account.*

(v) the number, location and movement of vessels detected by radar;

*The greater the* ***number of contacts*** *showing on a radar screen, the greater likelihood that the inexperienced eye will not prioritise and correctly assess the greatest danger.*

(vi) the more exact assessment of the visibility that may be possible when radar is used to determine the range of vessels or other objects in the vicinity.

*Visibility range is difficult to assess even by the most experienced seaman. It is good practice to note the radar range at which ships and other contacts can first be seen and adjust speed accordingly. In patchy fog or mist always adjust speed for the lowest* ***estimate of visibility.*** *It is important not to keep changing speed as erratic adjustments of your own vessel's speed can cause confusion to another vessel's radar plot.*

**TOP TIP**

*Safe speed is a favourite question amongst MCA oral examiners. You should be able to reel off the six factors to be taken into account by all vessels and then the six by those with operational radar.*

## RULE 7

### *Risk of collision*

(a) Every vessel shall use all available means appropriate to the prevailing circumstances and conditions to determine if risk of collision exits. If there is any doubt such risk shall be deemed to exist.

*It is possible for two vessels to be on a collision course with each other but to be so far apart that there is no real risk of collision. Taken to the extreme, two vessels could be on opposite sides of the Atlantic on collision courses and if they were to keep their courses and speeds they would eventually collide. Clearly a time must come when a real risk of collision starts to exist. It is however not as easy as one might imagine to define this instant. The master of a large ship will have a totally different perception of risk of collision to the skipper of a much smaller one. Much will depend on the size and speed of the vessels involved, the navigational constraints, weather conditions, and very importantly, the experience of the person in charge of the watch. Bearing in mind the spirit of the COLREGS, if there is any doubt whatsoever, it should be assumed that a risk of collision does exist and take action accordingly.*

*Risk of collision can only be assessed if a constant and proper look-out is kept as defined in Rule 5. On large ships there is a requirement that there should be at least two people on watch, with a look-out forward and an officer of the watch on the bridge. Unfortunately, for all sorts of reasons, this is not always the case and one can never guarantee that the other vessel is keeping a proper look-out, or that you have been seen.*

*The MCA warn against the use of VHF in a situation where a risk of collision exists. Positive identification, especially in restricted visibility, is frequently difficult to establish and valuable time can be wasted and intentions misunderstood if proper procedures are not followed. Any action that proposes a deviation from the Rules is liable to lead to confusion and any contravention of the COLREGS, which is not clearly understood by both parties, may lead to serious consequences.*

(b) Proper use shall be made of radar equipment if fitted and operational, including long-range scanning to obtain early warning that risk of collision exists. If there is any doubt such risk shall be deemed to exist.

*A radar plot should kept in order to assess the risk of collision. This Rule is in Part B Section 1 and therefore applies to vessels in any state of visibility. It is therefore not satisfactory only to use radar in restricted visibility. If you have an operational radar on board, you should be using it at all times. Radar should be used to give early warning of a risk of collision, and a guide to traffic density. This can be of great assistance to the experienced watchkeeper not only in restricted visibility but also at night. However as radar sophistication improves, take care to ensure that you understand the difference between 'sea' and 'ground' stabilisation of automatic radar plotting aid (ARPA) information.*

**TOP TIP**

*Ground stabilisation of the radar image should not be relied upon for collision avoidance.*

**(c)** Assumptions shall not be made on the basis of scanty information, especially scanty radar information.

*It is common practice in good visibility to line up a vessel with the land to see whether the bearing against the land is changing over a period of time. This will only work well if the land is sufficiently far away and its bearing remains constant during that interval. But if the bearing of the land is not steady and is changing, the method is fundamentally flawed. Great care should be taken before using this method as a means of establishing a risk of collision. The only failsafe way is to take a series of compass bearings to assess risk of collision.*

*Placing an Electronic Bearing Marker (EBL) on a contact does not constitute a radar plot and is classed as scanty radar information. Rule 19(d) states that if a vessel detects another by radar alone she 'shall determine if a close quarter situation is developing and/or a risk of collision exists.' This can only be ascertained with any degree of accuracy by constructing a radar plot. If it is not possible to construct a proper radar plot either by paper plotting or by using an automatic radar plotting aid (ARPA), the Watchkeeper should navigate with extreme caution, proceed at a safe speed and avoid alterations of course, which may confuse other vessels with automatic plotting (ARPA) equipment.*

**(d)** In determining if risk of collision exists, the following considerations shall be among those taken into account:

(i) such risk shall be deemed to exist if the compass bearing of an approaching vessel does not appreciably change;

*The only sure visual way of determining whether a risk of collision exists is to take compass bearings of an approaching vessel. The taking of relative bearings or lining up a vessel with a guardrail or shroud are not reliable means of determining a risk of collision.*

(ii) such risk may sometimes exist even when an appreciable bearing change is evident, particularly when approaching a very large or a tow or when approaching a vessel at close range.

*An appreciable change in bearing is particularly important when assessing risk of collision with large vessels and vessels engaged in towing, especially when they are at close range. It is quite possible that the bow of a large vessel or tug might be drawing right whilst the stern of the vessel or last vessel towed is drawing left and this is not a happy state of affairs!*

*It is paramount that 'all available means' be used to determine if a risk of collision exists. This includes using radar (if fitted and operational). Therefore if you have radar on onboard but choose not to turn it on and a collision occurs, you could be held partly responsible for not using 'all available means.'*

*If there is any doubt at all whether a risk of collision exists, you should assume that it does and act accordingly.*

## RULE 8

### *Action to avoid collision*

*An understanding of Rule 8 is paramount to safe navigation. Any action to avoid a collision must be early, clear, bold, positive and based upon good seamanship. Small nibbling alterations to slip around another vessel's stern must be avoided. Every effort must be made to make actions clear to the other vessel at an early stage. Remember that a super tanker will need to make a decision at 6–8 miles whereas a superyacht may wrongly wait until 2–3 miles when it will be too late for the larger ship to take the necessary action should the superyacht get it wrong.*

(a) Any action taken to avoid collision shall be taken in accordance with the Rules of this Part and shall, if the circumstances of the case admit, be positive, made in ample time and with due regard to the observance of good seamanship.

*Action taken to avoid collision applies not only to the give-way vessel but also to the stand-on vessel if the former does not appear to be taking appropriate avoiding action. The stand-on vessel must not allow a risk of collision to increase to the point at which a collision is imminent and unavoidable.*

*Action taken to avoid a collision must be readily apparent to the other vessel. For vessels in sight of each other, this is best demonstrated by an alteration of course such that the other vessel sees a different aspect. Alterations of speed alone are not readily apparent but may in many cases be a safe course of action. In these cases, it may be prudent to slow down much more than is necessary in order to make the action more obvious earlier.*

*The Master of a merchant ship has a very different perception of a risk of collision developing than the skipper of a yacht. Manoeuvring a large vessel is a slow process and requires careful planning whereas small craft are more manoeuvrable and decisions can be left until much later. When the skipper of a small craft is the give-way vessel to a larger ship, he should bear in mind that the officer on the bridge of the large ship may be getting very anxious long before he might normally consider taking avoiding action.*

*When altering course to avoid another vessel it is considered 'good seamanship' to pass under the stern of the other vessel so as to avoid crossing ahead of her (Rule 15).*

(b) Any alteration of course and/or speed to avoid collision shall, if the circumstances of the case admit, be large enough to be readily apparent to another vessel observing visually or by radar; a succession of small alterations of course and/or speed should be avoided.

*This paragraph reinforces the requirement that any action taken to avoid a collision must be positive. Collisions have occurred where vessels have made a series of small alterations of course based on scanty radar information. It is particularly important to make bold alterations of course and/or speed when taking avoiding action in reduced visibility so that it may be more readily apparent to another vessel observing on radar.*

**(c)** If there is sufficient sea-room, alteration of course alone may be the most effective action to avoid a close quarters situation provided that it is made in good time, is substantial and does not result in another close quarters situation.

*In a visual situation, alterations of course are much more apparent than changes in speed. A vessel which is keeping a look-out by a relative display radar set (Head Up) will find that alterations of course and/or speed by other vessels are not readily apparent, since the motion of a target on the radar display is a combination of the observing vessel's true motion combined with that of the radar contact. Due to the slightly historical nature of this information, there is always some delay between the action taken by a contact and what appears on the radar screen. An ARPA system goes some way to resolving this problem, but there is still a processing delay, so that alterations of course or speed by a radar contact are not instantly apparent.*

*In multi-ship situations, it is important to check that an alteration of course or speed to keep clear of one vessel does not result in creating a risk of collision with another vessel.*

**(d)** Action taken to avoid collision with another vessel shall be such as to result in passing at a safe distance. The effectiveness of the action shall be carefully checked until the other vessel is finally past and clear.

*It is often assumed that once avoiding action has been taken, that is the end of the story. It is important that any action taken continues to be carefully monitored to ensure that the alteration is having the desired effect. This is particularly important when operating in high-density traffic.*

**(e)** If necessary to avoid collision or allow more time to assess the situation, a vessel shall slacken her speed or take all way off by stopping or reversing her means of propulsion.

*Very often the best course of action in a complicated situation is to slow down or stop. If nothing else it will allow more thinking time!*

**(f)** (i) A vessel which, by any of these Rules, is required not to impede the passage or safe passage of another vessel shall, when required by the circumstances of the case, take early action to allow sufficient sea-room for the safe passage of the other vessel.

(ii) A vessel required not to impede the passage or safe passage of another vessel is not relieved of this obligation if approaching the other vessel so as to involve risk of collision and shall, when taking action, have full regard to the action which may be required by the Rules of this Part.

(iii) A vessel the passage of which is not to be impeded remains fully obliged to comply with the Rules of this Part when the two vessels are approaching one another so as to involve risk of collision.

*Paragraph 8f introduces the concept of the 'not to be impeded' vessel. This refers to:*
*(a) a vessel constrained by her draft which is still a power-driven vessel in the COLREGS and if impeded may take action as a power-driven vessel,*

*(b) a power-driven vessel navigating in a Traffic Separation Zone should not be impeded by crossing power-driven vessels under 20m or sailing vessels, and fishing vessels should not impede any vessel navigating in a Traffic Separation Zone.*
*(c) a vessel which can only navigate within a narrow channel should not be impeded by power-driven vessels under 20m or by sailing vessels and crossing vessels. Fishing vessels should not impede* ***any*** *vessel navigating in a narrow channel.*

*So what does not impede mean? It is not specifically defined anywhere in the Rules.*

*Vessels which 'should not impede' another vessel must, as far as possible keep clear and take avoiding action before a risk of collision develops. Any action taken to 'not impede' must take full regard that the vessel 'not to be impeded' may take avoiding action herself as a power-driven vessel at any time if she considers it necessary. Therefore the 'not to impede' vessel must not take any action which would prevent the 'not to be impeded' vessel taking her own action as detailed in Rules 14, 15 and 17c. As a vessel constrained by her draught is still classed as a power-driven vessel under the COLREGS it is very, very unlikely that an alteration to port for a vessel that is 'not to be impeded' would be the correct course of action unless it was the only action left to the vessel which is not to impede which would prevent a collision.*

*This is quite different from the action that a power-driven vessel should take when faced with a risk of collision with:*
*(a) sailing vessel*
*(b) fishing/trawling vessel*
*(c) vessel restricted in her ability to manoeuvre*
*(d) vessel not under command*

*These vessels will expect to be given a clear passage and there is no Rule that details what action they should specifically take if another vessel fails to keep out of the way. They would revert to common sense and good seamanship. Therefore in practical terms there is no reason to avoid going to port to keep clear of these vessels if there is sufficient sea room.*

## RULE 9

### *Narrow channels*

(a) A vessel proceeding along the course of a narrow channel or fairway shall keep as near to the outer limit of the channel or fairway which lies on her starboard side as is safe and practicable.

*The implications of this Rule are obvious but frequently ignored by small craft, especially sailing boats. It is important to keep to the starboard side of a narrow channel (unlike a Traffic Separation Scheme (TSS) where you should avoid straddling the edges.) It is often good practice for small vessels to navigate outside narrow channels, and there are often local regulations to this effect when large vessels are using a narrow channel.*

**(b)** A vessel of less than 20m in length or a sailing vessel shall not impede the passage of a vessel which can safely navigate only within a narrow channel or fairway.

*Where a vessel is not to be impeded, avoiding action is required to be taken before any risk of collision develops. It may be difficult for the small vessel to determine whether or not a larger vessel can only navigate within the channel. If in doubt, it is best to assume she can only use the marked channel.*

**(c)** A vessel engaged in fishing shall not impede the passage of any other vessel navigating within a narrow channel or fairway.

*Fishing vessels (and trawlers which are still classed as fishing vessels) are required to avoid impeding the passage of any vessel navigating within a narrow channel irrespective of whether such vessel is able to navigate outside the main channel or not.*

**(d)** A vessel shall not cross a narrow channel or fairway if such crossing impedes the passage of a vessel which can safely navigate only within such channel or fairway. The latter vessel may use the sound signal prescribed in Rule 34(d) if in doubt as to the intention of the crossing vessel.

*This Rule applies to **any** vessel crossing a narrow channel or fairway.*

*Sailing boats are often guilty of breaking this Rule by tacking up narrow channels and expecting other traffic to keep clear. A sailing boat should, if she is unable to comply with this Rule, start her engine, become a power-driven vessel and navigate on the starboard side of a narrow channel.*

**(e)** (i) In a narrow channel or fairway when overtaking can take place only if the vessel to be overtaken has to take action to permit safe passing, the vessel intending to overtake shall indicate her intention by sounding the appropriate signal prescribed by Rule 34(c)(i). The vessel to be overtaken shall, if in agreement, sound the appropriate signal prescribed in Rule 34(c)(ii) and take steps to permit safe passing. If in doubt she may sound the signals prescribed in Rule 34(d).

*It is important to appreciate that when overtaking another vessel in a narrow channel **and you require the overtaken vessel to take action to allow sufficient sea room**, you are required to give sound signals to explain your intentions and await agreement before proceeding. Two prolonged blasts followed by a short blast indicates a desire to overtake to starboard and two prolonged blasts followed by two short blasts indicates a desire to overtake to port. If in agreement, the vessel to be overtaken will sound a prolonged blast and short blast followed by a second prolonged blast and a second short blast (Morse 'C'). If it is not agreed and the vessel to be overtaken cannot move out of the way for some reason, five or more rapid short blasts will be sounded by that vessel.*

(ii) This rule does not relieve the overtaking of her obligation under Rule 13.

*The overtaking Rule still applies even when the vessel being overtaken has signalled that she agrees to the manoeuvre and has moved aside to assist the manoeuvre.*

**(f)** A vessel nearing a bend or an area of a narrow channel or fairway where another vessel may be obscured by an intervening obstruction shall navigate with particular alertness and caution and shall sound the appropriate signal prescribed in Rule 34(e).

*When approaching a blind bend in a narrow channel if other on-coming vessels could be obscured, a prolonged blast (4–6 seconds) should be sounded. If another vessel is obscured but hears the sound, she should respond with a prolonged blast (4–6 seconds).*

**(g)** Any vessel shall, if the circumstances of the case admit, avoid anchoring in a narrow channel.

*No anchoring other than in an emergency, in which case make sure that the appropriate authority is advised.*

## RULE 10

### *Traffic separation schemes*

**(a)** This Rule applies to traffic separation schemes adopted by the Organisation and does not relieve any vessel of her obligation under any other Rule.

*This explains that although the COLREGS only strictly apply to IMO recognised traffic separation schemes, they do not relieve the master of his obligations under any other Rule.*

**(b)** A vessel using a traffic separation scheme shall:
(i) proceed in the appropriate traffic lane in the general direction of traffic flow for that lane;
(ii) so far as practicable keep clear of a traffic separation line or separation zone;
(iii normally join or leave a traffic lane at the termination of the lane, but when joining or leaving from either side shall do so at as small an angle to the general direction of traffic flow as practicable.

*This Rule outlines the general requirement for vessels following a TSS. It emphasises the requirement to join or leave at as small an angle as possible if it is not possible to join at the beginning or end of the lane.*

*A vessel should keep clear of the separation zone between the two lanes and the separation line that defines the outer boundary of a lane. Unlike a narrow channel where the obligation is to keep to the right side, in a TSS it is a requirement not to keep to the sides.*

*Vessels using TSS have a tendency to programme the centre of the TSS as a waypoint. This causes bunching of ships proceeding towards a single point and has contributed to collisions.*

**(c)** A vessel shall, so far as practicable, avoid crossing traffic lanes but if obliged to do so shall cross on a heading as nearly as practicable at right angles to the general direction of traffic flow.

*It may be difficult to avoid crossing a TSS in an area such as the Dover Straits where the scheme extends for many miles, but there are many instances where short TSSs are located, for example passing headlands, and vessels should pass clear of the scheme without having to deviate unduly from her intended course.*

*If obliged to cross a TSS, vessels should do so with the* ***heading*** *(not the ground track [COG]) as close as possible to right angles to the traffic flow.* ***No allowance should be made to counteract the effect of tidal stream or current.*** *This is done to prevent ambiguity of aspect.*

*It should be noted that when crossing a TSS and altering (correctly) in accordance with Rule 8, Rule 10 will be required to be put in abeyance and every effort should be made to return to crossing at right angles when it is safe to do so.*

**(d)** (i) a vessel shall not use an inshore traffic zone when she can safely use the appropriate traffic lane within the adjacent traffic separation scheme. However, vessels of less than 20m in length, sailing vessels and vessels engaged in fishing may use the inshore traffic zone.

(ii) Notwithstanding sub-paragraph (d)(i), a vessel may use an inshore traffic zone when en route to or from a port, offshore installation or structure, pilot station or any other place situated within the inshore traffic zone, or to avoid immediate danger.

*Through traffic should always use the appropriate TSS lane. Fishing vessels, sailing vessels and vessels less than 20m in length may use the inshore traffic zone. Vessels bound for a port, or other destination within the inshore zone, are also permitted to use the inshore zone as are vessels avoiding immediate danger.*

**(e)** A vessel other than a crossing vessel or a vessel joining or leaving a lane shall not normally enter a separation zone or cross a separation line except:

(i) in cases of emergency to avoid immediate danger.

(ii) to engage in fishing within a separation zone.

*This Rule gives fishing vessels permission to fish within a separation zone and other vessels to enter or leave a TSS other than joining at the beginning or crossing in the case of an emergency.*

**(f)** A vessel navigating in areas near the terminations of traffic separation schemes shall do so with particular caution.

*The termination of a TSS will generally represent an area of high traffic density and all vessels not entering or leaving the TSS are well advised to avoid these areas if possible and in any case to navigate with extreme caution.*

**(g)** A vessel shall so far as practicable avoid anchoring in a traffic separation scheme or in areas near its terminations.

*This Rule prevents anchoring in a TSS or in the approaches to it other than in an emergency. In practical situations, asking for assistance in the form of a tow may be preferable to anchoring.*

**(h)** A vessel not using a traffic separation scheme shall avoid it by as wide a margin as is practicable.

*This reiterates Rule 10(f); TSSs are safe places once all the shipping has settled into them. However other vessels which do not intend to use them should not navigate close to them as they may cause confusion to ships using the TSS.*

**(i)** A vessel engaged in fishing shall not impede the passage of any vessel following a traffic lane.

*A fishing boat is required to avoid impeding the passage of any vessel* ***following*** *a traffic lane, but it does not specify the action to be taken by a fishing vessel that encounters a crossing vessel. In this case, the normal steering and sailing rules apply.*

**(j)** A vessel of less than 20m in length or a sailing vessel shall not impede the safe passage of a power-driven vessel following a traffic lane.

*This Rule is of particular importance to smaller craft whether under power or sail. It requires vessels of less than 20m and all sailing vessels to 'avoid impeding the safe passage of a power-driven vessel following a traffic lane'. Action must be taken before a risk of collision develops to allow the power-driven vessel sufficient sea room for her safe navigation. Her navigation should not be hindered or obstructed.*

*If the power-driven vessel in the lane determines that a risk of collision does exist, she should sound at least five short blasts on her whistle. The smaller craft is still not relieved of her duty to avoid impeding the safe passage of the other vessel, and should take whatever action is necessary to avoid a collision under the steering and sailing Rules, such as slowing down, stopping, going astern or altering course away from the danger. The power-driven vessel now becomes either the give-way or stand-on vessel and is required to take action under Rule 16 or 17, as appropriate to avoid a collision. The skipper of a vessel under 20m contravening this Rule could incur a penalty for impeding a vessel using the lane.*

**(k)** A vessel restricted in her ability to manoeuvre when engaged in an operation for the maintenance of safety of navigation in a traffic separation scheme is exempted from complying with this Rule to the extent necessary to carry out the operation.

**(l)** A vessel restricted in her ability to manoeuvre when engaged in an operation for the laying, servicing or picking up of a submarine cable, within a traffic separation scheme, is exempted from complying with this Rule to the extent necessary to carry out the operation.

*These last two parts of Rule 10 allow vessels that are restricted in their ability to manoeuvre (RAM [or RIATM]) to carry out maintenance on buoys for the safety of navigation or to lay, recover or service underwater cables in a TSS without regard to Rule 10. It is not uncommon to see these types of operations being performed and mariners normally receive advance notice in* Notices to Mariners *and regular local radio warnings whilst the work is being carried out. This relaxation does not however apply to all RAM (OR RIATM) activities. Other RAM (OR RIATM) activities may sometimes be in progress under a localised rule rather than an International one.*

## Section II – Conduct of vessels in sight of one another

### RULE 11

*Application*

Rules in this section apply to vessels in sight of one another.

*The Rules in Section II apply only to vessels in sight of each other. They do not apply to vessels that are unable to see each other; see Section 3, Rule 19. If a vessel is initially detected by radar alone, Rule 19 applies, however if visual contact is subsequently established, vessels must then comply with the Rules of Section II. It is essential that a good visual look-out is maintained in restricted visibility as the Rules change from Section III to Section II if another vessel becomes visible.*

### RULE 12

*Sailing vessels*

**(a)** When two sailing vessels are approaching one another, so as to involve risk of collision, one of them shall keep out of the way of the other as follows:

(i) when each has the wind on a different side, the vessel which has the wind on the port side shall keep out of the way of the other;

(ii) when both have the wind on the same side, the vessel which is to windward shall keep out of the way of the vessel which is to leeward;

*This Rule is often summarised as 'port tack keeps out of the way of starboard tack', and when they both have the wind on the same side, the windward boat keeps out of the way of the leeward boat. It is important to appreciate that when sailing vessels are racing they must still comply with the COLREGS when they are in a risk of collision with another vessel that is not involved in the race.*

*It is frequently difficult to determine on which side a vessel to windward has the wind especially at night. When this situation arises, a boat with the wind on her port side should assume that she should keep clear.*

*Part 2, Section A of the ISAF international yacht racing rules actually defines one boat as having the* ***'right of way'*** *over another. I always thought that the only person with a legal right of way was a pedestrian on a pedestrian crossing (other than in France, Spain, Italy and Greece in my personal experience!)*

***However, it is very important to note that this is not the case in the international COLREGS. Nowhere is the expression 'RIGHT OF WAY' used and all vessels must take whatever action is deemed necessary to prevent a collision.***

**(b)** For the purposes of this Rule the windward side shall be deemed to be the side opposite to that on which the mainsail is carried or, in the case of a square-rigged vessel, the side opposite to that on which the largest fore-and-aft sail is carried.

*In order to determine which tack a vessel is on, note should be made of the position of her mainsail or in the case of a square-rigger, the position of the largest fore-and-aft sail.*

*Don't forget that when a sailing boat is overtaking another vessel, she must keep clear of the vessel being overtaken, regardless of its type.*

## RULE 13

### *Overtaking*

(a) Notwithstanding anything contained in the Rules of Part B, Sections I and II, any vessel overtaking any other shall keep out of the way of the vessel being overtaken.

***Any** vessel overtaking another vessel shall keep out of the way of the vessel being overtaken. It is important to note that this Rule is in Section II and therefore only applies to vessels in sight of one another; it does not apply to vessels that are detected by radar alone, ie with no visual contact.*

*There is, however, something of an anomaly in that 'not under command' vessels (NUC) and vessels 'restricted in ability to manoeuvre' (RAM [or RIATM]) are also required to keep out of the way of any vessel they are overtaking. However, Rule 3(f) and (g) states that such vessels are 'unable to keep out of the way of another vessel.' The official answer indicates that the overtaking vessel should be able to take some form of avoiding action even if it is to slow down. A vessel being overtaken in this situation should navigate with extreme caution and be prepared to take avoiding action if necessary. This does emphasise the necessity to keep an **all-round** look-out.*

(b) A vessel shall be deemed to be overtaking when coming up with another vessel from a direction more than 22½° abaft her beam, that is, in such a position with reference to the vessel she is overtaking, that at night she would be able to see only the stern light of that vessel but neither of her sidelights.

*To be an overtaking vessel, a vessel must be closing on another from a direction more than 22½° abaft the beam of the overtaken vessel. Side and steaming lights should not be visible at night from this sector. Only the stern light can be seen if the navigation lights are properly screened. The definition used to refer to 'two points abaft the beam', a compass point being 11¼° (32 points on a 360° compass rose), hence 'two points' being translated into the current equivalent of 22½°.*

(c) When a vessel is in any doubt as to whether she is overtaking another, she shall assume that this is the case and act accordingly.

*It is often difficult in daylight for a vessel to determine whether she is within the overtaking arc (135°) of another vessel. If she is in any doubt, she should assume that she is the overtaking vessel and keep clear. At night the situation can more easily be resolved by observing the other vessel's navigation lights, but once again if there is any doubt a vessel should assume she is overtaking and keep clear.*

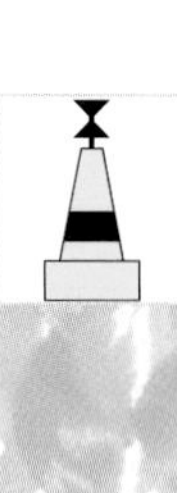



(d) Any subsequent alteration of the bearing between the two vessels shall not make the overtaking vessel a crossing vessel within the meaning of these Rules or relieve her of the duty of keeping clear of the overtaken vessel until she is finally past and clear.

*The vessel being overtaken is in a privileged position within the context of the COLREGS. The overtaking vessel must keep clear until she is* ***finally past and clear.*** *In a narrow channel where a vessel has signalled her agreement to be overtaken, and has actually pulled over and reduced speed, the overtaking vessel still carries this full responsibility to keep clear.*

**TOP TIP**

*The Overtaking Rule (Rule 13) does not apply in restricted visibility when vessels are not in visual contact with one another.*

## RULE 14

### *Head-on situation*

(a) When two power-driven vessels are meeting on reciprocal or nearly reciprocal courses so as to involve risk of collision each shall alter her course to starboard so that each shall pass on the port side of the other.

*This Rule applies* ***only to power-driven*** *vessels meeting head-on. It is the only Rule that actually tells each vessel which way to alter course, namely to starboard. It is important to make a positive alteration in ample time.*

(b) Such a situation shall be deemed to exist when a vessel sees the other ahead or nearly ahead and by night she would see the mast head lights of the other in a line or nearly in a line and/or both sidelights and by day she observes the corresponding aspect of the other vessel.

(c) When a vessel is in any doubt as to whether such a situation exists she shall assume that it does exist and act accordingly.

*By day a head-on situation can be recognised from the other vessel's aspect and by night the visibility of both sidelights. It is often difficult, say, due to yawing, to ascertain exactly whether another vessel is head-on, in which case it must be assumed that it is and alter course accordingly. This situation may be difficult at night with smaller vessels with a single masthead light (<50m) and poor sidelight screening.*

## RULE 15

### *Crossing situation*

When two power-driven vessels are crossing so as to involve risk of collision, the vessel which has the other on her own starboard side shall keep out of the way and shall, if the circumstances of the case admit, avoid crossing ahead of the other vessel.

*Like Rule 14, this Rule **only refers to power-driven** vessels and since the Rule advises against crossing ahead of another power driven vessel on her own starboard side (this is in the arc of the starboard navigation light 112½°), the best course of action is to alter course to starboard to show the other vessel a change of aspect and pass under her stern. At night the stand-on vessel must be able to see a change in the colour of the sidelights of the give-way vessel, thus giving a positive indication of her action.*

## RULE 16

### *Action by give-way vessel*

Every vessel which is directed to keep out of the way of another vessel shall, so far as possible, take early and substantial action to keep well clear.

*'Early and substantial' are important words to remember. If you are required to take action to avoid another vessel, it should be early and substantial, obvious and if necessary reinforced by a manoeuvring signal and supplemented by an all round white manoeuvring light.*

## RULE 17

### *Action by stand-on vessel*

(a) (i) Where one of two vessels is to keep out of the way the other shall keep her course and speed.

*When a risk of collision exists between two vessels and one vessel is required to give way to the other, the stand-on vessel, shall maintain her course and speed. This Rule applies to vessels that are in sight of one another, and does not apply in restricted visibility. **There is no such thing as a stand-on vessel in restricted visibility**; see Rule 19.*

(ii) The latter vessel may, however, take action to avoid collision by her manoeuvre alone, as soon as it becomes apparent to her that the vessel required to keep out of the way is not taking appropriate action in compliance with these Rules.

*When it becomes apparent that the give-way vessel is not taking appropriate action, the stand-on vessel **may** take action to avoid a collision, and is then relieved of her duty to stand-on. When in doubt as to the other vessel's intentions, the stand-on vessel should initially sound five or more short and rapid blasts, (the 'wake up' signal) augmented by a white all-round manoeuvring light at the masthead and take action so as not to prevent the other vessel taking action herself under these Rules.*

(b) When, from any cause, the vessel required to keep her course and speed finds herself so close that collision cannot be avoided by the action of the give-way vessel alone, she shall take such action as will best aid to avoid collision.

*A situation should never be allowed to deteriorate to the extent that a collision is imminent, however, if it appears that collision cannot be avoided by the action of the give-way vessel alone, the stand-on vessel* **must** *now take whatever action she considers necessary. This* **might** *justify an alteration of course to port for a power-driven vessel on the port bow, if an alteration to starboard would offer the port side of one's own vessel to a beam-on collision. It may be preferable to meet another vessel end-on rather than beam-on. This will minimise the target area and might result in a glancing blow rather than a 90° 'T' bone. It is impossible to lay down hard and fast rules in this situation, but it is worth remembering that decisions made under pressure, may have to be justified at a later date.*

*Smaller power-driven vessels have huge astern power and in most circumstances can avoid a collision by going full astern to stop.*

**(c)** A power-driven vessel which takes action in a crossing situation in accordance with sub-paragraph (a)(ii) of this Rule to avoid collision with another power-driven vessel shall, if the circumstances of the case admit, not alter course to port for a vessel on her own port side.

*This Rule refers only to power-driven vessels in a crossing situation within the meaning of Rule 15. Having given at least five short and rapid blasts augmented by a white all-round manoeuvring light at the masthead, the stand-on vessel should allow the give-way vessel time to react to the warning signal. It is mandatory to sound this signal when in doubt as to another vessel's intentions; see Rule 34(d). She may then take action as follows:*

*1 Slow down*
*2 Stop*
*3 Reverse*
*4 Alter to starboard*

*She should not at this stage consider an alteration to port as this would preclude the give-way vessel taking the action appropriate for her.*

**(d)** This Rule does not relieve the give-way vessel of her obligation to keep out of the way.

*The give-way vessel cannot escape her responsibility to keep out of the way by waiting for the stand-on vessel to take avoiding action. It is unusual for either vessel to be totally exonerated from all blame in the event of a collision.*

## RULE 18

### *Responsibilities between vessels*

Except where Rules 9, 10 and 13 otherwise require:

*The requirements of Rule 9 (Narrow Channels), Rule 10 (Traffic Separation Schemes) and Rule 13 (Overtaking) must be complied with in interpreting Rule 18.*

**(a)** A power-driven vessel underway shall keep out of the way of:
(i) a vessel not under command;
(ii) a vessel restricted in her ability to manoeuvre;
(iii) a vessel engaged in fishing;
(iv) a sailing vessel.

**(b)** A sailing vessel underway shall keep out of the way of:
(i) a vessel not under command;
(ii) a vessel restricted in her ability to manoeuvre;
(iii) a vessel engaged in fishing.

**(c)** A vessel engaged in fishing when underway shall, so far as possible, keep out of the way of:
(i) a vessel not under command;
(ii) a vessel restricted in her ability to manoeuvre.

*Rule 18(a), (b) and (c) define what may be considered as priorities between various types of vessels meeting so as to involve risk of collision, a sort of 'pecking order'. The Rule defines who gives way to whom. The pecking order is as follows:*

- *(Vessel at anchor)*
- *(Sea plane or WIG craft on the water)*
- *Power-driven vessel*
- *Sailing vessel*
- *Fishing vessel*
- *RAM (or RIATM) and NUC*

*Note that no differentiation is made between RAM (or RIATM) and NUC. If they encounter each other, each should endeavour to keep clear of the other. This is often misunderstood with many thinking that NUC is superior to RAM (or RIATM). This is not the case and each is required to do her best to keep clear of the other.*

**(d)** (i) Any vessel other than a vessel not under command or a vessel restricted in her ability to manoeuvre shall, if the circumstances of the case admit, avoid impeding the safe passage of a vessel constrained by her draught, exhibiting the signals in Rule 28.
(ii) A vessel constrained by her draught shall navigate with particular caution having full regard to her special condition.

*A vessel constrained by draught (CBD) is mentioned but only in the context of not being impeded. The impede Rule is often misunderstood. A vessel that is not to impede, should take action not to impede before a risk of collision develops. If the CBD vessel considers that she is being impeded and a risk of collision is developing, she should sound at least five short and rapid blasts augmented by a white all-round manoeuvring light at the masthead. She is now required to comply with either Rule 16 or Rule 17 as the give-way or stand-on vessel. The other vessel is never relieved of her obligation to avoid impeding the safe passage of the vessel constrained by draught and should take whatever action is appropriate under the Rules by altering course, slowing down or stopping. A vessel constrained by her draught can only ever be a power-driven vessel within the meaning of these Rules.*

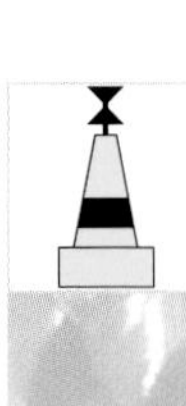



**(e)** A sea plane on the water shall, in general, keep well clear of all vessels and avoid impeding their navigation. In circumstances, however, where risk of collision exists, she shall comply with the Rules of this Part.

*Sea planes on the water are to keep clear of all vessels. Landing and take-off areas are allocated for sea plane operation and other vessels should keep well clear.*

**(f)** (i) A WIG craft, when taking off, landing and in flight near the surface, shall keep well clear of all other vessels and avoid impeding their navigation;

*WIG craft (Wing-in-Ground) on the water are to keep clear of all vessels. In the future, landing and take-off areas will be allocated for WIG craft operation and other vessels should keep well clear.*

(ii) A WIG craft operating on the water surface shall comply with the Rules of this Part as a power driven vessel.

*WIG craft that are afloat are to be treated as power-driven craft.*

## Section III – Conduct of vessels in restricted visibility

### RULE 19

*Conduct of vessels in restricted visibility*

**(a)** This Rule applies to vessels not in sight of one another when navigating in or near an area of restricted visibility.

*This Rule applies to vessels not in visual sight of one another, and in this case, none of the Rules of Section II apply. This Rule must also be complied with when navigating near an area of restricted visibility, for example in patchy fog.*

**(b)** Every vessel shall proceed at a safe speed adapted to the prevailing circumstances and condition of restricted visibility. A power-driven vessel shall have her engines ready for immediate manoeuvre.

*Safe speed is defined in Rule 6. At one time a safe speed was proposed as a speed at which a vessel could be stopped in half the visible distance. In dense fog this went on to imply that the vessels in thick fog should be stopped. With the advent of operational radar, this criterion no longer applies.*

*Power-driven vessels shall have their engines ready for immediate manoeuvre.*

*Most highly manoeuvrable small vessels can stop within a ship's length or so if necessary and this might be considered a 'safe' speed under most circumstances of restricted visibility. One consideration usually forgotten in determining a safe speed in small vessels is the noise generated by their engines and their reduced ability to detect*

*the sound signals of other vessels over the top of this noise.*

*An auxiliary sailing vessel should consider starting her engine so that she is more manoeuvrable or at the very least have it ready to start in an emergency.*

**(c)** Every vessel shall have due regard to the prevailing circumstances and conditions of restricted visibility when complying with the Rules of Section I of this Part.

*This paragraph draws attention to the fact that the Rules of Section I still apply and that, in complying with them, due regard shall be taken of the conditions imposed by restricted visibility. In a narrow channel, a small vessel might be well advised to navigate in shallow water in order to avoid getting into close-quarter situations with larger vessels.*

**(d)** A vessel which detects by radar alone the presence of another vessel shall determine if a close-quarters situation is developing and/or risk of collision exists. If so, she shall take avoiding action in ample time, provided that when such action consists of an alteration of course, so far as possible the following shall be avoided:

*The implications of this paragraph are best appreciated with the benefit of some knowledge of radar plotting.*

*If a vessel is detected by radar alone, ie with no visual sighting, the radar observer is required to ascertain by means of a paper radar plot or an automatic radar plotting aid (ARPA) or a mini automatic radar plotting aid (MARPA) whether a close-quarters situation and risk of collision exists. A close-quarters situation is not always easy to define as much depends on the circumstances such as the state of visibility, the vessels involved, the quality of the radar equipment and the experience of the operator. It is important to ensure that, if the option exists, the radar should be 'sea stabilised' and NOT 'ground stabilised' when using radar for aspect recognition upon which the COLREGS are to be interpreted.*

*Rule 19 requires that if a radar contact is deemed to pose a risk of collision, avoiding action shall be taken in ample time. Note that the vessel is not given an option; Rule 19 states that she shall take avoiding action.*

**TOP TIP**

*There is no such thing as a stand-on vessel in restricted visibility. Everyone has to take appropriate action.*

(i) an alteration of course to port for a vessel forward of the beam, other than for a vessel being overtaken;

*In taking avoiding action, as far as possible a vessel should avoid altering her course to port for a vessel forward of her beam, other than for a vessel being overtaken. This poses a potential problem. With a relative motion radar image, which most vessels use, it is not easy to determine whether you are overtaking as the radar information you see is in relative motion. If you are lucky enough to have an ARPA or MARPA this may assist but care needs to be taken to understand the limitations of ARPA and MARPA, particularly recognising the differences between true and relative vectors and perhaps more importantly the differences of 'sea' and 'ground' stabilisation of the image and the*

*misleading information which can be construed by the inexperienced.*

*It is important to remember that the requirements of Rule 13 (Overtaking) are not relevant in restricted visibility.*

**TOP TIP**

*If you have a radar contact that appears to be overtaking you, you are still required to take avoiding action. The overtaking Rule (13) does not apply in restricted visibility.*

(ii) an alteration of course towards a vessel abeam or abaft the beam.

*As far as possible you should avoid altering course towards a vessel that is abeam or abaft the beam.*

*As ARPA (and MARPA) are becoming more common on commercial yachts, it should be understood that small and frequent alterations by vessels in restricted visibility add confusion to information given by automatic plotting equipment. Therefore it is recommended that alterations in heading or changes in speed are made boldly and as infrequently as possible.*

**(e)** Except where it has been determined that a risk of collision does not exist, every vessel which hears apparently forward of her beam the fog signal of another vessel, or which cannot avoid a close-quarters situation with another vessel forward of her beam, shall reduce her speed to the minimum at which she can be kept on her course. She shall if necessary take all her way off and in any event navigate with extreme caution until danger of collision is over.

*When a vessel hears a fog signal of another vessel apparently forward of the beam, she is required to reduce to minimum steerageway, and if necessary take all way off. This assumes that in spite of any prior action that may have been taken to avoid a close-quarters situation she is now too close to carry on at the present speed and too close to consider a course alteration.*

*In a pilotage situation, it is often determined from a radar plot that a contact forward of the beam will pass relatively close but even so, no risk of collision should exist. In this situation a vessel should continue to proceed with extreme caution.*

*If another power-driven vessel in the vicinity sounds two prolonged blasts, this indicates that she is stopped in the water. In which case the safest course of action is to turn away from her. Only return to your initial heading once the fog signal has drawn clear or is no longer heard. It is very easy to fall into the trap of associating a sound signal with a particular radar contact. This is a dangerous practice and would be viewed as scanty information.*

*Avoid making any attempt to contact the other vessel by VHF; see MGN 167(M+F).*

*It is worth noting that although power-driven vessels have a different sound signal for making way and stopped, all hampered vessels (sailing, fishing, CBD, RAM [or RIATM] and NUC) do not change their fog signal when they stop making way.*

**TOP TIP**

*Do not make any manoeuvring signal to indicate that you are altering course in restricted visibility as these should only be used by power-driven vessels in sight of other vessels.*

# Part C: Lights and Shapes

## RULE 20

### *Application*

**(a)** Rules in this Part shall be complied with in all weathers.

**(b)** The Rules concerning lights shall be complied with from sunset to sunrise and during such times no other lights shall be exhibited, except such lights as cannot be mistaken for the lights specified in these Rules or do not impair their visibility or distinctive character, or interfere with the keeping of a proper look-out.

**(c)** The lights prescribed by these Rules shall, if carried, also be exhibited from sunrise to sunset in restricted visibility and may be exhibited in all other circumstances when it is deemed necessary.

**(d)** The Rules concerning shapes shall be complied with by day.

**(e)** The lights and shapes specified in these Rules shall comply with the provisions of Annex I to these Regulations.

## RULE 21

### *Definitions*

**(a)** 'Masthead light' means a white light placed over the fore-and-aft centreline of the vessel showing an unbroken light over an arc of the horizon of 225° and so fixed as to show the light from right ahead to $22\frac{1}{2}$° abaft the beam on either side of the vessel.

**(b)** 'Sidelights' means a green light on the starboard side and a red light on the port side each showing an unbroken light over an arc of the horizon of $112\frac{1}{2}$° and so fixed as to show the light from the right ahead to $22\frac{1}{2}$° abaft the beam on its respective side. In a vessel of less than 20m in length the sidelights may be combined in one lantern carried on the fore-and-aft centreline of the vessel.

**(c)** 'Stern light' means a white light placed as nearly as practicable at the stern showing an unbroken light over an arc of the horizon of 135° and so fixed as to show the light $67\frac{1}{2}$° from right aft on each side of the vessel.

**(d)** 'Towing light' means a yellow light having the same characteristics as the 'stern light' defined in paragraph (c) of this Rule.

**(e)** 'All round light' means a light showing an unbroken light over an arc of the horizon of 360°.

**(f)** 'Flashing light' means a light flashing at regular intervals at a frequency of 120 flashes or more per minute.

## RULE 22

### *Visibility of lights*

The lights prescribed in these Rules shall have an intensity as specified in Section 8 of Annex I to these Regulations so as to be visible at the following minimum ranges:

**(a)** In vessels of 50m or more in length:
- a masthead light . . . . . . . . 6 miles
- a side light . . . . . . . . 3 miles
- a stern light . . . . . . . . 3 miles
- a towing light . . . . . . . . 3 miles
- a white, red, green or yellow all-round light . . . . . . . . 3 miles.

**(b)** In vessels of 12m or more in length but less than 50m in length:
- a masthead light . . . . . . . . 5 miles
  (except that where the length of the vessel is less than 20m) . . . . . . . . 3 miles
- a sidelight . . . . . . . . 2 miles
- a stern light . . . . . . . . 2 miles
- a towing light . . . . . . . . 2 miles
- a white, red, green or yellow all-round light . . . . . . . . 2 miles.

**(c)** In vessels of less than 12m in length:
- a masthead light . . . . . . . . 2 miles
- a sidelight . . . . . . . . 1 mile
- a stern light . . . . . . . . 2 miles
- a towing light . . . . . . . . 2 miles
- a white, red, green or yellow all-round light . . . . . . . . 2 miles.

**(d)** In inconspicuous, partly submerged vessels or objects being towed:
- a white all round light . . . . . . . . 3 miles.

## RULE 23

### *Power-driven vessels underway*

**(a)** A power-driven vessel underway shall exhibit:
(i) a masthead light forward;
(ii) a second masthead light abaft of and higher than the forward one; except that a vessel of less than 50m in length shall not be obliged to exhibit such light by may do so;
(iii) sidelights;
(iv) a stern light.

**(b)** An air-cushion vessel when operating in the non-displacement mode shall, in addition to the light prescribed in paragraph (a) of this Rule, exhibit an all-round flashing yellow light.

(i) a power-driven vessel of less than 12m in length may in lieu of the lights prescribed in paragraph (a) of this Rule exhibit an all-round white light and sidelights;

(ii) a power-driven vessel of less than 7m in length whose maximum speed does not exceed 7 knots may in lieu of the lights prescribed in paragraph (a) of this Rule exhibit an all-round white light and shall, if practicable, also exhibit sidelights;

(iii) the masthead light or all-round white light on a power-driven vessel of less than 12m in length may be displaced from the fore-and-aft centreline of the vessel if centreline fitting is not practicable, provided that the sidelights are combined in one lantern which shall be carried on the fore-and-aft centreline of the vessel or located as nearly as practicable in the same fore-and-aft line as the masthead light or the all-round white light.

**(c)** A WIG craft only when taking off, landing and in flight near the surface shall, in addition to the lights prescribed in paragraph (a) of this Rule, exhibit a high-intensity all-round flashing red light.

## RULE 24

### *Towing and pushing*

**(a)** A power-driven vessel when towing shall exhibit:

(i) instead of the light prescribed in Rule 23(a)(i) or (a)(ii), two masthead lights in a vertical line. When the length of the tow, measuring from the stern of the towing vessel to the aft end of the tow exceeds 200m, three such lights in a vertical line;

(ii) sidelights;

(iii) a stern light;

(iv) a towing light in a vertical line above the stern light;

(v) when the length of the tow exceeds 200m, a diamond shape where it can best be seen.

**(b)** When a pushing vessel and a vessel being pushed ahead are rigidly connected in a composite unit they shall be regarded as a power-driven vessel and exhibit the lights prescribed in Rule 23.

**(c)** A power-driven vessel when pushing ahead or towing alongside, except in the case of a composite unit, shall exhibit:

(i) instead of the light prescribed in Rule 23(a)(i) or (a)(ii), two masthead lights in a vertical line;

(ii) sidelights;

(iii) a stern light.

**(d)** A power-driven vessel to which paragraph (a) or (c) of this Rule applies shall also comply with Rule 23(a)(ii).

**(e)** A vessel or object being towed, other than those mentioned in paragraph (g) of this Rule, shall exhibit:

(i) sidelights;

(ii) a stern light

(iii) when the length of the tow exceeds 200m, a diamond shape where it can best be seen.

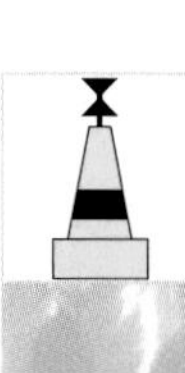



**(f)** Provided that any number of vessels being towed alongside or pushed in a group shall be lighted as one vessel,
(i) a vessel being pushed ahead, not being part of a composite unit, shall exhibit at the forward end sidelights;
(ii) a vessel being towed alongside shall exhibit a stern light and at the forward end, sidelights.

**(g)** An inconspicuous, partly-submerged vessel or object, or combination of such vessel or objects being towed, shall exhibit:
(i) if it is less than 25m in breadth, one all-round white light at or near the forward end and one at or near the after end except that dracones need not exhibit a light at or near the forward end;
(ii) if it is 25m or more in breadth, two additional all-round white lights at or near the extremities of its breadth;
(iii) if it exceeds 100m in length, additional all-round white lights between the lights prescribed in sub-paragraph (i) and (ii) so that the distance between the lights shall not exceed 100m;
(iv) a diamond shape at or near the aftermost extremity of the last vessel or object being towed and if the length of the tow exceeds 200m, an additional diamond shape where it can best be seen and located as far forward as is practicable.

**(h)** Where from any sufficient cause it is impracticable for a vessel or object towed to exhibit the lights or shapes prescribed in paragraph (e) of (g) of this Rule, all possible measures shall be taken to light the vessel or object towed or at least to indicate the presence of such vessel or object.

**(i)** Where from any sufficient cause it is impracticable for a vessel not normally engaged in towing operations to display the lights prescribed in paragraph (a) or (c) of this Rule, such vessel shall not be required to exhibit those lights when engaged in towing another vessel in distress or otherwise in need of assistance. All possible measures shall be taken to indicate the nature of the relationship between the towing vessel and the vessel being towed as authorised by Rule 36; in particular by illuminating the towline.

## RULE 25

### *Sailing vessels underway and vessels under oars*

**(a)** A sailing vessel underway shall exhibit:
(i) sidelights;
(ii) a stern light.

**(b)** In a sailing vessel of less than 20m in length the lights prescribed in paragraph (a) of this Rule may be combined in one lantern carried at or near the top of the mast where it can best be seen.

**(c)** A sailing vessel underway may, in addition to the lights prescribed in paragraph (a) of this Rule, exhibit at or near the top of the mast, where they can best be seen, two all-round lights in a vertical line, the upper being red and the lower green, but these lights shall not be exhibited in conjunction with the combined lantern permitted by paragraph (b) of this Rule.

**(d)** (i) A sailing vessel of less than 7m in length shall, if practicable, exhibit the lights prescribed in paragraph (a) or (b) of this Rule, but if she does not, she shall have ready at hand an electric torch or lighted lantern showing a white light which shall be exhibited in sufficient time to prevent collision.
(ii) A vessel under oars may exhibit the lights prescribed in this Rule for sailing vessels, but if she does not, she shall have ready at hand an electric torch or lighted lantern showing a white light which shall be exhibited in sufficient time to prevent collision.

**(e)** A vessel proceeding under sail when also being propelled by machinery shall exhibit forward, where it can best be seen, a conical shape, apex downwards.

## RULE 26

### *Fishing vessels*

**(a)** A vessel engaged in fishing, whether underway or at anchor, shall exhibit only the lights and shapes prescribed in this Rule.

**(b)** A vessel when engaged in trawling, by which is meant the dragging through the water of a dredge net or other apparatus used as a fishing appliance, shall exhibit:
(i) two all-round lights in a vertical line, the upper being green and the lower white, or a shape consisting of two cones with their apexes together in a vertical line one above the other;
(ii) a masthead light abaft of and higher than the all-round green light; a vessel of less than 50m in length shall not be obliged to exhibit such a light but may do so;
(iii) when making way through the water, in addition to the lights prescribed in this paragraph, sidelights and a stern light.

**(c)** A vessel engaged in fishing, other than trawling, shall exhibit:
(i) two all-round lights in a vertical line, the upper being red and the lower white, or a shape consisting of two cones with apexes together in a vertical line one above the other;
(ii) when there is outlying gear extending more than 150m horizontally from the vessel, an all-round white light or a cone apex upwards in the direction of the gear;
(iii) when making way through the water, in addition to the lights prescribed in this paragraph sidelights and a stern light.

**(d)** The additional signals described in Annex II to these Regulations, apply to a vessel engaged in fishing in close proximity to other vessel engaged in fishing.

**(e)** A vessel when not engaged in fishing shall not exhibit the lights or shapes prescribed in this Rule, but only those prescribed for a vessel of her length.

**TOP TIP**

*Fishing vessels other than trawlers do NOT show a steaming light in addition to their red/white fishing lights even if they are over 50m in length whereas a trawler does!*

## RULE 27

### *Vessels not under command or restricted in their ability to manoeuvre*

**(a)** A vessel not under command shall exhibit:
(i) two all-round red lights in a vertical line where they can best be seen;
(ii) two balls or similar shape in a vertical line where they can best be seen;
(iii) when making way through the water, in addition to the lights prescribed in this paragraph sidelights and a stern light.

**(b)** A vessel restricted in her ability to manoeuvre, except a vessel engaged in mine-clearance operations, shall exhibit:
(i) three all-round lights in a vertical line where they can best be seen. The highest and lowest of these lights shall be red and the middle light shall be white.
(ii) three shapes in a vertical line where they can best be seen. The highest and lowest of these shapes shall be balls and the middle one a diamond;
(iii) when making way through the water, a masthead light or lights, sidelights and a stern light, in addition to the lights prescribed in sub-paragraph (i);
(iv) when at anchor, in addition to the lights or shapes prescribed in sub-paragraph (i) and (ii), the light, lights or shape prescribed in Rule 30.

**(c)** A power-driven vessel engaged in a towing operation such as to severely restrict the towing vessel and her tow in their ability to deviate from their course shall, in addition to the lights or shapes prescribed in Rule 24 (a), exhibit the lights or shapes prescribed in sub-paragraphs (b)(i) and (ii) of this Rule.

**(d)** A vessel engaged in dredging or underwater operations, when restricted in her ability to manoeuvre, shall exhibit the lights and shapes prescribed in sub-paragraphs (b)(i), (ii) and (iii) of this Rule and shall in addition, when an obstruction exists, exhibit:
(i) two all-round red lights or two balls in a vertical line to indicate the side on which the obstruction exists;
(ii) two all-round green lights or two diamonds in a vertical line to indicate the side on which another vessel may pass;
(iii) when at anchor, the lights or shapes prescribed in this paragraph instead of the lights or shape prescribed in Rule 30.

**(e)** Whenever the size of a vessel engaged in diving operations makes it impracticable to exhibit all lights and shapes prescribed in paragraph (d) of this Rule, the following shall be exhibited:
(i) three all-round lights in a vertical line where they can best be seen. The highest and lowest of these lights shall be red and the middle light shall be white;

**TOP TIP**

*A towing tug that is restricted in her ability to manoeuvre (RAM or RIATM) does not turn off any lights if she stops in the water, as do other RAM (or RIATM) vessels.*

**TOP TIP**

*Pass on the diamonds' side (diamonds are forever), don't pass on the balls' side otherwise it's a balls-up!*

(ii) a rigid replica of the International Code flag 'A' not less than 1m in height. Measures shall be taken to ensure its all-round visibility.

**(f)** A vessel engaged in mine-clearance operations shall in addition to the lights prescribed for a power-driven vessel in Rule 23 or the lights or shape prescribed for a vessel at anchor in Rule 30 as appropriate, exhibit three all-round green lights or three balls. One of these lights or shapes shall be exhibited near the foremast head and one at each end of the fore yard. These lights or shapes indicate that it is dangerous for another vessel to approach within 1000m of the mine-clearance vessel.

**(g)** Vessels of less than 12m in length, except those engaged in diving operations, shall not be required to exhibit the lights and shapes prescribed in this Rule.

**(h)** The signals prescribed in this Rule are not signals of vessels in distress and requiring assistance. Such signals are contained in Annex IV to these Regulations.

## RULE 28

### *Vessels constrained by their draught*

A vessel constrained by her draught may, in addition to the lights prescribed for power-driven vessels in Rule 23, exhibit where they can best be seen three all-round red lights in a vertical line, or a cylinder.

**TOP TIP**

*Whilst the three vertical red lights are very conspicuous, the cylinder is extremely difficult to see, even with binoculars.*

## RULE 29

### *Pilot vessels*

**(a)** A vessel engaged on pilotage duty shall exhibit:
(i) at or near the masthead, two all-round lights in a vertical line, the upper being white and the lower red;
(ii) when underway, in addition, sidelights and a starlight.
(iii) when at anchor, in addition to the lights prescribed in sub-paragraph (i), the light, lights or shape prescribed in Rule 30 for vessels at anchor.

**(b)** A pilot vessel when not engaged in pilotage duty shall exhibit the lights or shapes prescribed for a similar vessel of her length.

## RULE 30

### *Anchored vessels and vessels aground*

**(a)** A vessel at anchor shall exhibit where it can best be seen:
(i) in the fore part, an all-round white light or one ball;

(ii) at or near the stern and at a lower level than the light prescribed in sub-paragraph (i), an all-round white light.

**(b)** A vessel of less than 50m in length may exhibit an all-round white light where it can best be seen instead of the lights prescribed in paragraph (a) of this Rule.

**(c)** A vessel at anchor may, and a vessel of 100m and more in length shall, also use the available working or equivalent lights to illuminate her decks.

**(d)** A vessel aground shall exhibit the lights prescribed in paragraph (a) or (b) of this Rule and in addition, where they can best be seen:
(i) two all-round red lights in a vertical line;
(ii) three balls in a vertical line.

**(e)** A vessel of less than 7m in length, when at anchor, not in or near a narrow channel, fairway or anchorage, or where other vessel normally navigate, shall not be required to exhibit the lights or shape prescribed in paragraph (a) and (b) of this Rule.

**(f)** A vessel of less than 12m in length, when aground, shall not be required to exhibit the lights or shapes prescribed in sub-paragraphs (d)(i) and (ii) of this Rule.

## RULE 31

### *Sea planes and WIG craft*

Where it is impracticable for a sea plane or a WIG craft to exhibit lights and shapes of the characteristics or in the positions prescribed in the Rules of this Part she shall exhibit lights and shapes as closely similar in characteristics and position as is possible.

# Part D: Sound and Light Signals

## RULE 32

### *Definitions*

**(a)** The word 'whistle' means any sound signalling appliance capable of producing the prescribed blasts and which complies with the specifications in Annex III to these Regulations.

**(b)** The term 'short blast' means a blast of about one second's duration.

**(c)** The term 'prolonged blast' means a blast of from four to six seconds duration.

## RULE 33

### *Equipment for sound signals*

**(a)** A vessel of 12m or more in length shall be provided with a whistle, a vessel of 20m or more in length shall be provided with a bell in addition to a whistle and a vessel of 100m or more in length shall, in addition, be provided with a gong, the tone and sound of which cannot be confused with that of the bell. The whistle, bell and gong shall comply with the specification in Annex III to these Regulations. The bell or gong or both may be replaced by other equipment having the same respective sound characteristics, provided that manual sounding of the prescribed signals shall always be possible.

**(b)** A vessel of less than 12m in length shall not be obliged to carry the sound signalling appliances prescribed in paragraph (a) of this Rule but if she does not, she shall be provided with some other means of making an efficient sound signal.

## RULE 34

### *Manoeuvring and warning signals*

**(a)** When vessels are in sight of one another, a power-driven vessel underway, when manoeuvring as authorised or required by these Rules, shall indicate that manoeuvre by the following signals on her whistle:

- one short blast to mean 'I am altering my course to starboard';
- two short blasts to mean 'I am altering my course to port';
- three short blasts to mean 'I am operating astern propulsion'.

*When manoeuvring under Section II of the Rules, the use of sound signals is mandatory by power-driven vessels. The sounding of the appropriate signal costs nothing but it may help to clarify a situation and will prove invaluable in any subsequent investigation!*

**(b)** Any vessel may supplement the whistle signals prescribed in paragraph (a) of this Rule by light signals, repeated as appropriate, whilst the manoeuvre is being carried out:

(i) these light signals shall have the following significance
- one flash to mean 'I am altering my course to starboard';
- two flashes to mean 'I am altering my course to port';
- three flashes to mean 'I am operating astern propulsion';

(ii) the duration of each flash shall be about one second, the interval between flashes shall be about one second, and the interval between successive signals shall be not less than ten seconds;

(iii) the light used for this signal shall, if fitted, be an all-round white light, visible at a minimum range of five miles, and shall comply with the provisions of Annex I to these Regulations.

**(c)** When in sight of one another in a narrow channel or fairway:

(i) a vessel intending to overtake another shall in compliance with Rule 9(e)(i) indicate her intention by the following signals on her whistle.
- two prolonged blasts followed by one short blast to mean 'I intend to overtake you on your starboard side';

- two prolonged blasts followed by two short blasts to mean 'I intend to overtake you on your port side'.

(ii) the vessel about to be overtaken when acting in accordance with Rule 9(e)(i) shall indicate her agreement by the following signal on her whistle:
- one prolonged, one short, one prolonged and one short blast, in that order.

**(d)** When vessels in sight of one another are approaching each other and either vessel fails to understand the intentions or actions of the other, or is in doubt whether sufficient action is being taken by the other to avoid collision, the vessel in doubt shall immediately indicate such doubt by giving at least five short and rapid blasts on the whistle. Such signals may be supplemented by a light signal of at least five short and rapid flashes.

**(e)** A vessel nearing a bend or an area of a channel or fairway where another vessel may be obscured by an intervening obstruction shall sound one prolonged blast. Such a signal shall be answered with a prolonged blast by any approaching vessel that may be within hearing around the bend or behind the intervening obstruction.

**(f)** If whistles are fitted on a vessel at a distance apart of more than 100m, one whistle only shall be used for giving manoeuvring and warning signals.

## RULE 35

### *Sound signals in restricted visibility*

In or near an area of restricted visibility, whether by day or night, the signals prescribed in this Rule shall be used as follows:

**(a)** A power-driven vessel making way through the water shall sound at intervals of not more than two minutes one prolonged blast.

**(b)** A power-driven vessel underway but stopped and making no way through the water shall sound at intervals of not more than two minutes two prolonged blasts in succession with an interval of about two seconds between them.

**(c)** A vessel not under command, a vessel restricted in her ability to manoeuvre, a vessel constrained by her draught, a sailing vessel, a vessel engaged in fishing and a vessel engaged in towing or pushing another vessel shall, instead of the signals prescribed in paragraphs (a) or (b) of this Rule, sound at intervals of not more than two minutes three blasts in succession, namely one prolonged followed by two short blasts.

**(d)** A vessel engaged in fishing, when at anchor, and a vessel restricted in her ability to manoeuvre when carrying out her work at anchor, shall instead of the signals prescribed in paragraph (g) of this Rule sound the signal prescribed in paragraph (c) of this Rule.

**(e)** A vessel towed, or if more than one vessel is towed, the last vessel of the tow, if manned, shall at intervals of not more than two minutes sound four blasts in succession, namely one

prolonged followed by three short blasts. When practicable, this signal shall be made immediately after the signal made by the towing vessel.

**(f)** When a pushing vessel and a vessel being pushed ahead are rigidly connected in a composite unit they shall be regarded as a power-driven vessel and shall give the signals prescribed in paragraphs (a) or (b) of this Rule.

**(g)** A vessel at anchor shall at intervals of not more than one minute ring the bell rapidly for about five seconds. In a vessel of 100m or more in length the bell shall be sounded in the forepart of the vessel and immediately after the ringing of the bell, the gong shall be sounded rapidly for about five seconds in the after part of the vessel. A vessel at anchor may, in addition, sound three blasts in succession, namely one short, one prolonged and one short blast, to give warning of her position and of the possibility of collision to an approaching vessel.

**(h)** A vessel aground shall give the bell signal and if required the gong signal prescribed in paragraph (g) of this Rule and shall, in addition, give three separate distinct strokes on the bell immediately before and after the rapid ringing of the bell. A vessel aground may in addition sound an appropriate whistle signal.

**TOP TIP**

*Although this rule doesn't indicate what sound signal would in fact be appropriate, try UNIFORM in Morse – 'you are heading into danger' – dit, dit, dah.*

**(i)** A vessel of 12m or more but less than 20m in length shall not be obliged to give the bell signals prescribed in paragraphs (g) and (h) of this Rule. However, if she does not, she shall make some other efficient sound signal at intervals of not more than two minutes.

**(j)** A vessel of less than 12m in length shall not be obliged to give the above-mentioned signals but, if she does not, shall make some other efficient sound signal at intervals of not more than two minutes.

**(k)** A pilot vessel when engaged on pilotage duty may in addition to the signals prescribed in paragraphs (a), (b) or (g) of this Rule sound an identity signal consisting of four short blasts.

## RULE 36

### *Signals to attract attention*

If necessary to attract the attention of another vessel, any vessel may make light or sound signals that cannot be mistaken for any signal authorised elsewhere in these Rules, or may direct the beam of her searchlight in the direction of the danger, in such a way as not to embarrass any vessel. Any light to attract the attention of another vessel shall be such that it cannot be mistaken for any aid to navigation. For the purpose of this Rule the use of high intensity intermittent or revolving lights, such as strobe lights, shall be avoided.

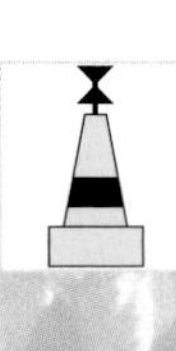



## RULE 37

### *Distress signals*

When a vessel is in distress and requires assistance she shall use or exhibit the signals described in Annex IV to these Regulations.

# Part : Exemptions

## RULE 38

### *Exemptions*

Any vessel (or class of vessels) provided that she complies with the requirements of the International Regulations for Preventing Collisions at Sea, 1972 (a), the keel of which is laid or which is at a corresponding stage of construction before the entry into force of these Regulations may be exempted from compliance therewith as follows:

**(a)** The installation of lights with ranges prescribed in Rule 22, until four years after the date of entry into force of these Regulations.

**(b)** The installation of lights with colour specification as prescribed in Section 7 of Annex I to these Regulations, until four years after the date of entry into force of these Regulations.

**(c)** The repositioning of lights as a result of conversion from Imperial to metric units and rounding off measurement figures, permanent exemption.

**(d)** (i) The repositioning of masthead lights on vessels of less than 150m in length, resulting from the prescriptions of Section 3(a) of Annex I to these Regulations, permanent exemption.

(ii) The repositioning of masthead lights on vessels of 150m or more in length, resulting from the prescriptions of Section 3(a) of Annex I to these Regulations, until nine years after the date of entry into force of these Regulations.

**(e)** The repositioning of masthead lights resulting from the prescriptions of Section 2(b) of Annex I to these Regulations, until nine years after the date of entry into force of these Regulations.

**(f)** The repositioning of sidelights resulting from the prescriptions of Section 2(g) and 3(b) of Annex I to these Regulations, until nine years after the date of entry into force of these Regulations.

**(g)** The requirements for sound signal appliances prescribed by Annex III to these Regulations, until nine years after the date of entry into force of these Regulations.

**(h)** The repositioning of all-round lights resulting from the prescription of Section 9(b) of Annex I to these Regulations, permanent exemption.

# Annex I

## Positioning and technical details of lights and shapes

### 1 Definition

The term 'height above the hull' means height above the uppermost continuous deck. This height shall be measured from the position vertically beneath the location of the light.

### 2 Vertical positioning and spacing of lights

**(a)** On a power-driven vessel of 20m or more in length the masthead lights shall be placed as follows:

(i) the forward masthead light, or if only one masthead light is carried, then the light, at a height above the hull of not less than 6m, and, if the breadth of the vessel exceeds 6m, then at a height above the hull not less than such breadth, so however that the light need not be placed at a greater height above the hull than 12m;

(ii) when two masthead lights are carried the after one shall be at least 4.5m vertically higher than the forward one.

**(b)** The vertical separation of the masthead lights of power-driven vessels shall be such that in all normal conditions of trim, the after light will be seen over, and separate from, the forward light at a distance of 1,000m from the stern when viewed from sea-level.

**(c)** The masthead light of a power-driven vessel of 12m but less than 20m in length shall be placed at a height above the gunwale of not less than 2.5m.

**(d)** A power-driven vessel of less than 12m in length may carry the uppermost light at a height of less than 2.5m above the gunwale. When however a masthead light is carried in addition to sidelights and a stern light or the all-round light prescribed in Rule 23(d)(i) is carried in addition to sidelights, then such masthead light or all-round light shall be carried at least 1m higher than the sidelights.

**(e)** One of the two or three masthead lights prescribed for a power-driven vessel when engaged in towing or pushing another vessel shall be placed in the same position as either the forward masthead light of the after masthead light; provided that, if carried on the after mast, the lowest after masthead light shall be at least 4.5m vertically higher than the forward masthead light.

**(f)** (i) The masthead light or lights prescribed in Rule 23(a) shall be so placed as to be above and clear of all other lights and obstructions except as described in sub-paragraph (ii).

(ii) When it is impracticable to carry the all-round lights prescribed by Rule 27(B)(i) or Rule 28 below the masthead lights, they may be carried above the after masthead light(s) or vertically in between the forward masthead light(s) and the after masthead light(s) provided that in the latter case the requirement of Section 3(c) of this Annex shall be complied with.

**(g)** The sidelights of a power-driven vessel shall be placed at a height above the hull not greater than three quarters of that of the forward masthead light. They shall not be so low as to be interfered with by deck lights.

**(h)** The sidelights, if in a combined lantern and carried on a power-driven vessel of less than 20m in length, shall be placed not less than 1m below the masthead light.

**(i)** When the Rules prescribe two or three lights to be carried in a vertical line, they shall be spaced as follows:

(i) on a vessel of 20m in length or more, such lights shall be spaced not less than 2m apart, and the lowest of these lights shall, except where a towing light is required, be placed at a height of not less then 4m above the hull;

(ii) on a vessel of less than 20m in length, such lights shall be spaced not less than 1m apart and the lowest of these lights shall, except where a towing light is required, be placed at a height of not less than 2m above the gunwale;

(iii) when the three lights are carried they shall be equally spaced.

**(j)** the lower of the two all-round lights prescribed for a vessel when engaged in fishing shall be at a height above the sidelights not less than twice the distance between the two vertical lines.

**(k)** The forward anchor light prescribed in Rule 30(a)(i), when two are carried, shall not be less than 4.5m above the after one. On a vessel of 50m or more in length this forward anchor light shall be placed at a height of not less than 6m above the hull.

### 3 Horizontal positioning and spacing of lights

**(a)** When two masthead lights are prescribed for a power-driven vessel, the horizontal distance between them shall not be less than one-half of the length but need not be more than 100m. The forward light shall be placed not more than one-quarter of the length of the vessel from the stem.

**(b)** On a power-driven vessel of 20m of more in length, the sidelights shall not be placed in front of the forward masthead lights. They shall be placed at or near the side of the vessel.

**(c)** When the lights prescribed in Rule 27(b)(i) or Rule 28 are placed vertically between the forward masthead light(s) and the after masthead light(s) these all-round lights shall be placed at a horizontal distance of not less than 2m from the fore-and-aft centreline of the vessel in the athwartship direction.

**(d)** When only one masthead light is prescribed for a power-driven vessel, this light shall be exhibited forward of amidships; except that a vessel of less than 20m in length need not exhibit this light forward of amidships but shall exhibit it as far forward as is practicable.

### 4 Details of location of direction-indicating lights for fishing vessels, dredgers and vessels engaged in underwater operations

**(a)** the light indicating the direction of the outlying gear from a vessel engaged in fishing as prescribed in Rule 26(c)(ii) shall be placed at a horizontal distance of not less than 2m and not more

than 6m away from the two all-round red and white lights. This light shall be placed not higher than the all-round white light prescribed in Rule 26(c)(i) and not lower than the sidelights.

**(b)** The lights and shapes on a vessel engaged in dredging or underwater operations to indicate the obstructed side and/or the side on which it is safe to pass, as prescribed in Rule 27(d)(i) and (ii), shall be placed at the maximum practical horizontal distance, but in no case less than 2m from the lights or shapes prescribed in Rule 27(b)(i) and (ii). In no case shall the upper of these lights or shapes be at a greater height than the lower of the three lights or shapes prescribed in Rule 27(b)(i) an d(ii).

## 5 Screens for sidelights

The sidelights of vessels of 20m or more in length shall be fitted with inboard screens painted matt black, and meeting the requirements of Section 9 of this Annex. On vessels of less than 20m in length the sidelights, if necessary to meet the requirements of Section 9 of this Annex, shall be fitted with inboard matt black screens. With a combined lantern, using a single vertical filament and a very narrow division between the green and red sections, external screens need not be fitted.

## 6 Shapes

**(a)** Shapes shall be black and of the following sizes:

(i) a ball shall have a diameter of not less than 0.6m;

(ii) a cone shall have a base diameter of not less than 0.6m and a height equal to its diameter;

(iii) a cylinder shall have a diameter of at least 0.6m and a height of twice its diameter;

(iv) a diamond shape shall consist of two cones as defined in (ii) above having a common base.

**(b)** The vertical distance between shapes shall be at least 1.5m.

**(c)** In a vessel of less than 20m in length, shape of lesser dimensions but commensurate with the size of the vessel may be used and the distance apart may be correspondingly reduced.

## 7 Colour specification of lights

The chromaticity of all navigation lights shall conform to the following standards, which lie within the boundaries of the area of the diagram specified for each colour by the International Commission on Illumination (CIE). The boundaries of the area for each colour are given by indicating the corner co-ordinates, which are as follows:

| | | | | | | |
|---|---|---|---|---|---|---|
| (i) White | x 0.525 | 0.525 | 0.452 | 0.310 | 0.310 | 0.443 |
| | y 0.382 | 0.440 | 0.440 | 0.348 | 0.283 | 0.382 |
| (ii) Green | x 0.028 | 0.009 | 0.300 | 0.203 | | |
| | y 0.385 | 0.723 | 0.511 | 0.356 | | |
| (iii) Red | x 0.680 | 0.660 | 0.735 | 0.721 | | |
| | y 0.320 | 0.320 | 0.265 | 0.259 | | |
| (iv) Yellow | x 0.612 | 0.618 | 0.575 | 0.575 | | |
| | y 0.382 | 0.382 | 0.425 | 0.406 | | |

## 8 Intensity of lights

**(a)** The minimum luminous intensity of lights shall be calculated by using:

$$I = 3.43 \times 10^6 \times T \times D^2 \times 5\text{-}D$$

*where*

I is luminous intensity in candelas under service conditions,
T is threshold factor 2 x $10^{-7}$ lux,
D is the range of visibility (luminous range) of the light in nautical mile,
K is the atmospheric transmissivity.
For prescribed lights the value of K shall be 0.8, corresponding to a meteorological visibility of approximately 13 nautical miles.

**(b)** A selection of figures derived from the formula is given in the following table:

| *Range of visibility (luminous range) of light in nautical miles* | *Luminous intensity of light in candelas for K–0.8* |
|---|---|
| D | I |
| 1 | 0.9 |
| 2 | 4.3 |
| 3 | 12 |
| 4 | 27 |
| 5 | 52 |
| 6 | 94 |

**Note**: The maximum luminous intensity of navigation lights should be limited to avoid undue glare. This shall not be achieved by a variable control of the luminous intensity.

## 9 Horizontal sectors

**(a)** (i) In the forward direction, sidelights as fitted on the vessel shall show the minimum required intensities. The intensities shall decrease to reach practical cut-off between 1° and 3° outside the prescribed sectors.

(ii) For stern lights and masthead lights at 22.5° abaft the beam for sidelights, the minimum required intensities shall be maintained over the arc of the horizon up to 5° within the limits of the sectors prescribed in Rule 21. From 5° within the prescribed sectors the intensity may decrease by 50% up to the prescribed limits; it shall decrease steadily to reach practical cut-off at not more than 5° outside the prescribed sectors.

**(b)** (i) All-round lights shall be so located as not to be obscured by masts, topmasts or structures within angular sectors of more than 6°, except anchor lights prescribed in Rule 30, which need not be placed at an impracticable height above the hull.

(ii) If it is impracticable to comply with paragraph (b)(i) of this section by exhibiting only one all-round light, two all-round lights shall be used suitably positioned or screened so that they appear, as far as practicable, as one light at a distance of one mile.

## 10 Vertical sectors

**(a)** The vertical sectors of electric lights as fitted, with the exception of lights on sailing vessels underway shall ensure that:

(i) at least the required minimum intensity is maintained at all angles from 5° above to 5° below the horizontal;

(ii) at least 60% of the required minimum intensity is maintained from 7.5° above to 7.5° below the horizontal.

**(b)** In the case of sailing vessels underway, the vertical sectors of electric lights as fitted shall ensure that:

(i) at least the minimum intensity is maintained at all angles from 5° above to 5° below the horizontal;

(ii) at least 50% of the required minimum intensity is maintained from 25° above to 25° below the horizontal.

**(c)** In the case of lights other than electric, these specifications shall be met as closely as possible.

## 11 Intensity of non-electric lights

Non-electric lights shall so far as practicable comply with the minimum intensities, as specified in the table given in Section 8 of this Annex.

## 12 Manoeuvring light

Notwithstanding the provisions of paragraph 2(f) of this Annex the manoeuvring light described in Rule 34(b) shall be placed in the same fore-and-aft vertical plane as the masthead light or lights and, where practicable, at a minimum height of 2m vertically above the forward masthead light, provided that it shall be carried not less than 2m vertically above or below the after masthead light. On a vessel where only one masthead light is carried the manoeuvring light, if fitted, shall be carried where it can be seen, not less than 2m vertically apart from the masthead light.

## 13 High-speed Craft*

**(a)** The masthead light of high-speed craft may be placed at a height related to the breadth of the craft lower than that prescribed in paragraph 2(a)(i) of this Annex, provided that the base angle of the isosceles triangles formed by the sidelights and masthead light, when seen in end elevation, is not less than 27°.

(a) On high-speed craft of 50m or more in length, the vertical separation between foremast and mainmast light of 4.5m required by paragraph 2(a)(ii) of this Annex may be modified provided that such distance shall not be less than the value determined by the following formula (*see key page 108*):

(b) $$y = \frac{(a + 17\psi)C}{1000} + 2$$

* Refer to the International Code of Safety for High-Speed Craft, 1994 and the International Code of Safety for High-Speed Craft, 2000.

*where*:

- y is the height of the mainmast light above the foremast light in metres
- a is the height of the foremast light above the water surface in service condition in metres
- ψ is the trim in service condition in degrees
- C is the horizontal separation of masthead lights in metres

### 14 Approval

The construction of lights and shapes and the installation of lights on board the vessel shall be to the satisfaction of the appropriate authority of the State whose flag the vessel is entitled to fly.

# Annex II

## Additional signals for fishing vessels fishing in close proximity

### 1 General

The lights mentioned herein shall, if exhibited in pursuance of Rule 26(d), be placed where they can best be seen. They shall be at least 0.9m apart but at a lower level than lights prescribed in Rule 26(b)(9i) and (c)(i). The lights shall be visible all round the horizon at a distance of at least one mile but at a lesser distance than the lights prescribed by these Rules for fishing vessels.

### 2 Signals for trawlers

**(a)** Vessels of 20m or more in length when engaged in trawling, whether using demersal or pelagic gear, shall exhibit:

(i) when shooting their nets, two white lights in a vertical line;
(ii) when hauling their nets, one white light over one red light in a vertical line;
(iii) when the net has come fast upon an obstruction, two red lights in a vertical line.

**(b)** Each vessel of 20m or more in length engaged in pair trawling shall exhibit:

(i) by night, a searchlight directed forward and in the direction of the other vessel of the pair;
(ii) when shooting or hauling their nets or when the nets have come fast upon an obstruction the lights prescribed in 2(a) above.

**(c)** A vessel of less than 20m in length engaged in trawling, whether using demersal or pelagic gear or engaged in pair trawling, may exhibit the lights prescribed in paragraphs (a) or (b) of this Section, as appropriate.

### 3 Signals for purse seiners

Vessels engaged in fishing with purse seine gear may exhibit two yellow lights in a vertical line. These lights shall flash alternately every second and with equal light and occultation duration. These lights may be exhibited only when the vessel is hampered by its fishing gear.

# Annex III

## Technical details of sound signal appliances

### 1 Whistles

(a) Frequencies and range of audibility.
The fundamental frequency of the signal shall lie within the range 70–700Hz. The range of audibility of the signal from a whistle shall be determined by those frequencies which may include the fundamental and/or one or more higher frequencies, which lie within the range 180–700Hz (±1%) for a vessel of 20m or more in length, or 180–2100Hz (±1%) for a vessel of less than 20m in length and which provide the sound pressure levels specified in paragraph 1(c) below.

(b) Limits of fundamental frequencies.
To ensure a wide variety of whistle characteristics, the fundamental frequency of a whistle shall be between the following limits:
(i) 70–200Hz, for a vessel 200m or more in length;
(ii) 130–350Hz, for a vessel 75m but less than 200m in length;
(iii) 250–750Hz, for a vessel less than 75m in length.

(c) Sound signal intensity and range of audibility
A whistle fitted in a vessel shall provide, in the direction of maximum intensity of the whistle and at a distance of 1m from it, a sound pressure level in at least one ⅓ octave band within the range of frequencies 180–700Hz (±1%) for a vessel of 20m or more in length, or 180–2100Hz (±1%) for a vessel of less than 20m in length, of not less than the appropriate figure given in the table below.

| *Length of vessel in metres* | *⅓ octave band level at 1m in dB referred to 2 x 10-5 N/m2* | *Audibility range in nautical miles* |
|---|---|---|
| 200 or more | 143 | 2 |
| 75 but less than 200 | 138 | 1.5 |
| 20 but less than 75 | 130 | 1 |
| Less than 20 | 120* | 0.5 |
| | 115† | |
| | 111‡ | |

* When the measured frequencies lie within the range 180–450Hz
† When the measured frequencies lie within the range 450–800Hz
‡ When the measured frequencies lie within the range 800–2100Hz

**TOP TIP**

*There is little chance of you hearing a sound signal from another vessel more than two miles away.*

The range of audibility in the table above is form information and is approximately the range at which a whistle may be heard on its forward axis with 90% probability in conditions of still air on board a vessel having average background noise level at the listening posts (taken to be 68dB in the octave centred on 250Hz and 63dB in the octave centred on 500Hz). In practice, the range at which a whistle may be heard is extremely variable and depends critically on weather conditions; the values given can be regarded as typical but under conditions of strong wind or high ambient noise level at the listening post the range may be much reduced.

(d) Directional properties
The sound pressure level of a directional whistle shall be not more than 4dB below the prescribed sound pressure level on the axis at any direction in the horizontal plane within +45° of the axis. The sound pressure level at any other direction in the horizontal plane shall be not more than 10dB below the prescribed sound pressure level on the axis, so that the range in any direction will be at least half the range on the forward axis. The sound pressure level shall be measured in that ⅓ octave band which determines the audibility range.

(e) Positioning of whistles
When a directional whistle is to be used as the only whistle on a vessel, it shall be installed with its maximum intensity directed straight ahead. A whistle shall be placed as high as practicable on a vessel, in order to reduce interception of the emitted sound by obstructions and also to minimise hearing damage risk to personnel. The sound pressure level of the vessel's own signal at listening posts shall not exceed 110dB(A) and so far as practicable should not exceed 100dB(A).

(f) Fitting of more than one whistle
If whistles are fitted at a distance apart of more than 100m, it shall be so arranged that they are not sounded simultaneously.

(g) Combined whistle systems
If due to the presence of obstructions the sound field of a single whistle or one of the whistles referred to in paragraph 1(f) above is likely to have a zone of greatly reduced signal level, it is recommended that a combined whistle system be fitted so as to overcome this reduction. For the purposes of the Rules, a combined whistle system is to be regarded as a single whistle. The whistles of a combined system shall be located at a distance apart of not more than 100m and arranged to be sounded simultaneously. The frequency of any one whistle shall differ from those of the others by at least 10Hz.

### 2 Bell or gong

(a) Intensity of signal
A bell or gong, or other device having smaller sound characteristics shall produce a sound pressure level of not less than 110dB at a distance of 1m from it.

(b) Construction
Bells and gongs shall be made of corrosion-resistant material and designed to give a clear tone. The diameter of the mouth of the bell shall be not less than 300mm for vessels of 20m or more in length. Where practicable, a power-driven bell striker is recommended to ensure constant

force but manual operation shall be possible. The mass of the striker shall be not less than 3% of the mass of the bell.

### 3 Approval

The construction of sound signal appliances, their performance and their installation on board the vessel shall be to the satisfaction of the appropriate authority of the State whose flag the vessel is entitled to fly.

# Annex IV

## Distress signals

1 The following signals, used or exhibited either together or separately, indicate distress and need of assistance:

(a) gun or other explosive signal fired at intervals of about a minute;
(b) continuous sounding with any fog-signalling apparatus;
(c) rockets or shells, throwing red stars fired one at a time at short intervals;
(d) signal made by radiotelegraphy or by any other signalling method consisting of the group ...—-... (SOS) in the Morse Code;
(e) signal sent by radiotelephony consisting of the spoken word 'Mayday';
(f) International Code Signal of distress by 'NC';
(g) signal consisting of a square flag having above or below it a ball or anything resembling a ball;
(h) flames on a vessel (as from a burning tar barrel, oil barrel, etc)
(i) rocket parachute flare or a hand flare showing a red light;
(j) smoke signal giving off orange-coloured smoke;
(k) slowly and repeatedly raising and lowering arms outstretched to each side;
(l) radiotelegraph alarm signal;
(m) radiotelephone alarm signal;
(n) signals transmitted by emergency position-indicating radio beacons (EPIRB);
(o) approved signals transmitted by radio-communication systems, including survival craft radar transponders (SART).

2 The use or exhibition of any of the foregoing signals, except for the purpose of indicating distress and need of assistance and the use of other signals which may be confused with any of the above signals, is prohibited.

3 Attention is drawn to the relevant sections of the International Code of Signals, the Merchant Ship Search and Rescue Manual and the following signals:

**TOP TIP**

*Flying your ensign upside down is no longer an approved method of indicating distress. It confused the French!*

(a) a piece of orange-coloured canvas with either a black square and circle or other appropriate symbol (for identification from the air);
(b) a dye marker.

# Amendments to the 1972 COLREGS

(all of which are included in the text above)

**The 1981 amendments**
**Adoption**: 19 November 1981
**Entry into force**: 1 June 1983
A number of Rules were affected but perhaps the most important change concerned Rule 10, which was amended to enable vessels carrying out various safety operations, such as dredging or surveying, to carry out these functions in traffic separation schemes.

---

**The 1987 amendments**
**Adoption**: 19 November 1987
**Entry into force**: 19 November 1989
These amendments affected several Rules, including Rule 1(e) vessels of special construction: the amendment classifies the application of the Convention to such ships; Rule 3(h), which defines a vessel constrained by her draught; Rule 10(c) crossing traffic lanes.

---

**The 1989 amendments**
**Adoption**: 19 October 1989
**Entry into force**: 19 April 1991
The amendment concerned Rule 10 and was designed to stop unnecessary use of the inshore traffic zone.

---

**The 1993 amendments**
**Adoption**: 4 November 1993
**Entry into force**: 4 November 1995
These amendments were mostly concerned with the positioning of lights.

---

**The 2001 amendments**
**Adoption**: 29 November 2001
**Entry into force**: 29 November 2003
The amendments included new Rules relating to Wing-in-Ground (WIG) craft.
The following were amended:
(a) General Definitions (Rule 3) – to provide the definition of wing-in-ground (WIG) craft;
(b) Action to avoid collision (Rule 8(a)) – to make it clear that any action to avoid collision should be taken in accordance with the relevant Rules in the COLREGS and to link Rule 8 with the other steering and sailing Rules;
(c) Responsibilities between vessels (Rule 18) – to include a requirement that a WIG craft, when taking off, landing and in flight near the surface, shall keep clear of all other vessels and

avoid impeding their navigation and also that a WIG craft operating on the water surface shall comply with the Rules as for a power-driven vessel;

(d) Power-driven vessels underway (Rule 23) – to include a requirement that WIG craft shall, in addition to the lights prescribed in paragraph 23(a) of the Rule, exhibit a high-intensity all-round flashing red light when taking off, landing and in-flight near the surface;

(e) Seaplanes (Rule 31) – to include a provision for WIG craft;

(f) Equipment for sound signals, and sound signals in restricted visibility (Rules 33 and 35) – to cater for small vessels;

(g) Positioning and technical details of lights and shapes (Annex I) – amendments with respect to high-speed craft (relating to the vertical separation of masthead lights);

(h) Technical details of sound signal appliances (Annex III) – amendments with respect to whistles and bell or gong to cater for small vessels.

# 8 Navigation Aids

## Hyperbolic navigation aids

Hyperbolic navigation systems were first developed during the Second World War. In the post war years their civilian use was greatly extended until the 1980s by which time virtually every sea-going craft, large or small, carried such a device. They were a considerable improvement on the radio direction finding technologies that preceded them, since their errors could be more reliably predicted. The three most commonly used systems were Decca, Omega and Loran.

### **OMEGA** (discontinued)

Omega was a very low frequency hyperbolic navigation system that established position by phase comparison but it finally ceased transmissions on 30 September 1997.

### **DECCA** (discontinued)

Decca was also a phase comparison system operating between 70–130kHz and was initially saved from shut-down in the early 1990s due to protests from fishermen and small craft users unable to afford the satellite technology which was replacing it, but the Decca Navigator system finally ceased operation on 31 March 2000 after 55 years of service.

### **LORAN-C**

Loran-C is an all-weather, highly accurate and reliable hyperbolic radio navigation system which covers most of the northern hemisphere. It operates on 90–110kHz band and uses time differences between pulses to fix position. It has a repeatable accuracy down to 0.25nm and an operating range of up to 650 miles from its transmitter stations. The original system, known as Loran-A, proved not to be sufficiently accurate so it was replaced by Loran-C. Loran-B was an experimental system but it never went fully operational. The long-term prospects for Loran-C are questionable even though it is now modulated for use in conjunction with differential GPS. In Europe, the Loran-C system was managed by the North West European Loran-C System (NELS), a co-operation between the Governments of Denmark, France, Germany, Ireland, the Netherlands and Norway. This co-operation ended in January 2006 when the Norwegian, German and Danish stations went off the air leaving the future of Loran-C in Europe in the hands of the British and the French who are expected to support it until at least 2015.

A predicted accuracy of 463m (0.25nm) will extend up to 650nm off the coasts of Europe while an accuracy of greater than 100m is predicted closer inshore. The repeatable accuracy of Loran-C is impressive, allowing a return to a marked position with great accuracy time and time again. The maximum useable range of Loran-C is 800 to 1200nm. Information on Loran-C can be found in ALRS Vol II.

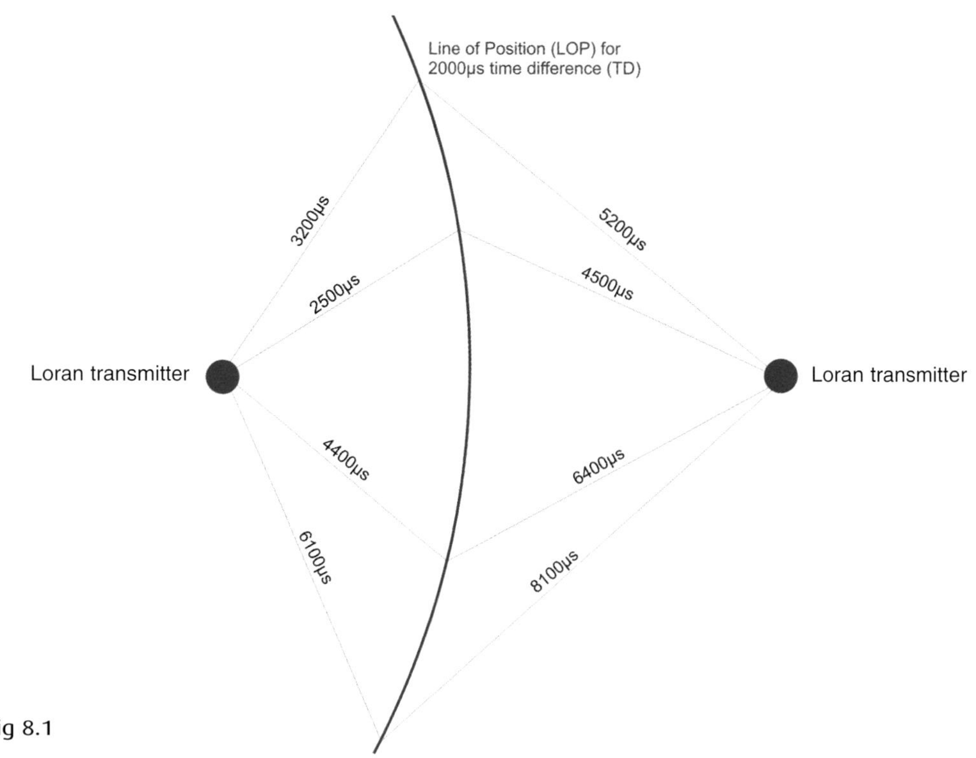


Fig 8.1

The ability to generate a position from the receipt of a series of radio signals is based upon the measurement of the time difference between the receipt time of each transmission. This time difference, measured in microseconds (µs), will be the same along a hyperbola-shaped position line between any two of the group stations (Figure 8.1). The problem for the receiver is differentiating between them. This is achieved by a known time delay between each station's transmissions.

Loran-C transmitters are organised into chains of three to five stations. Within a chain, one station is designated the master station (M) and the other secondary or slave stations (two to four) are identified by the letters W, X, Y and Z (Figure 8.2). The Loran-C navigation signal is carefully structured to make a sequence of brief radio frequency pulses on a carrier wave centred on a frequency of 100kHz. The secondary stations radiate pulses in groups of eight, whereas the master signal, for identification purposes, has an additional ninth pulse. The sequence of signal transmissions consists of a pulse group from the master station followed at precise time intervals by pulse groups from each of the secondary stations. The time interval between the reoccurrence of the master pulse is called the Group Repetition Interval (GRI). Each Loran-C chain has a unique GRI and since all Loran-C transmitters operate on the same frequency, the GRI is the key by which a Loran-C receiver can identify and isolate signal groups from a specific chain.

**Fig 8.2** Group Repetition Interval (GRI).

*Baselines and coverage* An imaginary line drawn between the master and each secondary station is called the *baseline*. The continuation of the baseline in either direction is called a *baseline extension* (Figure 8.3). Typical baselines in the Loran system are from 650 to 1025nm approximately. Effective chain coverage is determined by the power output from each transmitter in the chain, the distance between the transmitters and how they are positioned in relation to each other. This is known as the geometry of the chain.

When a chain of a master station (M) and two or more slave stations is active, the Loran-C receiver can measure two or more lines of position (LOP) with the expected time delays (TDs) and where they cross is the position of the fix (Figure 8.4).

The angle at which the LOPs cross has a significant bearing on the accuracy of position.

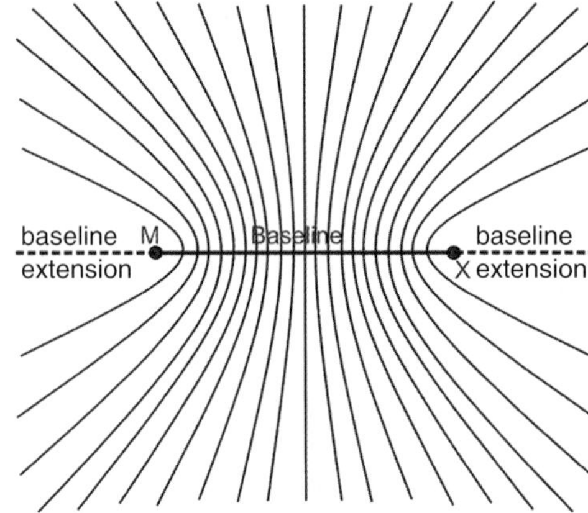

**Fig 8.3** Baseline extension.

*Base line extension error* The further away from the transmitting stations you get, the position lines will cut at more and more acute angles. This gives rise to positioning errors away from the ground station positions. This is known as the *diamond of error* (Figure 8.5). The more acute the angle of intersection of the hyperbolae, the greater is the potential position error. This error is particularly marked in position lines intersecting behind the stations and is often called the *base line extension error* (the base line being the line connecting two stations). In addition the lines are more widely spaced in these areas, which also reduces accuracy.

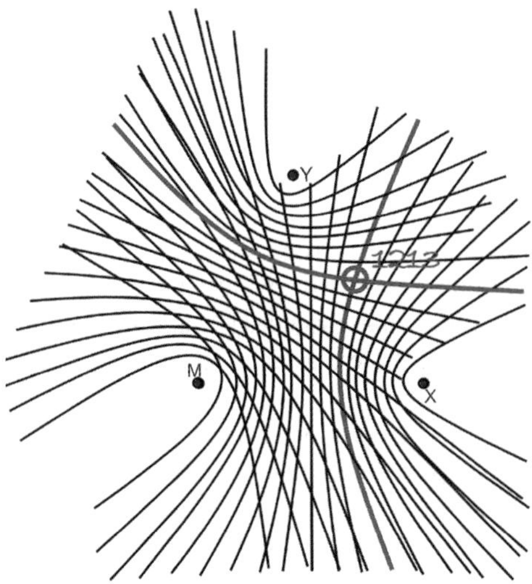

**Fig 8.4** position of a fix.

*Skywave rejection* A frequency of 100kHz is used for the Loran-C carrier wave to take advantage of propagation of the stable ground wave over long distances. However, sky waves reflected from the ionosphere are distorted by their 'bounce' off the ionosphere and the pulse shape returns to the surface with a different carrier phase within the pulses of the received signal. To avoid sky wave contamination, the Loran-C receiver looks carefully at the front end

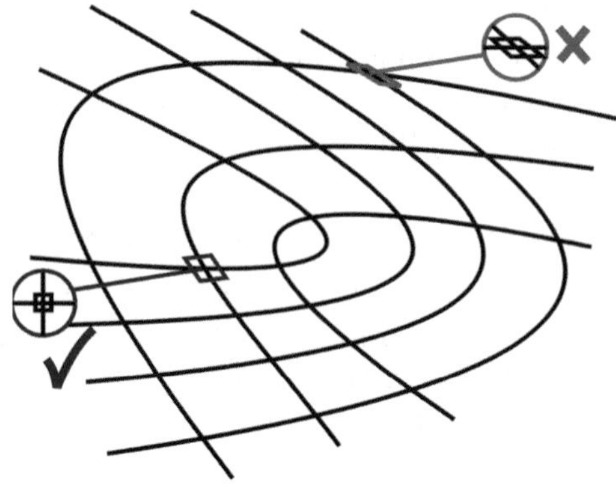
**Fig 8.5** Diamond error.

of the pulse transmitted by master and secondary stations. Usually the third cycle of the pulse (Figure 8.6) is employed to ensure that the time interval measurement is made using the uncontaminated part of the pulse. Precise control over the pulse shape at the transmitter ensures that the uncontaminated part of the pulse can be reliably identified by the receiver.

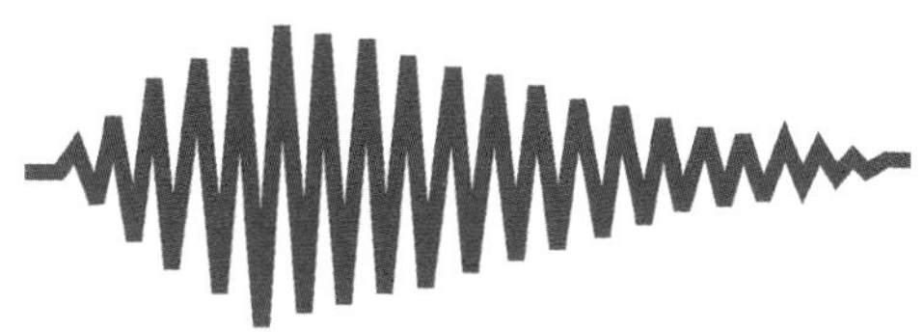

**Fig 8.6** Third cycle of the pulse.

*Phase coding* To reduce the effects of interference and noise on time difference measurements, and to assist in distinguishing between master and secondary stations, the carrier phase of selected transmitted pulses is reversed in a predetermined pattern. This pattern is repeated every two sets of pulses.

*Time difference measurement* The basic measurements made by Loran-C receivers are to determine the time difference (TD) in time-of-arrival between the master signal and the signals from each of the secondary stations of a chain. Each TD value is measured to a precision of about 0.1 microseconds (100 nanoseconds) or better. As a rule of thumb, a time accuracy of 100 nanoseconds corresponds to a geographical accuracy of around 30m.

*Automatic operation* Loran-C transmitters are set up for automatic operation with all vital transmitter functions being duplicated so that the result of any defect is minimised. These functions are monitored at each area control centre, each of which has the capability of initiating immediate corrective action should it be required. As a consequence, the individual transmitters are operated as unmanned stations except for caretakers.

*Precision clocks* To achieve high positioning accuracy within the service area, Loran-C transmitter stations are equipped with a suite of atomic clocks that provide the timing for the Loran-C signal transmissions. These clocks are caesium based with a typical stability of error of less than one second in 317,000 years.

*Time control* Precise navigation with Loran-C demands that the error in the timing system must not exceed a few tens of nanoseconds. In Europe it is specified that a station's clock shall not deviate by more than 30 nanoseconds from the clocks of the neighbouring stations. In achieving this timing precision it is necessary to measure continuously the time deviation between each of the clocks in the system. There are two basic methods in use for monitoring and adjusting the clocks in Loran-C systems, SAM Control and TOE Control:

### 1 System Area Monitor – SAM control

The most commonly used method is to measure the time difference between Loran-C signals received from a master and a secondary at a fixed location in the coverage area. Timing control includes making adjustments to the clock of the secondary station so that the measured TD is kept at a predetermined value. The measurement equipment at the fixed location is called a System Area Monitor (SAM); hence this method of timing control is referred to as 'SAM control'.

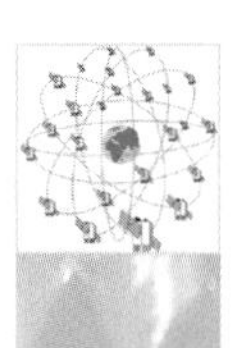



### 2 Time of Emission – TOE control

The alternative method for timing control (used in Europe) is to measure the arrival times of signals from adjacent transmitters relative to the local clock at each transmitter station. The measurements from all stations in the system are sent by permanent data-link to the control station where they are combined so that the time deviation of each transmitter's clock can be calculated. Computed adjustments are returned to the individual transmitter sites where they are used for clock synchronisation. This results in a common time reference for the Time Of Emission (TOE) of the Loran-C pulses from all transmitters and is called 'TOE control'.

***UTC time reference*** The common time reference is itself related to UTC using the UTC (Brest) time standard that is co-located with the Loran-C Control Centre at Brest in France. The time reference synchronisation to UTC (Brest) is maintained to within 100 nanoseconds.

## Fixed errors

***Land effect*** A Loran-C receiver computes distances from Loran-C transmitting stations using the time of arrival measurements and the propagation velocity of the radio ground wave to determine position. Small variations in the velocity of propagation between that over sea water and over different landmasses are known as the Additional Secondary Factor (ASF). The propagation of radio waves is distorted by the passage of the signal over land before passing over the sea. There is a change in the velocity of propagation between land and sea that changes the direction of the radio waves. Water has faster propagation characteristics whilst those of land are slower. Other factors such as urban development and ice can also effect propagation.

Corrections may be applied to compensate for this variation. Such corrections may improve the absolute accuracy of the Loran-C service in positions where the received Loran-C signal passes over anything but the sea surface on its way from transmitter to receiver. The values of ASF depend mainly on the conductivity of the Earth's surface along the signal paths. Sea water has high conductivity, and the ASFs of sea water are, by definition, zero. Dry soil, mountains or ice generally have low conductivity and radio signals travel over them more slowly, giving rise to substantial ASF delays and hence degradation of absolute accuracy. Fortunately, ASFs vary little with time, and it is therefore possible to calibrate the Loran-C service by measuring ASF values throughout the coverage area.

A program for mapping ASF in northern Europe is the basis for the production of ASF corrections. These corrections are distributed as electronic databases and can be found in the USHO 221 publication which gives fixed error corrections for receivers which only read out in latitude and longitude.

***Geometry of position lines*** The further you are from the master and slave stations, the greater the likelihood that the angle between the LOPs is acute and the distances between them becomes larger. The more acute and the further the distance between LOPs becomes, the less accurate the positions given will be. This is often referred to as *baseline extension error.*

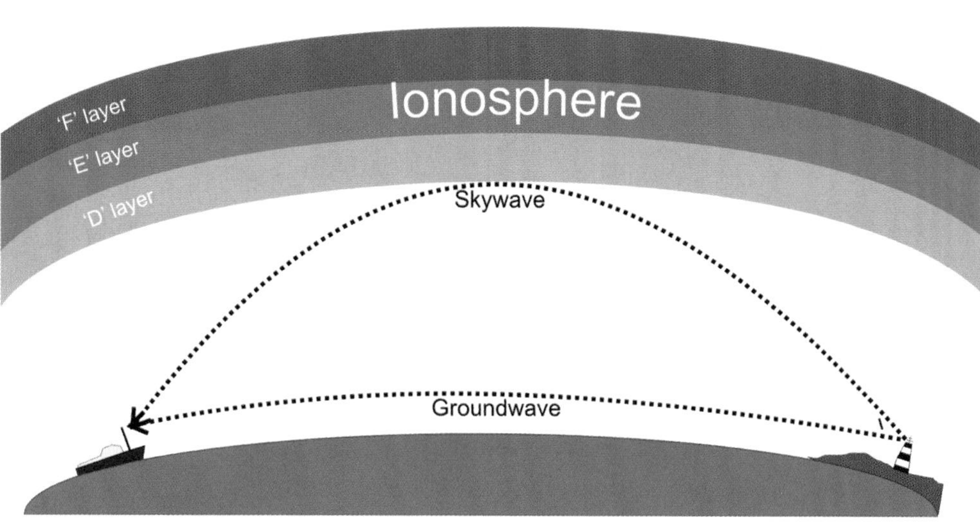


**Fig 8.7** Skywave signals can be prone to inaccuracies due to ionospheric layers.

## Variable errors

*Skywave effect* The speed and path of radio waves can vary according to various factors. Transmitted radio signals travel along the surface of the Earth as 'ground waves' but they can also be 'bounced' off the ionosphere and hence travel greater distances. As Loran-C is a time-based system, if the radio waves are 'bounced' off the ionosphere, then the time taken to reach a vessel will be longer which will in turn lead to inaccuracies.

Loran is able to use both ground wave and skywave signals, though with very different performance levels. It is able to correct for some of the skywave errors but, since these are so variable, the result is a considerable loss of accuracy. Skywave inaccuracies are at their worst at dawn and dusk since the ionosphere descends overnight and its layers, known as 'D', 'E' and 'F' layers split apart, making a more pronounced effect (Figure 8.7).

*Other variable errors* Other variable errors include delays in updating the clock information held by the receiver and interference from thunderstorms and static.

## Loran-C service integrity

Loran-C stations are constantly monitored to detect signal abnormalities, which would render the system unusable for navigation. 'Blink' is the prime means by which the user is notified that the transmitted Loran-C signal does not comply with the system specifications. Blink is a distinctive change in the group of eight Loran-C pulses that can be recognised automatically by a receiver so the user is notified instantly that the Loran-C chain blinking should not be used for navigation. Blink starts at a maximum of 60 seconds after detection of an abnormality. Automatic blink initiated within ten seconds of a timing abnormality may be added where Loran-C is extensively used for aviation purposes. Blink also indicates that the Control Centre cannot ensure that the signal complies with these specifications, for instance, as a result of discontinuation of data communications linking the Control Centre to the stations.

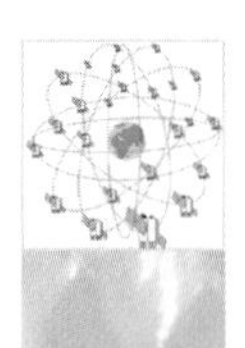



**Does Loran-C have advantages over GPS?**

- It is under civil rather than military control.
- The signal cannot be deliberately degraded.
- Signals can be received in cities and mountainous areas where GPS may not reliably penetrate.
- Loran-C has the ability to warn users of defects or loss of integrity in the system in real time (guaranteed within ten seconds). GPS does not do this in real time; there can be a 1½ to four hour delay.
- Unlike GPS with selective availability (SA) the repeatable accuracy of a Loran-C navigational fix is excellent.
- Capital and operational costs are a fraction of satellite costs.
- Loran-C may be used to supply long-range differential corrections to GPS.

# Satellite positioning systems

Global satellite navigation has proved to be an exciting technology, providing enhanced productivity and accuracy in a vast number of industries. It has added a new level of safety to a wide range of navigation, sports and recreational activities.

A Global Navigation Satellite System (GNSS) is a network of satellites transmitting high-frequency radio signals containing time and distance data that can be picked up by a receiver, allowing the user to pinpoint their location anywhere around the globe (Figure 8.8).

There are two Global Navigation Satellite Systems (GNSS) currently in operation: the US Global Positioning System (GPS) and the Russian GLObal NAvigation Satellite System (GLONASS). These systems are constantly being upgraded to meet higher standards of reliability. A third GNSS named GALILEO, after the Italian astronomer of the early 1600s, is currently being developed in Europe to specifically provide a higher standard of integrity and reliability, required to ensure the safety of lives during transport by air, land and sea without the use of additional systems as a cross check.

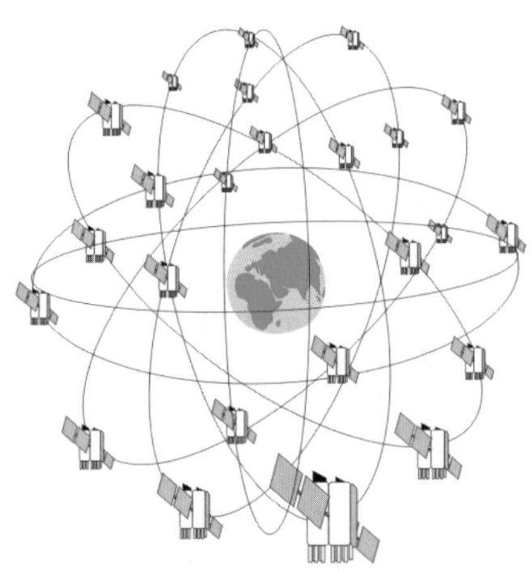

**Fig 8.8** The GPS satellite network.

The GPS and GLONASS satellite networks provide an excellent basis for positional accuracy but they can be far from totally accurate. The positioning systems can be further improved by Satellite-Based Augmentation Systems (SBAS). These provide differential signal corrections for GPS and GLONASS transmissions with the use of ground stations and geostationary satellites in specific regions. This is known as GNSS-1 and is the first phase in establishing a refined integrity for high-precision satellite navigation.

The second stage, GNSS-2, will require a series of new geostationary satellites and a complete upgrade of the existing satellite systems. This second phase is already well underway. GALILEO, the European system, is scheduled to begin service in 2008 and is being developed to meet the standards of GNSS-2 for rapid and reliable certified precision positioning.

## Global Positioning System (GPS)

GPS is the US GNSS. A network of 24 satellites (21 in use at any one time plus three spares) continuously transmits high-frequency radio signals, containing time and distance information that can be picked up by any GPS receiver, allowing the user to pinpoint their position anywhere on the Earth.

GPS was originally designated 'NAVSTAR' (NAVigation System with Timing And Ranging) and its development began in 1973. In 1978, the US Department of Defense launched the first GPS satellite, imposing Selective Availability (SA), an intentional degradation of GPS signals, to prevent the system being used by countries in attacks against the US. SA restricted GPS to 100m accuracy for non-US military users. In 2000, Selective Availability was turned off by Presidential Decree, giving all GPS receivers a potential accuracy of 15m without the use of signal correction. The signals are available 24 hours a day in any weather condition, everywhere around the world. When used with Wide Area Augmentation System (WAAS) or European Geostationary Navigation Overlay Service (EGNOS) receivers, GPS accuracy can be improved to 3m!

The GPS satellite network was completed with the launch of satellite number 24 in 1994. Replacement satellites continue to be launched, each having a life span of about 10 years. These satellites orbit the Earth at an altitude of 20,000km continuously broadcasting data on their positions. The user is equipped with a receiver capable of tracking these signals and determining the range from a particular satellite by measuring the time it takes for a signal to travel from the satellite to the receiver and multiplying this by the speed of the radio wave. Measuring the distances from four such satellites allows the user to fix his position uniquely in three dimensions and verify the receiver clock.

*Carrier waves* GPS satellites broadcast two carrier waves known as 'L1' and 'L2', which are frequency modulated with timing codes. Superimposed on these codes is a navigation message containing information regarding the transmitting satellite's position, correction parameters for the satellite's atomic clock, health and almanac data for all the satellites.

*Clock error analysis* From a pure positioning point of view, only three distances need to be determined to fix a three dimensional position (ie latitude, longitude and altitude). The fourth satellite signal is required so that the error in the measured distance caused by the receiver's clock being out of synchronisation with that of the satellites may be eliminated. This method of solution is known as the 'Navigation Mode' or alternatively 'Pseudo-range'. The term *pseudo-range* is used because the distance is derived by obtaining the time delay as measured by the receiver, which has been contaminated by clock error and refraction of the radio wave through the atmosphere. Using the range of a fourth satellite the receiver can analyse the small 'cocked hat' in the three point fix and work out what time adjustment needs to be applied to produce a perfect fix. In this way the unit can adjust minute variations in its clock. An error of 0.001 seconds can cause a 300km error in position. To get an accuracy of 3m, the clock needs to be accurate to 0.00000001 seconds! The effect of this is that the clock in a GPS receiver is almost as accurate as the phenomenally expensive caesium clock in the satellite.

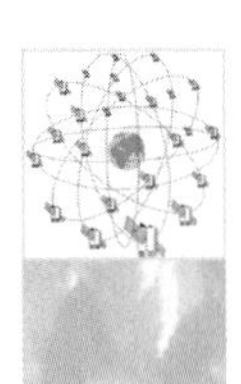



There are three major components to the GPS system, these being known as the Control Segment, Space Segment and User Segment.

***The Control Segment*** The control segment consists of five ground-based tracking or monitor stations which passively track all visible satellites. These stations track the satellites and record their positions. They also receive data concerning atmosphere conditions and clock data obtained from the satellite's caesium frequency atomic clock. This data is then transmitted to the master control station where the ephemeris data and clock status predictions for each satellite are generated. This data is then used in formulating the navigation messages that are uploaded to each satellite every hour from three ground transmitters. If the operational control system is ever disabled for any reason, pre-stored positional and timing information is available in each satellite to support a 14-day prediction span; after this the accuracy of the satellite's position will exceed 400m and the system will no longer be considered safe for navigation.

***The Space Segment*** The Space Segment consists of the 21 satellites plus three spares. They are in six orbital planes that are nearly circular, spaced 60° apart in longitude, and inclined at an angle of 55° to the equator. The height of each satellite is approximately 20,000km, and each one orbits twice per day. This configuration ensures that there is a minimum of four satellites continuously visible to any point on the Earth's surface. Each satellite transmits data on two different frequencies onto which is superimposed a coded signal. This signal contains information regarding the approximate position of all the satellites, (known as the *almanac*) and more precise information for the subject satellite known as its *ephemeris data*. There is also subsidiary information regarding the satellites status, clock corrections and the condition of the ionosphere.

***Precise (P) codes and course acquisition (C/A) codes*** Each satellite transmits a signal that carries a distinct code. The GPS receiver generates this same code internally, starting at exactly the same time. When it receives the code from the satellite it can measure the time difference between them. Since radio waves travel at the speed of light, the range can be accurately determined. The system of encoding is known as *pseudo-random noise* (PRN) and only receivers capable of generating their own replica code are capable of deciphering the signals.

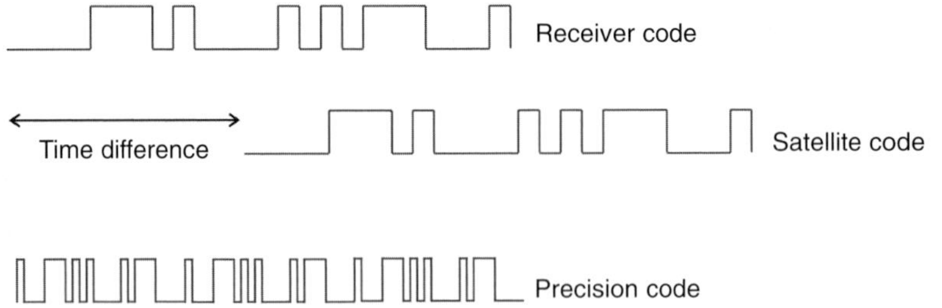


There are two types of code used, the course acquisition (C/A) code and the precise (P) code. The information contained is essentially the same for both codes. The C/A code only allows the user to access the standard positioning service whereas the P code gives access to the precise positioning service. The P code which was originally intended only for military use is more precise because there is much more complexity in the binary changes enabling a more precise comparison.

Two frequencies are used in the transmission of these codes. The higher frequency of 1575.47MHz, (known as the L1 frequency) carries both codes, while the lower frequency 1227.4MHz (known as the L2 frequency) carries only the P code. In order to minimise errors caused by refraction through the ionosphere, a military receiver wishing to use the precise code needs access to both frequencies on the basis that the errors caused by refraction are proportional to the frequency. Therefore transmissions on two frequencies enable the degree of refraction to be determined and corrections to be made.

*The User Segment* There are two distinct navigational solutions that may be computed depending upon which pseudo-random noise (PRN) sequence is used. Access to the precise (P) code forms the Precise Positioning Service (PPS) and is restricted to bona fide users only such as the US military and allies. The course acquisition (C/A) code that is broadcast on the L1 frequency only, forms the Standard Positioning Service (SPS) that is available to any user. The Standard Positioning Service is becoming more and more accurate with time as refinements are made to the services available to civilian users. Far from being restricted to ships and aircraft, users such as surveyors, explorers, hikers, bus and taxi companies and many others are now making use of GPS positioning. In addition, the precise timing is revolutionising such varied activities as telephone communication, data transfer, electrical power distribution and many other fields.

When initialising the GPS, it is a requirement to enter the height of the antenna.

*Accuracy* GPS accuracy is considered to be 33 metres for 95 per cent of the time. However, it is possible for the US government to reintroduce Selective Availability and to downgrade the accuracy of GPS by 100m in times of war.

Details of GPS can be found in the *Admiralty List of Radio Signals Volume 2.*

## Satellite-Based Augmentation Systems (SBAS)

Satellite-Based Augmentation Systems are networks of ground relay stations and geostatic satellites designed to receive satellite navigation signals and transmit corrected time and distance measurements that greatly improve accuracy. Observation and relay stations have been established at known positions all over the world, while their geostatic satellites continuously maintain a fixed position above the Earth. Using these known values for distance, SBAS corrects satellite navigation signals for atmospheric delays, incorrect satellite positioning and poor geometry (sometimes caused by inline or close alignment of satellites), increasing accuracy in specific regions. SBAS is vital to providing the reliability and precision required by aviation and other precision-critical applications. Using the same signal frequencies as satellite navigation, SBAS enabled receivers are inter-compatible. Three augmentation systems are currently in varying stages of operation and development covering North America, Europe and Asia. The incredibly accurate positioning capabilities of SBAS are being used in agriculture, development, mining and many other industries as well as hiking, boating, hunting, travel and a wide variety of other leisure and business activities.

*Wide Area Augmentation System (WAAS) – North America* In North America, WAAS provides satellite navigation correction and validation, making WAAS enabled GPS receivers at least five times more accurate than standard equipment. WAAS relay stations have been set at known positions throughout North America. SBAS enabled receivers do not require any additional equipment to use WAAS correction signals and, as with satellite navigation signals, there are no set-up or subscription fees. WAAS is accurate to within 3m (or less). System upgrades are currently being developed which will soon provide accuracy to well within one metre.

***European Geostationary Navigation Overlay System (EGNOS) – Europe*** EGNOS provides satellite navigation correction and validation throughout Europe, making EGNOS enabled receivers at least three times more accurate than standard devices. EGNOS relay stations have been set at known positions throughout Europe. SBAS-enabled receivers do not require any additional equipment to use EGNOS correction signals and, as with satellite navigation signals, there are no setup or subscription fees. Providing accuracy to within 5m or less, EGNOS represents the first step towards Europe's GALILEO global satellite navigation system (see page 130).

***Multifunctional Transport Satellite-based Augmentation System (MSAS) – Asia*** Throughout Asia, MSAS provides satellite navigation correction and validation, making SBAS enabled receivers at least three times more accurate than standard devices. MSAS relay stations have been set at known positions throughout Asia. SBAS enabled receivers do not require any additional equipment to use MSAS correction signals and, as with satellite navigation signals, there are no setup or subscription fees. Providing accuracy to within 5m or less, MSAS will expand safety and air-traffic capacity in the Asia Pacific regions.

***Differential Global Positioning System (dGPS)*** The Differential Global Positioning System (dGPS) is a system designed to improve the accuracy of Global Navigation Satellite Systems (GNSS) by measuring infinitesimal changes in variables to provide satellite positioning corrections. Two or more receivers observe the same set of satellites, taking similar measurements that produce similar errors when positioned closely together. A reference receiver, placed at a known location, calculates its known position and compares it to the position provided by the navigation satellite signals. The difference between the two values reveals the measurement error. The reference receiver then transmits a corrected signal to any number of receivers at unknown positions within the area covered by the dGPS. Accuracy of global satellite positioning is thereby increased from 15m to within a few metres. This technique compensates for errors in the satellite navigation system itself but may not always correct errors caused by the local environment when satellite navigation signals are reflected off tall buildings or nearby mountains, creating multi-path signals.

More sophisticated dGPS techniques can increase positioning accuracy to within a few millimetres. Raw measurements recorded by the reference receiver and one or more mobile receivers can be processed using specially designed software that calculates the errors. The corrections may then be transmitted in real time or after the fact (post-processing). By applying the corrections and recalculating the position, accuracy from within several metres to within a few millimetres is achieved, depending on the specific methodology used and the quality of the real-time data link.

**Warnings of malfunctions**

*dGPS reference stations also monitor the integrity of the GPS signals and can provide timely general warning of unscheduled satellite 'outages' when the orbit of a particular satellite fails to follow its predicted path. With further investigation at the reference station it is possible to develop a system capable of isolating the problematic satellite from those being monitored.*

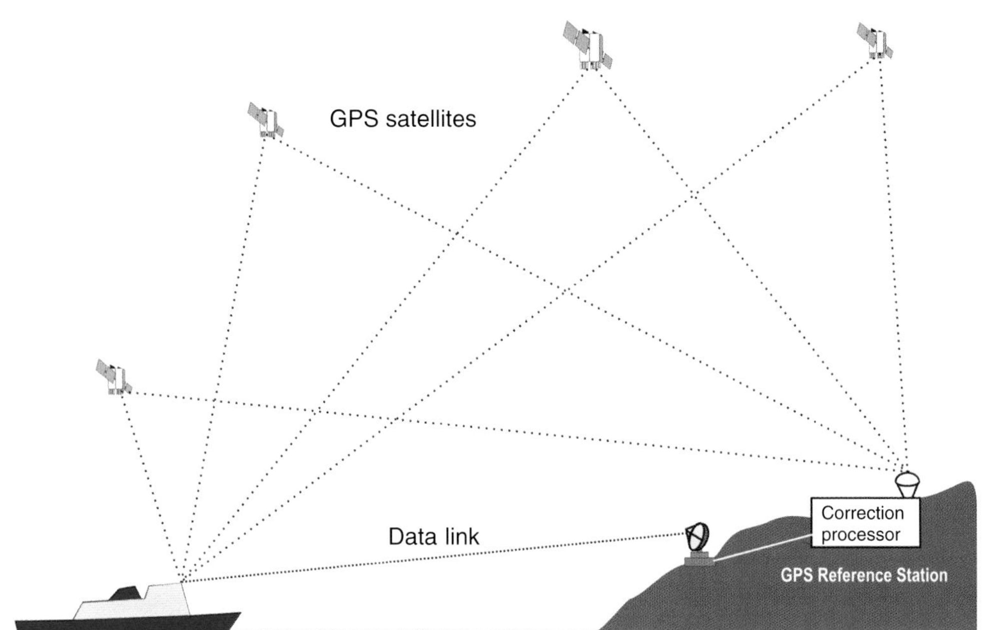


**Fig 8.9** Data links.

***Data links*** The term used for Differential Global Positioning System (dGPS) radio signals transmitted from a reference station or relay antenna at a known location to mobile receivers, to provide the positioning correction data that gives GPS systems maximum accuracy, up to within a centimetre. Data links allow reference stations, relay transmitters and mobile receivers to communicate calculations performed at each location to build a high proportion of data that is cross checked at every point for precision (Figure 8.9).

These data links are critical to collecting reliable GPS data. A number of factors including range, update rate and error correction rate determine the quality and specific application of a data link.

There are three types of data links used in differential GPS systems for high-performance accuracy:

1 HF data link operates in the HF frequency between 1.6MHz and 3.5MHz. Primarily designed for Local Area dGPS (LAdGPS) marine applications, HF data link is optimised for a metre accurate update rate and easy government frequency allocation. HF data link offers superior accuracy for marine applications with an operating range of 55–430nm.
2 UHF data link operates in the UHF frequency between 410MHz and 470MHz. Optimised for LAdGPS or Real-Time Kinematic (RTK) marine and land survey applications. UHF data link has a range of 44nm.
3 UHF bi-directional data link also operates in the UHF range and offers additional flexibility in configuring data processing functionality. Based on the Time Division Multiple Access (TDMA) principle, UHF bi-directional data link uses an MSK modulation optimised for relative positioning systems, used in marine seismic exploration and fleet management.

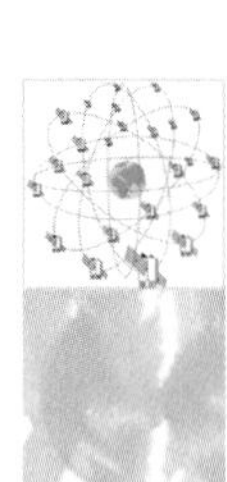



## Geodesy

One of the first things to learn about GPS is that it will give very accurate and highly repeatable information (if selective availability is switched off) but even with this information, it still may not be accurate once it is plotted on a chart. The problem is that the 'horizontal datum' (not to be confused with 'chart datum' which is the level beneath which all soundings are measured) set up in the GPS may not be the same datum as that used by the cartographer who created the chart. The 'datum' in this context means the reference points used to create the grid upon which the latitude and longitude is based.

Geodesy is concerned with measuring the shape of the Earth, that is to say measuring positions and heights (or depths) on the Earth's surface. Over the last decade or two, many new methods of making geodetic measurements have been developed that involve the use of artificial satellites. This was never a particularly interesting subject for the marine navigator but the arrival of satellite-based positioning systems and their incredibly increased accuracy has changed all that. In the past, the chart was more accurate than the navigator's ability to position himself but this is certainly no longer the case.

*The geoid* You may have heard that the Earth is not in fact a sphere but an 'oblate spheroid' (a sphere that has been squashed). Strictly speaking even that is not completely true as it's shape is much more complicated than that. It is an irregular oblate spheroid, called a *geoid* with mountains, sea beds, valleys, desert plains etc. The effect of this varied shape in the pre-satellite era was that different datums were developed as the basis for drawing charts. The problem is that cartographers construct their charts from distances between verticals at various datum points. Because of the irregularity of the Earth's surface and the different effects of gravity in different geographical locations, what is classed as 'vertical' in one place may not be the same 'vertical' in another!

*The spheroid* In the 1950s military technology reached a stage where a ballistic missile could be launched many thousands of miles and thus the relationships between the datum used in one area and that used in another started to become important. With the arrival of the space age and the launching of satellites capable of making accurate measurements of the Earth it was possible to create a 3D mathematical model of the shape of the Earth that more closely resembled reality. The World Geodetic System 1972 (WGS72), as it was known, became accepted as the main datum for marine cartography. Many charts were based on this datum and the original transit satellite navigation system also used this as its datum.

The current datum, however, uses a datum called WGS84 that is based on a more recent spheroid calculation of the Earth's shape called Geodetic Reference System 80 (GRS80). The important point to note is that many charts still in use are based on WGS72 and other regional datums, so extreme care needs to be taken when using satellite derived positions and relating them to positions on a chart (Figure 8.10).

The WGS84 datum is currently being subsumed into a common European Datum, namely the European Terrestrial Reference System 1989 (ETRS89) Datum. So in the future charts will be produced to ETRS89 standards rather than WGS84 although the charts themselves will remain unaltered.

To ensure that a GPS is set in the correct datum, choose the navigation setup section of the receiver and check which datum it is set to read. Even a small hand-held GPS will have over 100 different local datums worldwide to choose from, so it is imperative that the correct one is set. This should be checked against the chart(s) in use to ensure a correct match.

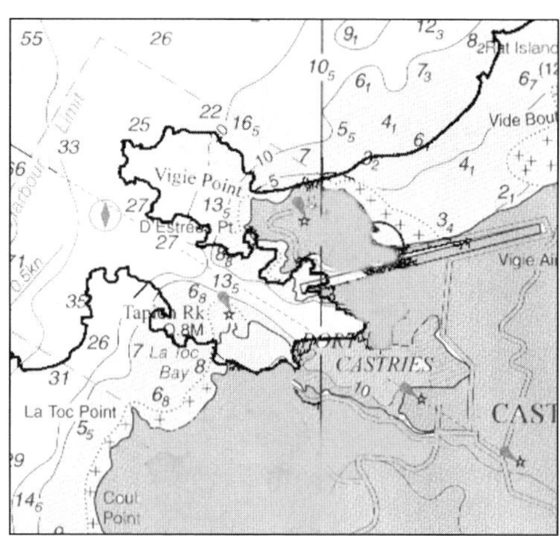


**Fig 8.10** This extract of chart 1273 shows the difference between the old astronomical datum and WGS84 (black outline). In this case the differences are nearly half a mile.

***Dilution of position*** GPS errors result from variations in the geometry of the tracked satellites. As the satellites orbit the Earth their position, relative to the receiver and to each other, is continually changing. The accuracy of any fix is dependent to a large extent on this geometry, ie upon the size of the intersecting angles. In a similar way the GPS position fix depends upon the size of the three-dimensional intersection angles made by the satellites and the receiver. Perfect GPS geometry would be provided by three satellites on the horizon, evenly spaced in azimuth with the fourth satellite directly overhead. The volume of the figure formed by the four satellites and the receiver is therefore an indication of the satellite geometry. It is exactly the same principle as with any fix: if the position lines cross at a fine angle there will be a large 'diamond of error'. If they cross close to 90° the diamond of error will be minimised.

*Measures of DOP* The dilution of precision parameters represent the geometrical distribution of the satellites with respect to the user's position. There are several measures of DOP which are specific to the user's particular requirements:

- GDOP: The Geometric Dilution of Position which integrates all four variables (lat, long, altitude and time). The GDOP parameter is a number which is small for high accuracy and large for low accuracy. Each four satellite group used for a fix will have an associated GDOP, also each satellite will have transmitted as part of its broadcast message an accuracy figure (URE) for the quality of its range measurement. This information can be found using the menu of your GPS receiver. Multiplying the GDOP by the accuracy figure will provide the user with the accuracy of the three dimensional position fix.

- PDOP: The Position Dilution of Position which integrates the three co-ordinates (lat, long and altitude).

- HDOP: The Horizontal Dilution of Position which integrates the horizontal co-ordinates (lat and long).

- VDOP: The Vertical Dilution of Position which integrates the vertical co-ordinate (altitude).

- TDOP: The Time Dilution of Position which integrates the time.

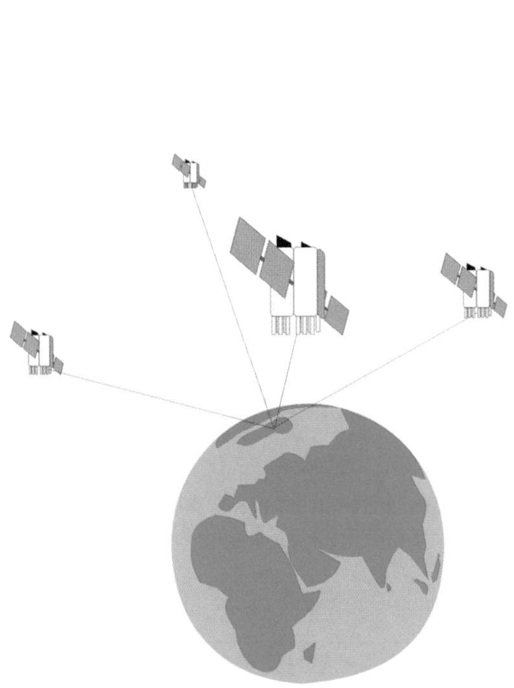

Fig 8.11 Good GDOP.

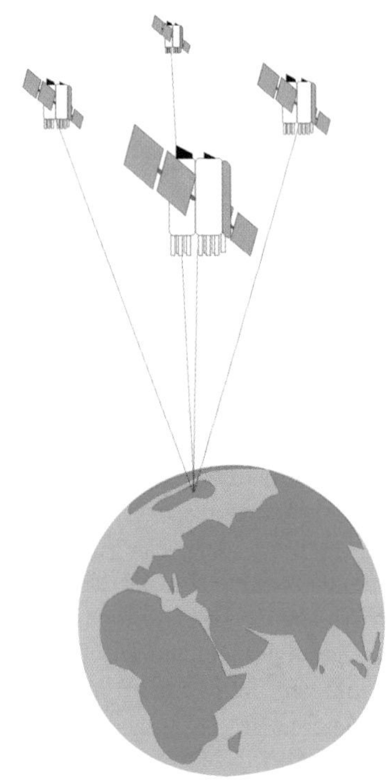

Fig 8.12 Poor GDOP.

## GPS errors

*Ephemeris error* Ephemeris (or orbital) data is constantly being transmitted by the satellites. Receivers maintain an almanac of data for all satellites and they continuously update this information as new data comes in. Typically, ephemeris (almanac) data is updated hourly. Within an hour, errors can creep in which will have an effect on accuracy.

*Ionospheric delay* The ionosphere is the layer of the atmosphere ranging in altitude from 50–500km. It consists largely of ionized particles which exert a delayed effect on GPS signals. While much of the error induced by the ionosphere can be removed through mathematical modelling, it is still one of the most significant error sources.

*Tropospheric delay* The troposphere is the lower part of the Earth's atmosphere that encompasses our weather. It's full of water vapour and varies in temperature and pressure.

*Receiver noise* Interfering radio transmissions can cause small errors to arise. The quality and efficiency of the receiver itself has a bearing on the degree of receiver noise.

*Multi-path error* Even when a signal reaches the ground it can still experience problems. Mountains, hills, buildings and bridges can all reflect the signal and cause the unit to receive a delayed signal.

| Summary of GPS errors (per satellite) | |
|---|---|
| Clock | 1.5m |
| Ephemeris errors | 2.5m |
| Ionosphere | 5.0m |
| Troposphere | 0.5m |
| Receiver noise | 0.3m |
| Multipath | 0.6m |
| Total | 10.4m |

When the total figure (given above) is multiplied by the GDOP, the result is the likely accuracy of the GPS position. For example, if the GDOP is 3 then the likely accuracy of each satellite is 31.2m, but if the GDOP were 1 then the likely accuracy would be 10.4m per satellite.

*GPS navigation* GPS has revolutionised navigation at sea in many ways. In its simplest form, it allows a passage to be entered in the form of waypoints which make up a route and, when set to follow the route, the GPS will monitor progress by displaying a simple screen showing the cross track error (XTE) demonstrating how far to port or starboard of the planned ground track the vessel is (Figure 8.13). In more complicated form, the GPS can provide the position basis for a navigation plotter or full electronic display and information system (ECDIS).

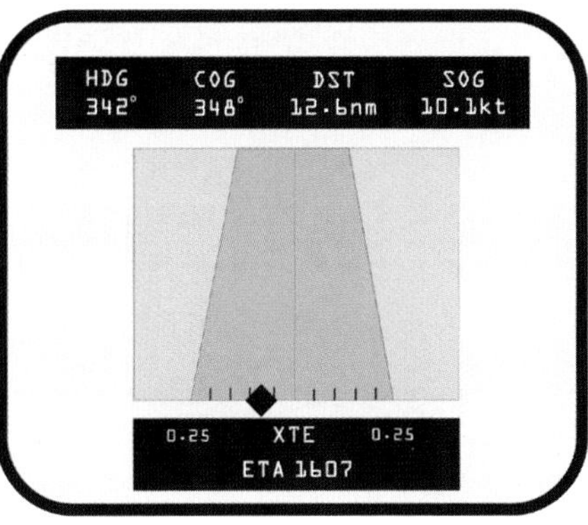


**Fig 8.13** Cross track error (XTE).

## Integrating GPS and Loran-C – Eurofix

It has generally been accepted that making the world's shipping rely on one stand-alone navigation system with only the sextant as backup is fundamentally flawed. As the future of Loran is assured, at least in the medium term (France has agreed to continue with it until at least 2015), it would seem sensible to devise a back-up system of Loran-C for GPS and vice-versa. There are several ways that these two systems can be combined to their mutual benefit. From a physical perspective, Loran and GPS have very different characteristics:

| Loran-C | GPS |
|---|---|
| Ground-based | Satellite-based |
| Low frequency | High frequency |
| High signal level | Low signal level |

Consequently they are unlikely to suffer from the same modes of failure. Such dissimilarities mean Loran can enhance GPS performance. This enhancement was developed in the Netherlands and is known as the Eurofix system. It uses the north European Loran system to distribute dGPS corrections from four Loran-C transmitters over a range of about 1000km.

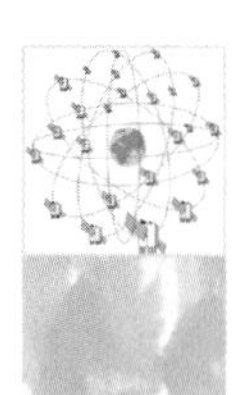



Comparatively, this coverage area is very much larger than that provided by the United States Coast Guard (USCG) marine radio beacon dGPS system. The four European Loran transmitters can offer the Eurofix service to the waters off Scandinavia, Holland, Germany, Belgium, France and Northern Spain.

***Pseudolites (land based satellites)*** A Loran transmitter can also be adapted relatively easily to transmit the same type of signal that a GPS satellite sends. This means it could function as an extra land-based satellite (so called 'pseudolite'), enhancing the GPS constellation. It can do this whilst simultaneously providing an alternative source of navigational information.

***GPS can also enhance Loran-C*** Loran, like GPS, is also a navigation system based on timing. If the Loran clocks were all calibrated using the GPS timing systems this alone would substantially improve the performance of Loran.

***The future – carrier wave GPS*** Projects now well into development are exploring the use of the 'L' band carrier wave used to carry the GPS codes (P & C/A) as a more precise timing reference. As technology develops, centimetre (or even millimetre!) accuracy may one day be possible.

## GLONASS (GLObal NAvigation Satellite System)

GLONASS is the Russian Global Navigation Satellite System (GNSS). It is based on a constellation of active satellites which continuously transmit coded signals in two frequency bands, which can be received by users anywhere on the Earth's surface to identify their position and velocity in real time based on ranging measurements. The system is a counterpart to the United States Global Positioning System (GPS) and both systems share the same principles in the data transmission and positioning methods. GLONASS is managed for the Russian Federation Government by the Russian Space Forces and the system is operated by the Coordination Scientific Information Center (KNITs) of the Ministry of Defense of the Russian Federation.

The first GLONASS satellite was launched in 1982 and the GLONASS network was completed with the launch of the 24th satellite in 1998. The GLONASS signals are available 24 hours a day in any weather conditions and include world coverage. The operational space segment of GLONASS consists of 21 satellites in 3 orbital planes, with 3 on-orbit spares. The three orbital planes are separated by 120°, and the satellites within the same orbit plane by 45°. Each satellite operates in circular 19,100km orbits at an inclination angle of 64.8° and each satellite completes an orbit in approximately 11 hours 15 minutes.

The ground control segment of GLONASS is entirely located within former Soviet Union territory. The ground control centre is located in Moscow and the telemetry and tracking stations are in St. Petersburg, Ternopol, Eniseisk and Komsomolsk-na-Amure.

## GALILEO

Named after the Italian astronomer of the early 1600s, the development of Europe's GALILEO Global Navigation Satellite System (GNSS) began in 1999. Galileo will be Europe's own global navigation satellite system, providing a highly accurate, guaranteed global positioning service but under civilian control. It will be inter-operable with GPS and GLONASS.

A user will be able to take a position with the same receiver from any of the satellites in any combination. By offering dual frequencies as standard, however, Galileo will deliver real-time positioning accuracy down to the metre range, which is unprecedented for a publicly available system. It will guarantee availability of the service under all but the most extreme circumstances and will inform users within seconds of a failure of any satellite. This will make it suitable for applications where safety is crucial.

The first experimental satellite was launched at the end of 2005. Thereafter up to four operational satellites are to be launched to validate the basic Galileo space and related ground segment. Once this in-orbit validation phase has been completed, the remaining satellites will be installed to reach the full operational capability (estimated 2008).

The fully deployed Galileo system will consist of 30 satellites (27 operational and 3 active spares), positioned in 3 circular planes at an altitude of 23,616km above the Earth. Once this is achieved, the Galileo navigation signals will provide good coverage up to 75° north. The large number of satellites, together with the optimisation of the constellation, and the availability of the three active spare satellites, will ensure that the loss of one satellite has no discernible degrading effect to the position signal.

Two Galileo Control Centres will be implemented in Europe to provide the control of the satellites and to perform navigation mission management. The data collected by a global network of 20 Galileo Sensor Stations will be sent to the Galileo Control Centres and they will use this data to compute the integrity of the system and synchronize the time signal of all satellites and of the ground station clocks. The exchange of the data between the Control Centres and the satellites will be performed through up-link stations.

As a further feature, Galileo will provide a global Search and Rescue (SAR) function, based on the current Cospas-Sarsat system. To do so, each satellite will be equipped with a transponder, which is able to transfer the distress signals from user transmitters to Rescue Co-ordination Centres, which will then initiate the rescue operation. At the same time, the system will provide a signal to the user, informing him that his predicament has been detected and that help is under way.

# 9 The Echo Sounder

## Measurement of depth

The only method for accurately taking soundings until well into this century was the lead-line. A line was marked off at fathom intervals with various knots, strips of leather and red, white and blue bunting (cloth). Tallow (a wax) was placed in an indentation in the bottom of the lead weight. The vessel proceeded at slow speed and the line was swung and dropped to the bottom so that it was vertical as the vessel passed over its lead weight resting on the sea bed. The tallow picked up samples of the bottom so when the line was recovered, not only was the depth measured but a knowledge of the sea bed was available also.

Lord Kelvin developed a more advanced version of the lead-line which was used until the 1930s: a sinker ran down a wire to the sea bed from a low-friction drum which measured the amount of cable as it ran out. As it hit the bottom, the length was noted and the navigator would use a table entering the length of the wire and speed of the vessel and the vertical depth was calculated. On some models, there was a chemical tube inside the sinker and as the sinker went deeper, more water would be forced into the tube and discoloured the chemical at a known rate. When it was recovered, the depth could be double checked by measuring how far up the tube the change of colour had progressed.

## Echo sounder

The concept of the echo sounder was developed by the Frenchman Paul Langevin, in 1917 and it still provides an extremely accurate method of determining a depth. Modern instruments are very different in the technology of their construction from early models but the principle of operation has really not changed in more than 80 years.

The principle is simple. In saltwater, sound travels at 1500 metres per second. A pulse of sound is transmitted from a transducer in the hull; it travels to the sea bed, bounces back and is recovered by a receiver (usually part of the transducer). The echo sounder measures the time difference between the transmission of the pulse of sound and the receipt of its echo and the depth can then easily be calculated using the formula:

$$\text{Distance} = \frac{\text{Velocity} \times \text{Time}}{2}$$

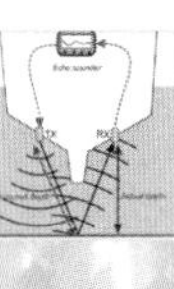



## The hardware

A pulse generator is fired by a timing control producing a pulse at a frequency in the range 10-250kHz and with a time duration of between 0.1–5.0 microseconds (µs). This pulse is converted into acoustic energy by a transducer which is normally fitted through the hull at approximately half to two thirds of the hull length from the bow. Occasionally a transducer may be fitted inside the hull. It directs the signal downwards through the water beneath. At the same moment that the pulse is released, the timing control sends a signal to the recording system to start a timing process.

A modern transducer is a single unit that combines the duties of transmitter and receiver. There are still some vessels with separate units for the two functions. These should not be confused with echo sounder systems having multi-transducer arrays, nor those in which two transducer signals are displayed on the same graph. A multi-transducer array provides the operator with optional transducers from which to select the most suitable position for the pertaining circumstances. Dual display systems may provide upwards of six transducers, any two of which may be selected at a time. This facility is particularly useful for wide-beam vessels that regularly operate in narrow channels.

The transducer can either be of the 'magnetic stiction' or 'piezo-electric' type. The former is a stack of nickel plates around which is an electro-magnetic coil and the latter a series of piezo-electric ceramic elements through which an alternating current is passed. Both types vibrate in sympathy with the alternating current and produce pulses of energy that the transducer converts into sound energy. This sound radiates from the transducer at 1500m/s and if reflected from the bottom, is received and sent to a built-in amplifier. This is then processed and passed to the display. Some models have a visual readout, which may be a neon bulb on a rotating arm, a digital read-out, a cathode ray tube or an LCD screen in black and white or colour. Alternatively, the information may be displayed on a scrolling paper roll.

The minimum depth that can be recorded is determined by the pulse length. The shorter the pulse length, the shallower the depth that can be recorded. Most navigation sounders are capable of reading depths greater than 1.5m. Maximum depth depends upon the power generated, the frequency of operation (the absorption of the energy by the water increases with frequency) and the reflective power of the sea bed, but in general is unlikely to exceed 2000m.

## Controls

*Range* A control which selects the limits of depth represented on the read-out. Modern systems commence at zero eg 0–30m, 0–100m, 0–300m, etc. The measuring scale changes with the maximum depth setting. Older models may have two or more ranges and the facility to zoom in on particular ranges eg 30–70m or 50–90m. Within these ranges there is a phasing system that gives windows of the displayed depth and enables the depth to be read off the paper record to a higher precision giving more detailed information. The MCA require that all depth scales read from 2m upwards, and do not allow phase ranging systems to be read.

**TOP TIP**

*Current statutory requirements state that every echo sounder range scale should start at zero whatever the maximum depth requirement setting. Does yours?*

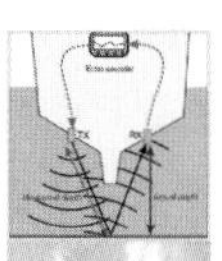



***Sensitivity*** This control adjusts amplification of the echoed signal and hence the strength of the mark that appears on the screen or paper trace. Sensitivity should be adjusted to give a distinct indication of the bottom, but avoiding excessive external noise. A time variable gain level can be provided to reduce the response from false echoes immediately after transmission is made from reverberations and cross-noise. This gradually increases with time until the level set by the sensitivity control is reached. It corresponds closely to the sea clutter control on a radar set.

***Discriminator*** A discriminator works in a similar manner to the rain clutter control on a radar set; it shortens the pulse length and hence the strength of each trace to assist the operator in differentiating between the bottom and returns from fish and spurious water noise.

***Fix marker*** A control which enables the operator to mark the paper at chosen times so that they can be reviewed later, eg when crossing expected sounding contours. Some paper trace echo sounders automatically print a time mark at given intervals and by noting a time against one of these marks, a subsequent time reference can be annotated to the depth record.

***Paper speed*** On scrolling paper-recorder echo sounders, the speed of the paper may be adjustable. This is helpful in survey work and gives a more detailed trace of the bottom. Conversely it can also be helpful in conserving the paper roll!

***Transmission mark setting*** A transmission mark may be displayed on paper-recording echo sounders simultaneously with emission of the sound pulse. This may be adjustable to give depth readings below the transducer, below the keel or below the waterline. It is important that the navigator knows for sure where the readings obtained by the echo sounder are measured from when checking depths during pilotage.

## Using the echo sounder

The depth indicated on the echo sounder as the default will be the measured depth of water below the transducer itself. (Some vessels may have more than one transducer). Thus it is essential to know where the transducer is positioned in relation to the water surface and the deepest part of the keel. Some echo sounders provide a correction facility to make an allowance so that the reading is adjusted to read from the waterline or from the bottom of the keel.

Although it makes water depth calculations easy if the echo sounder is adjusted to read below the waterline, it may lull you into a false sense of security if you forget

**Fig 9.1** Depth calculation.

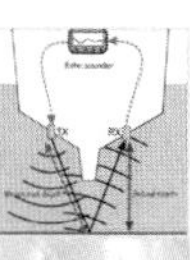

and think that the echo sounder reading is the depth under the keel. If an adjustment to the default reading is made, a notice to that effect should be mounted on the readout as a reminder and a note made in the Captain's Standing Orders. A sound pilotage plan will include the calculation of the least expected depth for each leg run. Modern echo sounders have alarms to provide warnings of unexpected shallow areas and of unexpectedly deep ones.

## Echo sounder errors

*Stylus error* On paper-recorder echo sounders, the rate of movement of the stylus across the paper must be correct and constant to ensure an accurate reading. The operating manual will contain details of how many passes or rotations of the stylus should be made in a fixed time period, enabling the operator to check, by counting, the average rate against the prescribed number. Any variation in the rate will cause an error; although a small deviation from the recommended rate will not make a significant difference.

*Index error* This is an error caused by the stylus not being zeroed when the pulse generator is activated. An off-zero index position may be set by the operator to compensate for readings other than directly from the transducer, ie below the waterline or below the keel. Care needs to be taken to ensure that any additions or subtractions to the index setting are adjusted as changes in the vessel's trim or draught are experienced. *Squat* (the difference in under-keel clearance of a vessel stopped and moving), which is generally not planned for, will affect the correct reading of an echo sounder.

*Separation error (also known as Pythagorean error)* If a separate transducer and receiver are fitted, the horizontal distance between them will cause an error in the indicated depth. This error is a function of the separation between the transmitter and receiver and the depth of water. This error increases as the depth decreases and can become misleading in shallow water (Figure 9.2).

## Propagation effects

*Aeration* As a vessel moves through the water, the bow wave causes air particles to be trapped in the sea water which are then carried as bubbles under the hull to cover the underwater surface for the first 25% or so of the hull length. These bubbles considerably reduce the output strength of the pulse and so it is important to site the transducer clear of these affected areas. In a bulbous bow vessel aeration

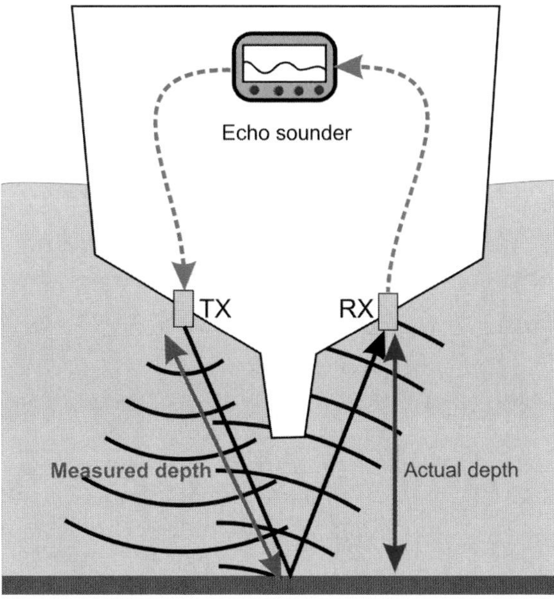


**Fig 9.2** Separation error. TX = transmit; RX = receive.

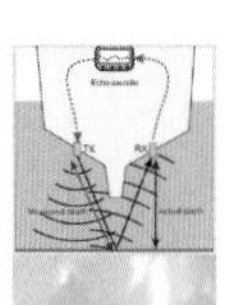



commences just aft of the bulb and so the optimum position for a transducer is in the bulb itself. Aeration can seriously affect performance and it will be exaggerated by high speed, pounding, shallow water, going astern, altering course and the interruption of the water flow by obstructions such as double-bottom caps, discharges, bilge keels and intakes.

*Reverberation and cross noise* These two effects cause spurious depth readings (unless reduced by the time variable gain control) near to and often indistinguishable from the index transmission mark. They are caused by reflections from hull obstructions or vibrations from the hull itself respectively. Reverberation can also be caused by air bubbles, particularly if the vessel is pitching violently.

*Propagation error* Transmission in the ocean is most unpredictable; from an acoustic point of view, the ocean is a stratified medium. The speed of sound in water changes with temperature, salinity and pressure. It thus changes significantly with the season, the time of day, depth, geographical position and the proximity to rivers, melting ice etc. Tables are available to take these variables into account to adjust the speed of sound in water and hence echo sounder depth readings. As an indication, the velocity of sound in water increases at the rate of 2.7m/sec for one degree rise in temperature; at 1.2m/sec for a change of one part per thousand in salinity and 0.007m/sec for one metre increase in depth. For example the Red Sea is hotter and more saline than average most of the time and so mariners in that area are advised to add about 5% to the recorded depth. In fresh water the echo sounder readings will appear deeper than is actually the case, possibly leading to a false sense of security. As this error is a percentage of the real depth, it is not significant in shallow water.

*Multiple echoes* These are caused by the reception of the signal echo after it has bounced successively between hull (or sea surface) and the sea bed a number of times. At each return some of the energy can be detected, progressively at weaker strength, and appearing as weaker responses at multiples of the actual depth. The effect is most noticeable in shallow water. It is for this reason that when a phased echo sounder is being used (one which reads ranges other than those starting at zero, 30–70m, for example), it should always be initiated using a zero-required range phase and a note made of the first echo return. Otherwise it is possible that the selected phase will not include the first echo return and switching on at one's expected depth may show one of the multiple echoes with the true depth being on a previous phase, hence the operator may believe that there is more water under the keel than is in fact the case.

*Multi-trace echoes* This occurs when the echo of a particular pulse returns from great depth at sufficient strength to be detected after the transmission of a subsequent pulse or pulses. It will show as a depth echo of apparently shallow depth and can easily be mistaken for a shoal.

*The cone effect* The transmission from the transducer is approximately conical in shape typically having a beam width of about 20° athwartships and slightly larger longitudinally. Whilst this reduces the chances of lost returns due to rolling and pitching, it can lead to incorrect readings when the sea bed shelves steeply. It can also mask depressions in the sea bed and, in deep water, can cause the soundings obtained to be displaced making the trace disappear in some cases.

*Side reflection* When passing through a narrow and shallow channel, side lobes of the pulses may bounce off the sides of the channel causing spurious readings which may be less than the

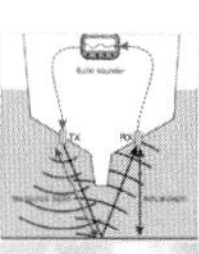

actual depth. Similarly mooring piles and channel marks may reflect pulses and display as small spikes under the vessel.

## Oceanographic influences

*Fish shoals* Some fish have swim bladders which can be distended or dilated in order to adjust their buoyancy. These bladders, being filled with gas, reflect sound waves in water and make an echo on the sounding trace. The nature of this echo will depend on the size, number and disposition of the fish concerned. In the open sea the echoes are easy to identify unless they are lying close to the bottom, where they will merge with bottom echoes. Echoes of fish swimming in the vicinity of rock pinnacles and coral heads can be extremely difficult to distinguish from echoes caused by weed and other growths.

*Water layers* As the pulse of sound passes through water of different densities, refraction takes place. In certain circumstances a partial reflection may occur, while in extreme cases the reflections may be complete giving a false reading. The higher the frequency of the echo sounder, the greater the chances of refraction and the greater the possibility of reflection taking place. In the open sea this is not common and it is unlikely to cause total reflections, so the bottom should be clearly distinguishable. Some types of coral exude a substance into the water immediately above and around them which gives the water a slightly opaque and milky appearance and this can cause partial reflections at its boundary.

*Deep scattering layer* Some forms of plankton can reflect sound waves quite effectively if they are present in sufficient numbers. The 'deep scattering layer' is thought to consist of plankton, which lie at a depth of about 1,000m in daylight. At night the layer is known to rise seeking warmer water towards the surface. It can produce strong echoes and is known as one of the most frequent causes of false echo soundings reported in deep water. The bottom is often invisible through this layer.

*Fresh water springs* Springs exist on the sea bed that have fresh water issuing from them. These springs can produce a marked echo on the readout which resembles a wreck or small shoal. It is usually possible to determine the sea bed through the water produced by the fresh water spring.

*Kelp or weed* This can be very difficult to identify on an echo sounder. The bottom is normally clearly visible through kelp and weed, although on occasions it may become obscured. Kelp is not common at depths greater than about 80m, but other weeds may be found at almost any depth in coastal waters.

*Turbulence* This is caused by the interaction of the tidal streams in the open sea or at the junction of a tributary. This may cause false echoes. The false echoes could be caused by reflections from the water layer and not from the turbulence itself.

*Sea bed characteristics* These will affect the appearance of the sounding on the recorder trace and this can often aid interpretation of the nature of the bottom. Rock will show as a thin hard line whilst mud on rock generates a smudge above the rock return. Sand gives a good firm line but mud alone is very indistinct, as are most types of seaweed. A steeply shelving bottom will reflect away a large part of the strength of the pulse and hence the image will appear very weak.

# 10 Measurement of Speed and Distance (Log)

**IN ORDER TO NAVIGATE SAFELY**, the minimum a mariner needs is a chart, a steering compass, an echo sounder and a means of measuring the distance travelled. For hundreds of years, navigation was carried out with these basic tools. Thus the ability to measure distance travelled is a vital element of navigation. In bygone days a reliable method was to cast a 'log' over the side at the bow and count how long it took to reach the stern. This was known as a Dutchman's log.

A more accurate method was developed in the 18th century that continued to be used until the turn of the 19th century where a kite-shaped plank was thrown overboard attached to a 100 fathom (180m) line. The plank was weighted so that it floated upright and provided drag on the line. As the ship moved away from the plank, the line was allowed to run out. The line was marked at intervals by knots and the number of knots pulled over the side in a time of 28 seconds as measured by an hourglass, (or 28-second glass, I guess,) gave the speed in 'knots', a term used to this day. A knot is a nautical mile per hour.

## Walker log

It was in 1838 that Thomas Walker came up with his towed log. This 19th century speed measuring device is still used today by yachtsmen and as a back up system on larger vessels. It is streamed astern of the vessel and measures the distance travelled.

The log line tows a 'rotator', which spins in the water in proportion to the vessel's speed. The rotator spins, turning its braided towing line which turns a spindle in a measuring device on deck that displays the distance run on a glass fronted display (Figure 10.1).

The Walker Log is susceptible to errors due to fouling of the rotator, a change of freeboard and adverse weather. The log does not perform well at slow speeds or in a following sea. The shiny brass rotator can attract large predatory fish! The line should be checked for deterioration on a regular basis. It is streamed once the passage is underway and recovered before the speed reduces too much to keep the rotator revolving. When streaming, the line is streamed first and the rotator is deployed once all the line is paid out in a bight. When recovering, the inboard end of the line is detached from the log recorder and, as the rotator is recovered, the inboard end is paid out over the stern otherwise the towing line ends up wound up in 'a right bunch of bastards', to coin a salty phrase!

# Pitometer or pressure tube log

The whole concept of measuring the speed of a ship changed in 1732 when Henri de Pitot, a French engineer, came out with a design of a machine for measuring the speed of running water and the wake of vessels. This log works on the principle that water pressure 'P' is proportional to the square of the ship's velocity 'V' times a coefficient 'K' where K depends upon the size, shape and speed of the ship and the length of the protruding part of the pitot tube. This is summarised by the formula:

$$P = K \times V^2$$

This log consists of a protruding tube or 'rodmeter' that extends 0.5m beyond the plating of the vessel with two openings in it. The tube is a hollow bronze rod of oval cross section with a flat end and an opening facing forward called the *impact opening*. Another two openings are located on the side of the tube and these are called the *static openings*. The impact and static openings are connected to two separate tubes running up through the tube. They are then connected to a pressure transducer that measures the pressure differential between them. As speed increases, the pressure in the chamber from the impact opening changes the pressure in the transducer and a reading of speed is obtained.

The relationship between the change in pressure and the movement of the indicating needle is not linear and has to be corrected. Speed accuracy is not reliable below one knot. A direct indication of speed is given by a pitometer log rather than a calculation from the distance travelled and the time taken. The log is less likely to be fouled than an impeller log as it has no external moving parts but is prone to blockage in silted waters or areas of heavy plankton activity. The major disadvantage of this log and all those mentioned thus far is that they are not reliable when used in shallow water.

This principle is still used in aircraft speed measurement today.

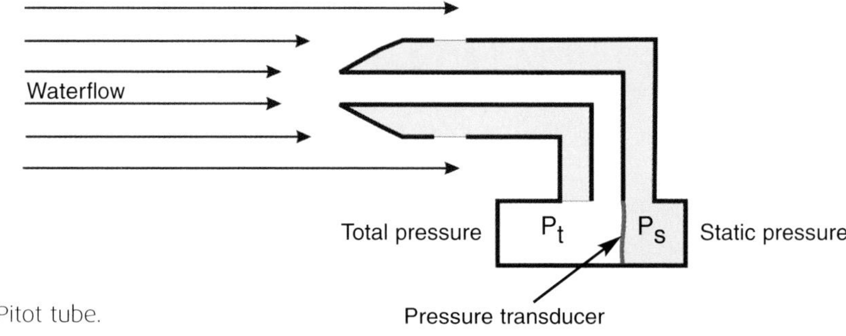


**Fig 10.2** Pitot tube.

# Impeller log

Sometimes referred to as the 'Chernikeeff log', this is operated by the flow of water passing along the hull. The water flow rotates an impeller which is mounted in a retractable housing and protrudes below the line of the hull. It can be retracted for cleaning should it become

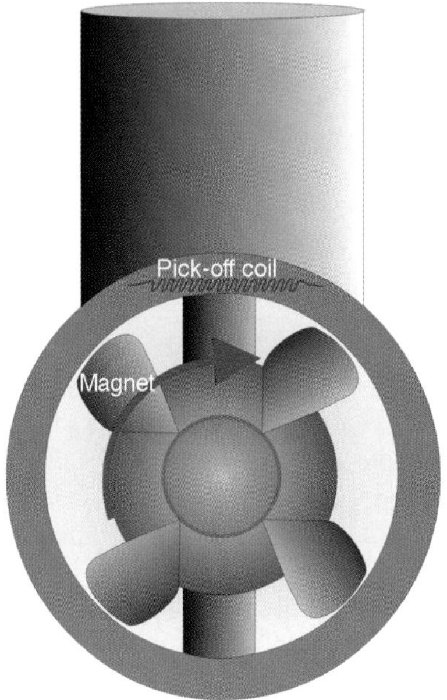


**Fig 10.3** Impeller log.

fouled. The impeller has a magnet in one of the vanes and, as it rotates, it induces an electromagnetic pulse through a pick-off coil. The induced pulses in the coil are counted by an electronic counter and fed to a speed indicator. The number of speed pulses is also recorded and their sum provides a record of the distance travelled. The equipment is intrinsically safe as the maximum output of the log is less than one volt and it is therefore safe for use on tankers. The log can be retracted if the vessel enters shallow water or is dry-docked. The impeller causes little drag and suffers very little slip or variable error.

# Electromagnetic log

The electromagnetic log works on the well proven electromagnetic principle of Faraday's law, which states that a voltage is induced in a conductor by a moving magnetic field. A sensor attached to the hull of the vessel produces an electromagnetic field by using the water as the conductor. An output is generated as the vessel progresses and water flows past the electrodes, which means that the output is generated relative to the ship's speed through the water. The coil and sensors are contained in a housing, which can be flush with the hull or may protrude up to 0.5m below the hull. The electronic signal generated is sent via a comparison transformer and amplifier to drive the speed indicator by means of a servomotor. This is then electronically integrated to compute the distance run.

# Doppler log

The Doppler effect is the change of frequency of the transmitted energy (acoustic or electromagnetic) resulting from the relative motion between a transmitter and receiver or reflector.

The Doppler log measures the change in frequency between the transmitted and reflected ultrasonic energy from the sea bed or water column, the change in frequency being proportional to the vessel's velocity.

The acoustic wave is directed ahead of the vessel at an angle of 60° to the horizontal. This has been found to be the optimum angle for the functioning of the transducer. The shape of the sea bed is not significant so long as it is not perfectly smooth, thus preventing any return of acoustic energy.

If the vessel is pitching, or trimmed, an error will be introduced. This can be overcome by two acoustic beams, one ahead and the other astern. This is referred to as the 'Janus Configuration' after the Roman God with two faces. The effect is to cancel out the errors induced by pitching and trim of the vessel.

The addition of a second transducer, placed at 90° to the first, enables an athwartships velocity to be indicated. This is referred to as a twin axis Doppler log. This log may work in either 'water' or 'ground' lock mode giving the navigator the choice of speed through the water or speed over the ground.

## Other methods of speed indication

If the log is malfunctioning there are other methods of determining speed that can be employed as a back up. ARPA radars often have a feature allowing the navigator to lock on to a radar conspicuous object and this will give a reading of the vessel's speed over the ground. The GPS will also display this. The engine revolutions can be calibrated to see what speed they produce and this can be used as a rough and ready *water* speed indicator. Ground speed can also be calculated from a succession of accurate fixes.

# 11 Radar

**THE WORD RADAR IS AN ACRONYM** and derives from RAdio Direction And Ranging. The development of the principle of using extremely high frequency radio waves to detect solid objects goes back as far as 1886 when Heinrich Rudolph Hertz proved conclusively that radio waves would be reflected when they came into contact with a solid object. Christian Hülsmeyer, from Düsseldorf, held a British Patent for a Hertzian Wave Projecting and Receiving Apparatus approved in London in 1904. Marconi promoted the feasibility of such equipment for use in ships in 1922, but the real breakthrough came during 1938 in the turbulent days before the start of World War II when the British Government poured money into research into what was perceived to be potential war-winning technology.

## Radar pioneers

The challenge for radar pioneers was to design a device that could fire a pulse of high frequency radio waves (microwaves) in a pre-determined direction and then catch any reflected echoes whilst measuring the time they had taken since they left the transmitter. The speed of a pulse of microwaves has been accurately measured at 161,860nm per second. To put that into perspective, a pulse could travel to the moon and back in just over 2½ seconds.

## Microwaves

Marine navigation radars use super high frequency microwaves known as 'X' or 'S' band:

X-band: 3cm wavelength, frequency between 9300 and 9500MHz.
S-band: 10cm wavelength, frequency between 2900 and 3100MHz.

Electromagnetic energy is generated by a magnetron and projected in the form of a fast continuous succession of pulses of radio waves from the radar antenna at the speed of 161,860nm per second. The pulses travel through the atmosphere until they encounter a solid mass when they are reflected and return to the antenna to be collected by a receiver and following various stages of amplification and video processing, they appear as a contact on the radar display. The time taken from the moment a pulse of microwaves leaves the antenna to the time the reflected pulse returns – multiplied by the speed at which microwaves travel equals the total distance the pulse has travelled, which, when divided by two, gives the range of the target.

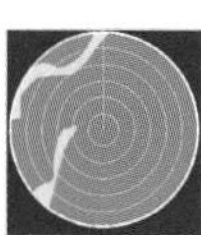

For example, if a pulse of microwaves was transmitted at time *t1* and they returned to the receiver at time *t2*, it could be calculated that, because of the known speed at which radio waves travel, the total distance they travelled would be: *161,860 x (t2 – t1)*. This answer in nautical miles (nm) then must be halved (because the microwaves have had to travel both ways) to give the distance between the transmitter/receiver and the target. This technology established conclusively that radar could be used to determine accurate ranges, but problems arose when the pioneers discovered that the short pulses did not contain much power and were only effective at short ranges, so longer, more powerful pulses were required to measure longer distances. At the same time they had to ensure that any potential return from each pulse must be received before the next one is transmitted, otherwise the interference would thoroughly confuse the display and the operator. This led to the development of longer ranges requiring longer and more powerful pulses and, at the same time, the interval between them needed to be lengthened. So, the longer the range-scale in use, the longer the pulse and the longer the interval

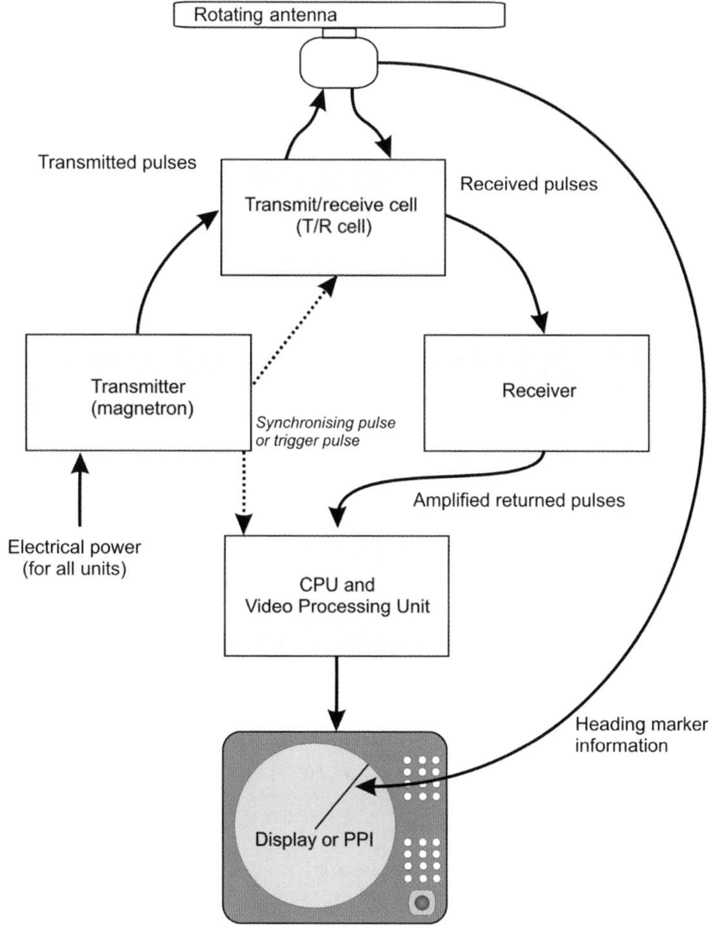


**Fig 11.1** Although this block diagram is simplified in the extreme, it clearly shows the relationship between the various component parts.

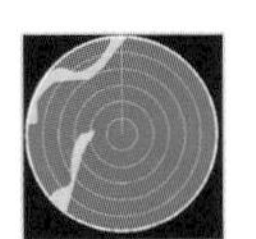



between pulses. On modern radar sets this is generally changed automatically with changes in range scale, however some sets give the operator the facility to select short, medium or long pulse according to their requirements.

The next problem that radar pioneers had was to be able to direct the pulses into a narrow beam in a pre-determined direction so that returning echoes could not only be timed, but the direction from which they returned could be determined. This was initially achieved firing the microwave pulses into a parabolic dish that directed them into a narrow horizontal beam. The narrower (in horizontal terms) the beam could be made, the more accurate the directional information could be determined. The parabolic dish had now been superseded by a slotted waveguide, of which more later.

## Components

The radar is composed of a number of parts as shown in Figure 11.1 (page 143).

## Transmitter or magnetron

The magnetron is the pulse generator. It has a cathode at the centre which is coated in a luminescence material that emits electrons. It is surrounded by a cylindrical copper anode into which are cut a series of cylindrical cavities. One of these cavities has a slot leading into a copper waveguide, allowing electrons to flow out of the magnetron into the waveguide, up to the antenna, which is itself just a horizontal piece of waveguide but with vertical slots cut at half wavelength intervals (Figure 11.2). The wider the antenna, the narrower the achievable horizontal beam width of electromagnetic energy being emitted.

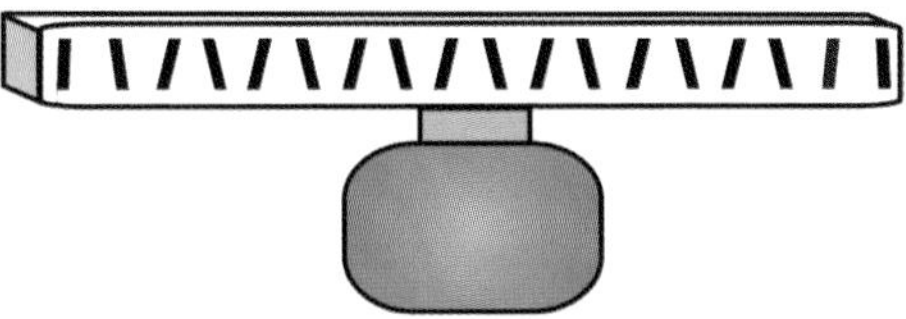

**Fig 11.2** Slotted waveguide.

An electrical current is generated by the pulse-modulator and 'triggered' at a precise moment. This passes through a HT coil (just like the ignition circuit in a basic petrol engine) and produces a large voltage difference between the cathode and the anode. The electrons move from the cathode to the anode, but they pass through a magnetic field created by a large magnet placed around the magnetron causing them to go in a long and circuitous route, with the magnetic field of each individual electron repelling each other, with the result that a big build-up of electrons occurs in the cavities in the anode. Those that end up in the single cavity that lead to a waveguide are then picked off by the pick-off probe and pass up the copper waveguide to the antenna (Figure 11.3).

When they reach the antenna, the waveguide along which they have travelled becomes slotted at half wavelength intervals allowing the emission of the radio waves into the atmosphere in the form of a beam with a narrow horizontal cross-section. During this operation, the magnetron becomes hot and requires cooling. This is achieved by fans or cooling fins built around the magnetron.

When the radar is first switched on, the magnetron needs to achieve operating temperature hence the built-in delay that is experienced. If the radar is left in stand-by mode for any period, a heater is used to maintain its operating temperature. The time that the trigger keeps the voltage across the cathode/anode dictates the length of the stream of electrons emitted, known as the *pulse length*. This technology that was developed in 1939, has since been refined but

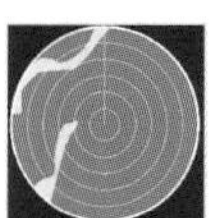

not dramatically improved upon. Although conventional wiring has not proved a satisfactory alternative to a waveguide for the transmission of radar pulses, some manufacturers now successfully use a shielded coaxial cable as an alternative.

The trigger which sets the operation in progress carries out three actions: it firstly switches off the receiver at the T/R cell to stop the transmission going straight to the receiver and blowing up the receiver; secondly it starts the transmission of electrons from the magnetron; and thirdly, starts the time base from the centre of the radar tube to the outside, at half the speed of sound. Each transmission from the magnetron makes up a very narrow section of the radar picture and each is known as a *radial line.*

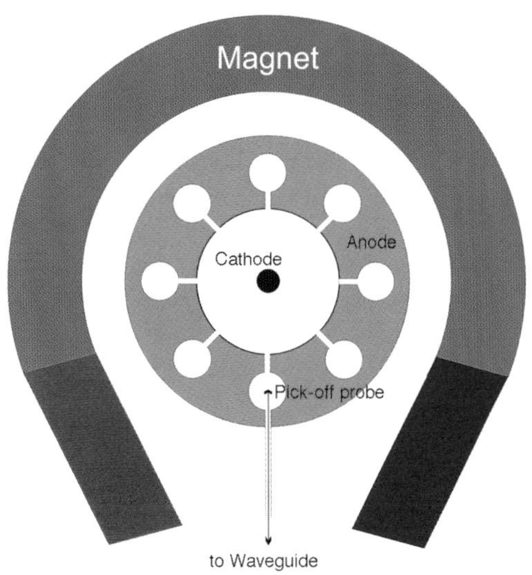


Fig 11.3

## Receiver

Electromagnetic energy in the form of pulses of radio waves is emitted from the antenna and, if the pulse strikes a reflective target, it is reflected back towards the antenna. The antenna catches the returning pulse, which is now a fraction of the power it was when it was originally transmitted, and passes it back down the waveguide through the transmit/receive cell (TX/RX) which is now open, allowing the reflected radio waves to enter the receiver. The reflected electromagnetic energy, although of much less power, is still at too high a frequency for a radio receiver to process in its raw state. The receiver therefore mixes the received microwaves with a low power frequency from a local oscillator in the receiver, forming a complex combined frequency. In order to adjust the tuning of the radar, the frequency of the local oscillator is changed so that the resulting frequency matches the preset intermediate frequency (IF) which was set in the receiver by the manufacturer. This combined lower frequency can then be amplified for use in the compilation of the image.

## Manual tuning or Auto Frequency Control (AFC)

As the magnetron warms up, it changes its size, and therefore its frequency output. The warm-up period is to enable the magnetron to reach its working frequency. A heater is used in the warm-up stage, and in 'standby mode' another heater keeps it at working temperature. To allow for any irregularities of the frequency of the magnetron, the manual tune or AFC control adjusts the local oscillator frequency to keep the mixed frequency exactly in tune with the amplifier. For a good radar picture it is absolutely essential that the radar is correctly tuned.

## Gain (linear amplification)

The relatively weak returning pulses are amplified in order that the video processor in the display unit can compile a useful image. This is done in six stages and could increase the strength of a pulse by up to $10^6$ or 1,000,000 times. However, care in adjusting the gain needs to be taken to ensure that the signal does not reach its saturation point before the last stage.

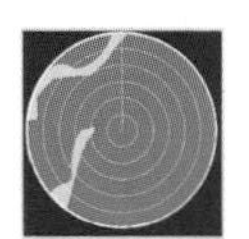



The operator has control of this linear amplification or *gain* on one of the earlier stages with the remaining ones being preset for optimum results.

It is possible for a large contact, sea clutter or precipitation to reach saturation before the final amplification stage, after which the amplitude of the signal remains the same. Thus if another contact reaches saturation at the final stage, both the contacts will appear to have the same image size.

### Gain (logarithmic amplification)

A logarithmic amplifier is more expensive than a linear amplifier, but has the advantage of amplifying the weak signal by a large amount to begin with, tailing off towards the sixth stage, and therefore avoiding the chance of the target reaching saturation. It copes with differentiating sea clutter and precipitation better than a linear amplifier. Some radars have the choice of selecting linear (LIN) or logarithmic (LOG) amplification.

### Threshold level

The threshold level is a setting made by the installer and cannot be adjusted by the operator. It sets how much receiver noise is removed, without cutting out small signal responses. It is based upon the average response from a target not reaching full amplitude or saturation when the gain is turned up to a point where there is a slight speckled background.

### Cathode ray tube

In older radar models, a cathode ray tube (CRT) was used to display the image taken directly from the raw data received from the receiver. To understand how that picture is displayed, it is simplest to look at how the CRT works. It is possible to amplify a very weak and intermittent electromagnetic response into an intelligible radio signal. This signal is converted into a voltage and fed into the cathode ray tube. A cathode ray tube has a cathode and an anode forming an electrostatic lens. A power supply is connected between the cathode and anode and a stream of electrons is fired at a phosphorescent screen. When the 'trigger' fires the transmission from the magnetron it also starts off the time base for this stream of electrons to be deflected from the centre of the display to the outside (by deflecting coils) at half the speed of sound. When the receiver senses a target response, it increases the voltage that is creating the electron beam. The higher the voltage, the more electrons hit the phosphorescent radar screen, causing a 'spot' to glow where the contact is to be found. The bigger the contact, the bigger the voltage increase and hence the bigger the spot target. So when using a radar with a cathode ray tube, it is more readily apparent to sense the size of the target from the size of the radar contact because it is formed from raw data, and not just a matter of illuminating a pixel on a modern LCD type.

## Spot size

Modern radars take information supplied from the receiver and amplify it, digitise it and then process it before it is displayed on what is, to all intents and purposes, a computer screen. The great advantage is that the image can be seen in daylight and that more sophisticated processing methods are possible. However, one does need to be careful to understand that a raster scan display screen is made up of thousands of minute pixels of which each one needs

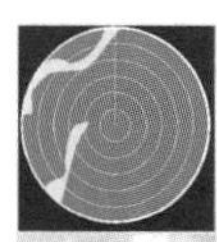

to be energised to make up its part of the image. If a contact is small and is between pixels it may not show at all, or it may illuminate all the surrounding pixels indicating a false size. There may therefore be a lack of correlation between the actual size of the contact and its spot size on the display. An inexpensive radar screen with a low pixel count is therefore less likely to display the smallest of contacts.

The horizontal beam width (HBW) of the radar will also have an effect upon the spot size. A contact large enough to be recognised by the radar will appear to have a spot size equivalent to its HBW. The further away it is, the larger it will appear.

## Transmitter power

When the transmission from a radar antenna hits a target there is a considerable loss in the reflected energy. After target bounce, the power of each pulse reduces by the fourth root so the reflected energy from a 16Kw transmitter is reduced to 2Kw and the reflected energy from a 4Kw transmitter is reduced to 1.4Kw.

It therefore follows that just transmitting huge amounts of power does not provide substantial increases in range. Appreciate that a small increase in range may produce a comparatively large decrease in response. A five-fold increase in power only yields an improvement in predicted detection range of approximately 50%.

When larger amounts of power are used, the interval between the pulses needs to be increased. This is known as the *pulse repetition interval* (PRI) and is increased to reduce the chance of a second trace echo occurring. Before the radar transmits again it is important to have waited long enough for all returning signals to have been received otherwise they may appear on a subsequent trace and cause confusion. With a radar set on a short pulse range, it is normal for the radar to delay sending the next pulse until a range of 41nm could have been reached, by which time the power of the pulse will have become attenuated or lost. When using a longer range with a long pulse, the radar will allow a longer period (PRI), in fact long enough for the pulse to travel 164nm before it too will have become attenuated or lost.

## Antenna rotation speed

It has been found in trials that there is a better chance of picking up a contact by hitting it a number of times consecutively with low power rather than hitting it once with high power. Therefore the speed that the antenna rotates is important in determining the chances of picking up a contact. The IMO require aerial rotation to be not less than 12rpm. However ,marine radar aerial rotation rates are usually in the region of 20–33rpm. With a pulse repetition frequency (PRF) in the region of 500–2000 times per second, and with a horizontal beam width in the region of 1°–2½°, an average radar will send off a pulse every 0.1° of aerial rotation, thus ensuring at least ten strikes of any contact in every pass.

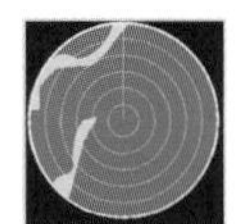

# Pulse Repetition Frequency (PRF) and Pulse Length (PL)

The number of pulse transmissions per second is known as the *pulse repetition frequency* (PRF) and is around 500 times per second when long pulse is selected, and up to 2000 times per second when using short pulses. Long pulses use more power and are required to achieve greater range and greater probability of detection. Short pulses give better definition and range discrimination. As the pulse length is increased so the interval between pulses is extended and, as there is no change in the speed of rotation, there will be less pulses per target pass. Therefore the shorter the pulse length, the shorter the dormant period between transmissions and the more pulses per target per pass and the better chance of identifying a small contact.

| | Pulse length | | | |
|---|---|---|---|---|
| | Short pulse | | Long pulse | |
| Range scale in use (nm) | Pulse Repetition Frequency (PRF) in Hertz or pulses per second | Pulse Length (PL) in micro seconds | Pulse Repetition Frequency (PRF) in Hertz or pulses per second | Pulse Length (PL) in micro seconds |
| 0.25 | 2000 | 0.05 | 2000 | 0.05 |
| 0.50 | 2000 | 0.05 | 1000 | 0.25 |
| 0.75 | 2000 | 0.05 | 1000 | 0.25 |
| 1.50 | 2000 | 0.05 | 1000 | 0.25 |
| 3.00 | 1000 | 0.25 | 500 | 1.00 |
| 6.00 | 1000 | 0.25 | 500 | 1.00 |
| 12.00 | 1000 | 0.25 | 500 | 1.00 |
| 24.00 | 500 | 1.00 | 500 | 1.00 |
| 48.00 | 500 | 1.00 | 500 | 1.00 |

Some radars are configured to use short, medium and long pulse lengths rather than just short and long. Some will change pulse length automatically with changes of range and others will allow the user to select short/medium/long pulse lengths.

# Radar antenna requirements

The IMO have set minimum standards for commercial navigational radars and require a maximum horizontal beam width of 2½°. This is easy to achieve with an X-band radar where an antenna width of 1.12m produces a beam width of 2°. X-band radar antennas on large merchant ships can achieve horizontal beam widths down to 0.65°.

On smaller radar models, particularly those with radomes rather than open array antennas, the X-band beam width may range as much as 4°–6°. When specifying a radar, it is important to consider the horizontal beam width as its size will be paramount to the quality of the bearing and the spot size of the image received.

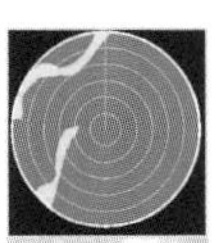

Antenna widths with S-band need to be 3.3 times wider than the equivalent X-band to achieve the same accuracy. As this is seldom possible, S-band antennas on large merchant ships have beam widths from 2° down to 1.7°. As an example, an S-band radar antenna achieving a 1.82° beam width requires an antenna width of 3.8m.

The IMO further require that any compass input to a commercial radar should be accurate to within ½°, and the thickness of the heading marker on the radar display should be no more than ½°. Additionally the heading marker should be able to be removed temporarily to ensure that it is not obscuring a contact, but should automatically reset itself once the removal switch is released.

The ship's heading marker should have an accuracy of 1° and the *electronic bearing line* (EBL) should have an accuracy of 1°. Although the scanner may physically look aligned with the heading marker this is often not the case because of the angle of squint caused by the way the main beam of the pulse leaves the slotted wave guide. To calibrate the alignment of the radar picture with the ship's head marker, select the 3nm range scale and point the vessel at a small contact on the outside of the radar picture, with Head Up mode selected (see page 153); if it is not immediately ahead select the calibration mode and adjust it accordingly.

The IMO require commercial radars to be fitted with range rings and a variable range marker (VRM). The accuracy is to be an error not exceeding 1.5% of maximum range scale in use, or 70m – whichever is the greater. To calibrate the range scale either:

(a) fix the vessel accurately alongside, taking account of the position of scanner and GPS aerial, and measure the distance to a cliff-like edge. Compare this with the chart, *or*

(b) when the ship passes between two fixed charted objects, compare the distance on the chart with the two ranges taken. The index error will be half the difference between the charted distance and the sum of the two ranges.

## Enhancing or echo stretching

The enhance control lengthens the contact radially on the screen so that it is easier to see. The range is not affected. All ranges should be measured from the inside edge of the contact, using the inside edge of the VRM. Enhancing or echo stretching a point contact makes sense in open water but take care if using this facility for coastal navigation as the coastline will become blurred and small inlets may disappear altogether.

## Comparisons of X-band and S-band

S-band wavelength is larger (10cm) so it is more powerful and will therefore travel further. The X-band wavelength (3cm) is very close to that of a large raindrop, so there is a serious loss of energy due to scattering and attenuation (power loss) in precipitation; so the reflected pulses from targets which might be expected to give a strong signal will be considerably reduced and masked by saturation within the receiver. Interestingly, drizzle does not cause attenuation to either radar type particularly. The S-band radar has a longer wavelength and so suffers less attenuation in precipitation.

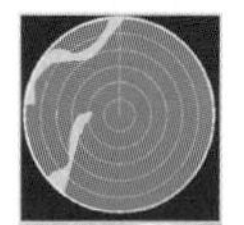



- S-band radar is better for looking for contacts in precipitation and through precipitation.
- The image response of an X-band radar for a target of a given size is better than an S-band radar.
- There is more sea-clutter response with an X-band radar than an S-band.
- For a given width, an S-band radar antenna is 3.3 times coarser, both horizontally and vertically than an X-band antenna.
- The radar horizon is marginally more distant with an S-band radar.
- X-band radar has better definition, range discrimination and bearing accuracy than S-band and is the preferred radar for accurate navigation, where long range scanning is generally not an important issue.

Having looked at both types, they both have important uses and if the vessel is of sufficient size to carry both, that is recommended; however if only one type can be carried then X-band should be the required option.

### Setting up a radar set

*Switch off*: Rain Clutter Control or Fast Time Constant (FTC)
Sea Clutter Control or Swept Gain
Automatic Clutter Control or Adaptive Gain
Interference Rejection (IR)

*Adjust in this (alphabetical) order*:
BRILLIANCE
GAIN until you can just see the speckles of background noise
RANGE to six or 12 miles
TUNING manually, or with AFC (Auto Frequency Control)

Then set CLUTTER controls
Turn on Interference Rejection (IR) if there is radar interference

## Sea clutter control or swept gain

Sometimes called 'Swept Gain' or 'Sensitive Time Control' (STC) because of time-related variation of gain. The control cuts the clutter to a greater extent at the centre of the radar, progressively reducing its effect out to 4–6nm. In older radars it was possible to remove the entire picture with this control, which makes it potentially the most dangerous of the adjustments that can be made to the image. If sea clutter removal is not really required – DO NOT USE IT. A searching technique should be used as the amount of sea clutter control needed varies on different radial lines. ***The incorrect use of sea clutter control can prove dangerous.*** Use only enough to break up the clutter, otherwise small contacts will be lost. Sea clutter control can also be used to see through rain clutter near the centre of the radar picture.

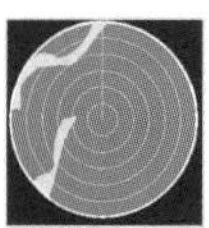

# Rain clutter

The rain clutter control uses a system of differentiation to leave just the leading edge of contacts. It is most effective for improving discrimination on shorter-range images. Another method (rather than adjusting the rain clutter control) which can be used to follow a contact through a rain cloud, is by reducing the gain. It is an academic argument whether to use rain clutter controls or simply suppress the gain when trying to discriminate contacts through rain clouds.

## Manual search for targets within precipitation

The masking effect of rain can be dealt with as follows:

(a) If the rain is close to the ship, searching with the sea clutter control may be effective.
(b) In general the most effective technique is to use the gain control in a searching fashion.
(c) If preferred, the rain clutter control may be used in a searching fashion, either alone or in combination with some suppression of the gain.
(d) Effectiveness may be assisted by overall reduction in response achieved by a short pulse length, a logarithmic receiver, selection of S-band TX, and/or selection of a low power transmitter.
(e) Use of adaptive gain provides automatic rain clutter suppression.

## Searching for targets beyond precipitation

Because of the attenuating effect of precipitation, it may be difficult to detect weak targets beyond areas of precipitation. This can be overcome by using an S-band radar or selecting a longer pulse length. It may be found useful to temporarily turn the gain control above the normal setting. The response of radar power from precipitation falls off in proportion to the square of the range.

# Automatic clutter control or adaptive gain

Ideally the clutter suppression should be set correctly for each radial line (each transmission) of the radar. No human operator can do this but a machine can, provided that a logarithmic amplifier is used which avoids saturation of the signal. This is called *adaptive gain*, because it adapts to the level of clutter experienced during the previous radial line (or transmission). When selected, the manual sea clutter and rain clutter controls are rendered inoperative; a fixed amount of differentiation is applied, and the gain is varied automatically, based on information received from the previous radial line.

The Constant False Alarm Rate (CFAR) refers to unwanted signals, such as noise and clutter, which cross the threshold and are referred to as false alarms. In the case of noise, which is a random phenomenon, the number of false alarms should be the same whatever the screen location, making the judgement of the threshold setting easy. With sea clutter, the false alarm rate is high at the centre, falling to a lower value with range. Adaptive gain seeks to simplify the problem of threshold setting by producing a constant false alarm rate, reducing the clutter to a noise-like response.

Depending on how well the threshold is set up, the radar has the ability to display *most* of the targets masked by clutter *most* of the time.

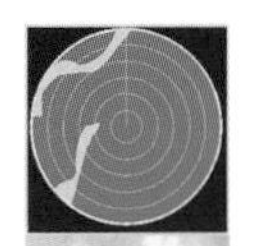



A prudent radar operator will switch off automatic clutter control from time to time and check the image manually, particularly when there is heavy clutter. The manual gain control remains operative.

Automatic clutter control should be switched off:

(a) To detect radar beacons.
(b) When carrying out a performance check.
(c) When attempting to identify coastlines.
(d) In rivers, narrow channels and enclosed dock areas.

### Rotation to rotation correlation

A further approach to automatic clutter suppression is available to systems that can store range and bearing data for more than a full antenna rotation or better still, for more than two or three rotations. The radar attempts to identify a weak target in clutter by the repetitive nature of its image when compared with random sea clutter responses. There is very little chance of a radar conspicuous wave remaining at the same range and bearing after one aerial rotation of approximately three seconds. If the comparison is made for three or more rotations, a correlation between the target can be made giving a greater or lesser chance of it being a contact.

The general effect of the correlation will be to favour consistent targets at the expense of clutter, but it must be borne in mind that targets that return an intermittent response, such as buoys or small vessels in a seaway, may be ignored.

Rotation to rotation correlation eliminates some of receiver noise and thus it is important to switch off the facility when setting the gain control.

## Interference Rejection (IR)

The receiver bandwidth of an X or S-band radar is as much as 20MHz, so there is a high probability of receiving energy transmissions from another radar as the total size of the radio band allocated to radar usage is only 200MHz. In this relatively narrow bandwidth, it is possible that pulses for another radar may be picked up by your own. It is relatively easy for your own radar to determine its own pulses by the strict timebase cycle in which it operates. If it receives other pulses which are not in sync with what it expects, it produces a random pattern on the display which often resembles spirals emanating out from the centre (Figure 11.4).

Whilst interference from another radar is tiresome, it does not actually degrade your own image and many mariners are happy to live with it. However, modern radars are fitted with an interference rejection facility which effectively looks at a succession of about ten consecutive radial lines and rejects any which do not follow the regular pattern of image which is being received. This is known as *line-to-line correlation.* Interference rejection should be turned off when initially setting the gain because it suppresses some noise and may lead to an incorrect gain setting which could mean that small contacts will be ignored. Certain types of step-sweep Racons may be also ignored by the radar when using IR.

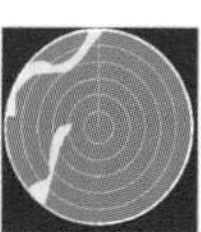

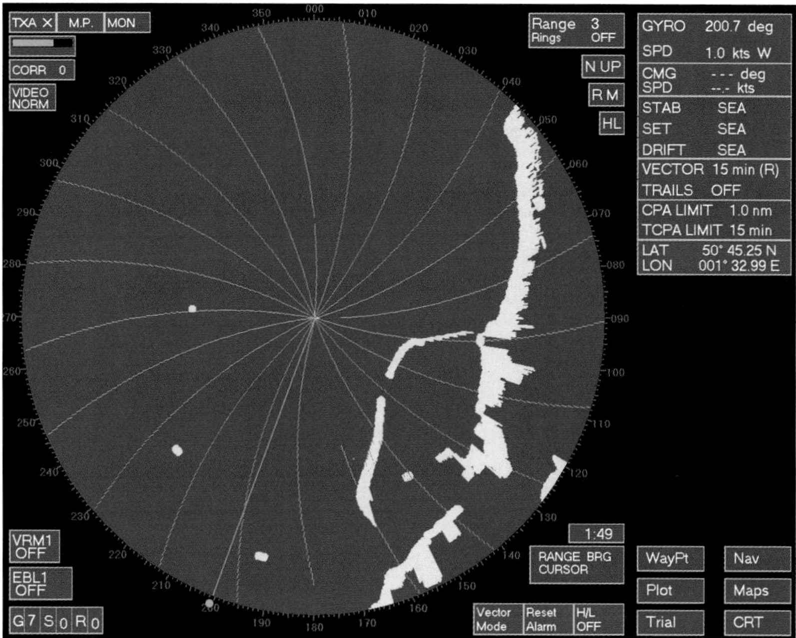


Fig 11.4 Interference rejection.

# Orientations of display (display modes)

## Head Up

A Head Up display is unstabilised by any external heading input and the heading marker points continuously up the radar screen (Figure 11.5, overleaf). Alterations of heading are shown by the entire image rotating away from the turn. It is difficult to take bearings in Head Up mode and in any case if there is no heading input, they will be relative to the ship's heading allowing plenty of opportunity for error. It is not feasible to attempt parallel indexing in Head Up mode.

**TOP TIP**

*Radar display orientation in the professional yachting industry varies from ship to ship and in some cases from watchkeeper to watchkeeper on the same ship. It is all too easy for an incoming watchkeeper to fail to recognise that the screen is not orientated to his or her normal preference and make a manoeuvring decision based on incorrect information. This is a dangerous practice and it is recommended that Masters' Standing Orders specify the way the screen is to be orientated and that all on board use the same orientation.*

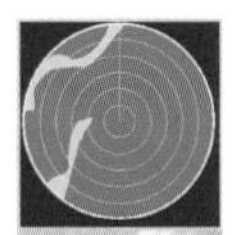

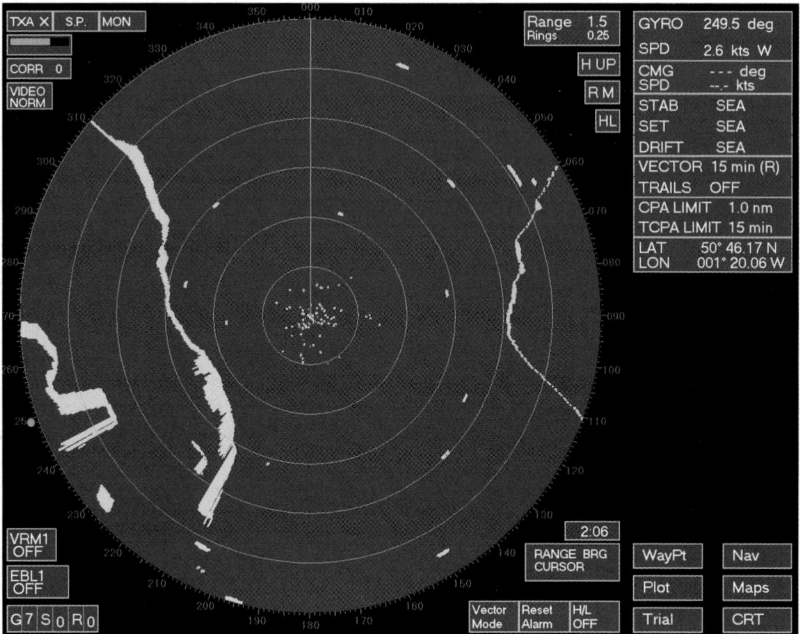


**Fig 11.5**
Head Up display.

## Course Up

A Course Up display is stabilised by an external heading input and whilst the heading marker still appears to point up the screen, any small alterations of heading are shown by the heading marker swinging from side to side (Figure 11.6 overleaf). The image on the screen is stabilised making it easier to take bearings that can be relative, magnetic or true according to the external input information.

## North Up

North Up orientation is the professionals' preferred choice. Not only is the image stabilised but any navigational points are orientated in the same way as a chart or plotter (Figure 11.7 overleaf). I have never been on a merchant ship or warship that did not have its radar in North Up mode and would not only recommend it, I would insist upon it!

# Relative motion or true motion

For collision avoidance, relative motion using relative vectors is the best way to give warning of a collision situation.

True motion has the advantage that it makes it much easier to identify manoeuvres of other vessels and the continuity of other target motion is not disrupted when the observing vessel manoeuvres.

True motion ground stabilised (see page 90) can lead to a mistaken interpretation of the target's true aspect in areas of strong tidal stream, in particular in head on situations, and should in any case not be used for collision avoidance.

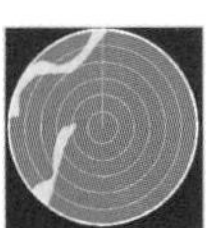

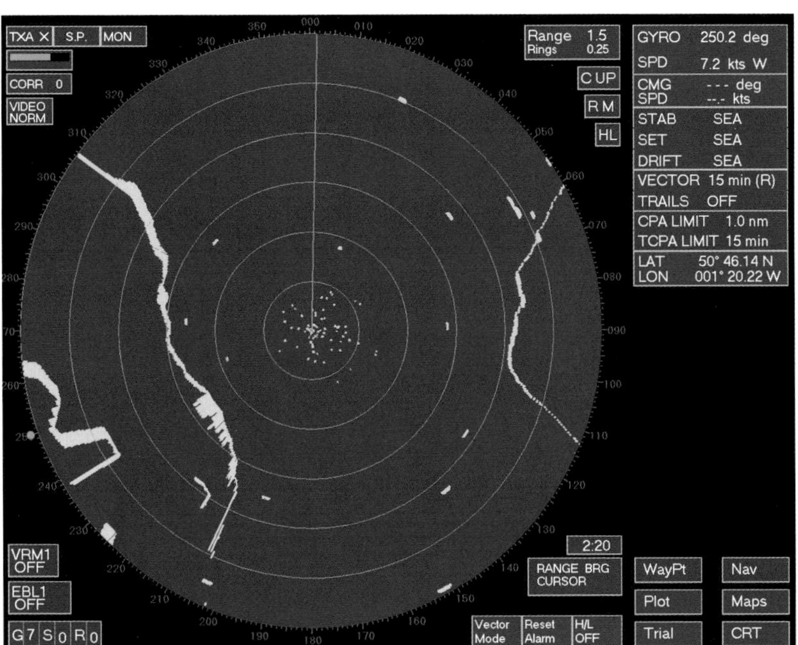


Fig 11.6
Course Up display.

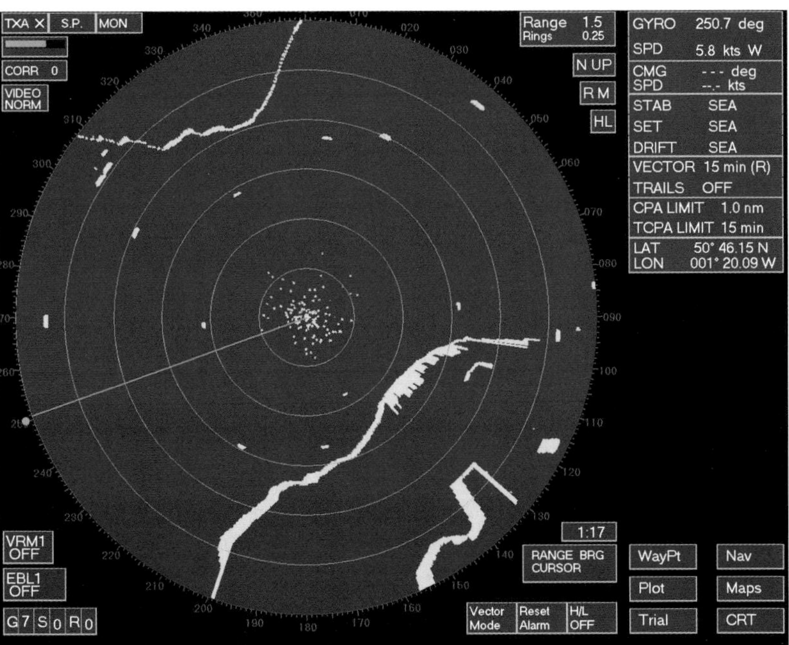


Fig 11.7
North Up display.

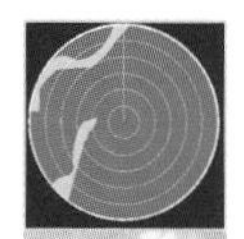



# Radar image limitations

## Vertical beam width

The IMO requires the vertical beam width to be no less than 20° to allow for ship's roll. In most radar specifications 25°–35° is quite normal. It further requires that specific target types be clearly displayed down to a minimum range of 50m. The least range that a radar set can receive a return signal is half the pulse length, and that also relies on the speed of the TR cell to change quickly enough from transmit to receive. A high mounted antenna will extend the maximum range but, at the same time extends the minimum range because the beam does not pass low enough to cover close-in objects. Sea clutter is more pronounced with a high mounted aerial. A low mounted aerial will achieve the closest minimum range provided the beam is not shadowed by the superstructure.

## Bearing discrimination

A wide horizontal beam width gives poor bearing discrimination and conversely a narrow horizontal beam width gives better bearing discrimination. The IMO set 2½° as the maximum acceptable horizontal beamwidth on commercial vessels. This means that in order for the radar to be able to discriminate between two objects at the same range, they need to be at least one horizontal beam width apart. If we look at the distance subtended by, say a 2° horizontal beamwidth at 10nm, it can be calculated that the ratio of the horizontal distance to range subtended by an angle of 2° is 3.5:100. Therefore at 10nm the width of the horizontal beam will be 3.5 cables or approximately 640m. So in practical terms, this radar will not be able to discriminate between two contacts less than 640m apart at a range of 10nm. They will appear as one target. At two and a half nautical miles they will need to be more than 160m apart to appear separately.

## Range discrimination

As the range is increased, so the pulse length needs to increase to contain sufficient power to cover the increased range. But by increasing the power and length of the pulse, its ability to discriminate between two contacts on the same bearing reduces. If the speed of radio waves is 161,860nm/sec which equates to 300 million m/sec, a pulse length of 1.0 micro-second will cover a distance of 300m; 0.25 micro-seconds will cover 75m; and 0.05 micro-seconds will cover 15m. This means that the radar will not be able to discriminate the range between two objects that are less than half a pulse length apart. Therefore using a radar on the 6M range with a long pulse, the pulse length will be 300m and a radar will not be able to discriminate range between two objects that are less than 150m apart.

## Formula for horizon range

Radio waves (microwaves) travel in virtually straight lines. Therefore the range is restricted by height of antenna, target and Earth's curvature.

Horizon range = 2.21 x sq root of antenna height (m)
(Radar horizon approximately 6% further than line of sight)

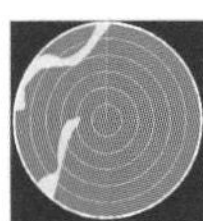

If the height of a coastline is known then the maximum range at which a coastline of determined height can be seen is given by the formula:

2.21 x sq root of antenna height (m) + 2.21 x sq root of coastline height (m)

## Sub refraction

Reductions in radar range can be caused by:

- Abnormal decrease in temperature with height.
- Increase of relative humidity with height.

Sub refraction can cause 40% reduction in range, particularly in Polar areas and in the warm sector of a depression.

## Super refraction

An increase in radar range can be caused by:

- Smaller than usual decrease in temperature with height.
- Decrease of relative humidity with height.

Sub refraction common in the tropics and in high pressure areas in temperate regions.

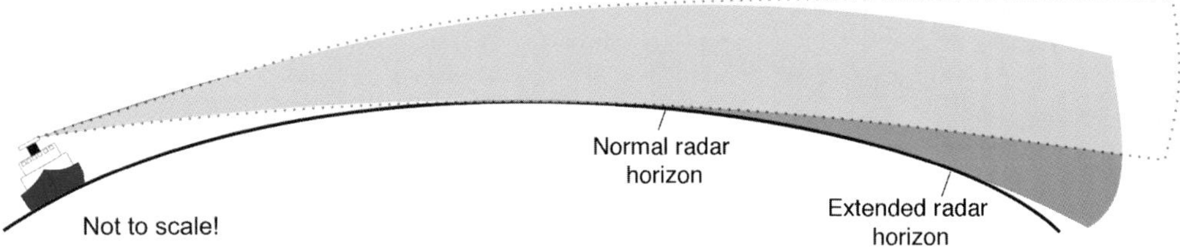


**Fig 11.8** Super refraction.

## Ducting or extra super refraction

This can cause increases of radar range up to 400nm! Ducting is caused by temperature inversion (air temperature rising with altitude and also a rapid decrease of humidity with height). This can cause a highly refractive layer as little as 30m above the Earth's surface and if the radar antenna is in or close to this layer, the radio waves get refracted by the duct and can travel through it for many hundreds of miles before being reflected and travelling back. This causes a second trace echo which should be ignored. The likely places associated with ducting are the Red Sea, Mediterranean with a southerly wind in summer, and the Canary Islands.

**Other reductions in range**

| | |
|---|---|
| *Rain*: | 25mm in 1 hour can reduce detection of up to 50%. |
| *Fog*: | 45m visibility can reduce detection up to 30%. |
| *Hail and snow*: | reduced detection up to 50% in heavy snow. |
| *Dust and sand*: | reduced detection up to 30% in sand storms. |

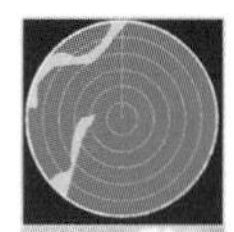

## Side lobes and side echoes

Although most of the pulse-generating effort goes into the main pulse, secondary pulses or side lobes are created as subsidiary beams of the main pulse (Figure 11.9). They become less strong the further they are from the direction of the main pulse. These side lobes can be reflected back from large passing contacts at relatively short range (up to about 3nm) and appear on the display as a series of decreasing echoes to the sides of the main contact. As they are all at the same range, they give the effect of a curved contact. Large bulk carriers in ballast or container ships beam-on are most likely to cause this effect. It is quite normal and cannot be adjusted out.

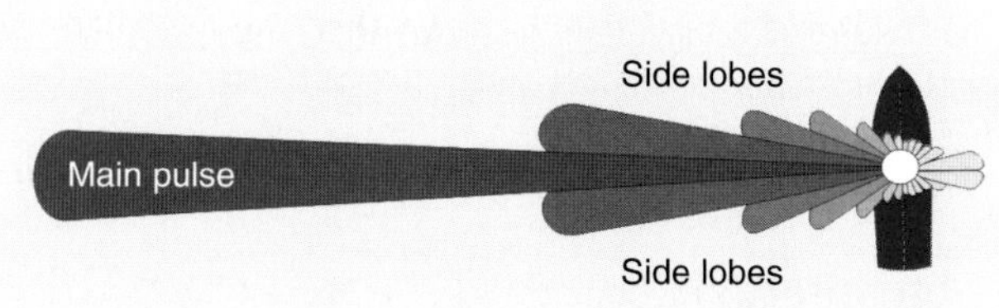


**Fig 11.9** Secondary pulses or side lobes are created as subscribing beams.

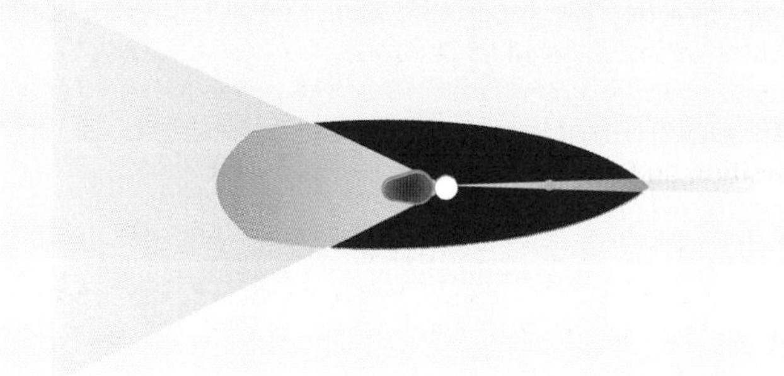

**Fig 11.10** Mounting a radar antenna in front of a funnel can cause a huge blind arc as can masts, superstructure, rigging etc.

## Blind arcs

Care needs to be taken when positioning radar antennae as parts of the ship's structure, masts and rigging can cause blind arcs (Figure 11.10). It is easy to get a blind arc without realising it. Most vessels have at least one blind arc and it is important to know from which direction you are least likely to see an approaching target.

## Shadowing

The radar image will suffer from both vertical and horizontal shadowing. This is because the radar cannot see around corners and promontories will obscure lower lying land behind them (Figure 11.11).

Similarly one vessel can be shadowed by being behind another and appear on the display as only one vessel (Figure 11.12).

## Indirect echoes

Indirect echoes are either caused by the radar pulses being reflected by the superstructure or cargo on one's own vessel

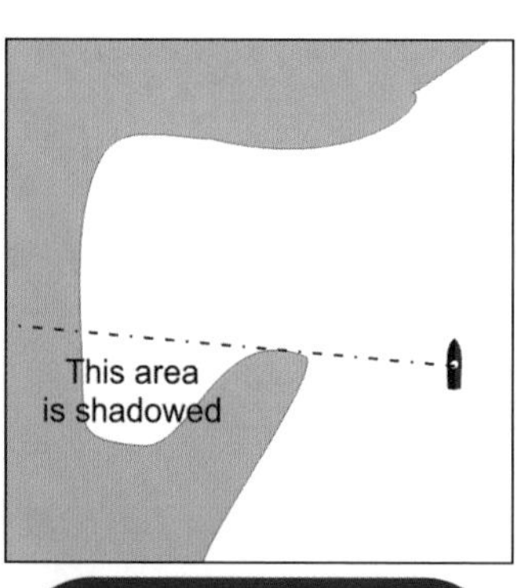


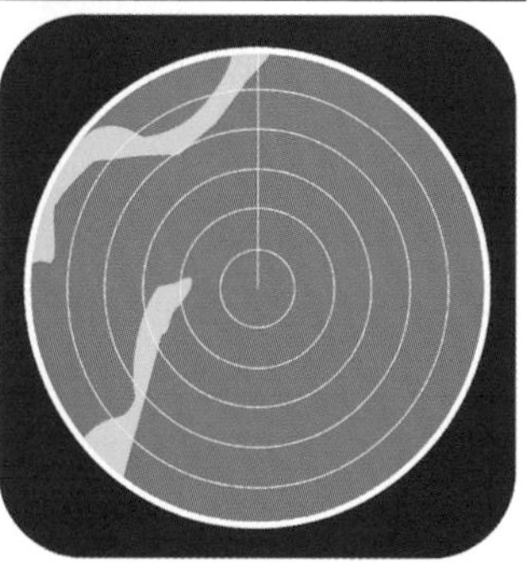

**Fig 11.11** Land shadowing.

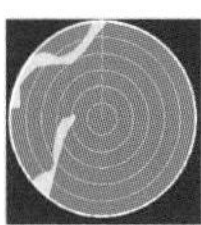

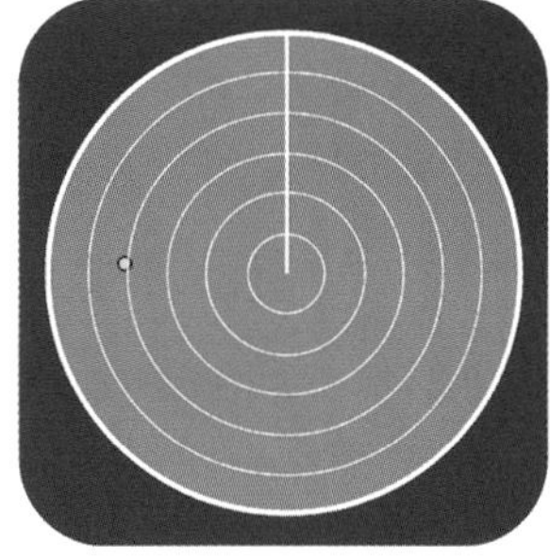

**Fig 11.12** Vessel 'A' will remain unseen by the radar whilst it is 'shadowed' behind vessel 'B'.

causing a contact to appear on the screen at the correct range but on the wrong bearing, or pulses to be reflected by the superstructure of another vessel causing a contact to appear on about the right bearing but at an incorrect range. Pulses can also be reflected by the hull or superstructure of a large ship, causing a double echo of a third target: once in its correct position and another in the direction of the large ship but at a greater range.

### Multi echoes and bridges

Multi echoes can be caused by pulses being reflected two or three times between your own vessel and a large target giving a series of contacts on the same bearing but at multiples of the correct distance.

A similar false echo can be caused as a ship approaches a bridge when radar pulses are reflected back by the bridge, hit the superstructure and are reflected again. This causes an apparent false target at the same range from the bridge as your own vessel but on the other side of it. This can be most disconcerting as the false echo will appear to be closing the bridge at the same speed as your own vessel and subsequent alterations of your heading to avoid it will be mirrored by the 'approaching' vessel.

## Coastal navigation using radar

### Radar fixing

Radar can be used most efficiently to fix the position of a vessel. We know that it is much better at measuring range than bearing and therefore by measuring three or more ranges and using a pair of compasses rather than a plotting device, a position can be established which should be without a 'cocked hat'. This is without doubt the most reliable way to fix a position in a pilotage or coastal navigation scenario as there is much less chance of operator error than there is when taking bearings. The fix is drawn with three arcs each having an arrow on each end as shown (Figure 11.13). It is not complete without the time being added.

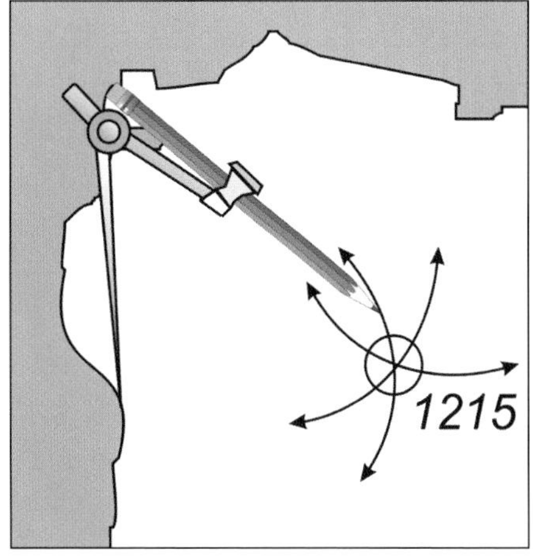


**Fig 11.13** Radar fixing.

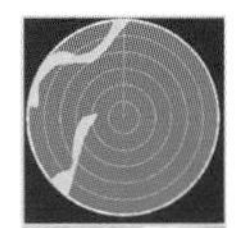



## Parallel indexing

If you are new to the concept of parallel indexing as a means of coastal navigation, prepare to be amazed at just how easily a radar in North Up mode can provide you with an accurate and efficient means of knowing whether you are on your planned track.

Setting up a simple parallel index is as follows:

***Stage One*** Decide on the tracks that you ideally want to follow. There is no need to buoy-hop in a navigational dot-to-dot game. Just simply decide where you would really like to go. Draw the tracks on the chart and mark them with their true courses (Figure 11.14).

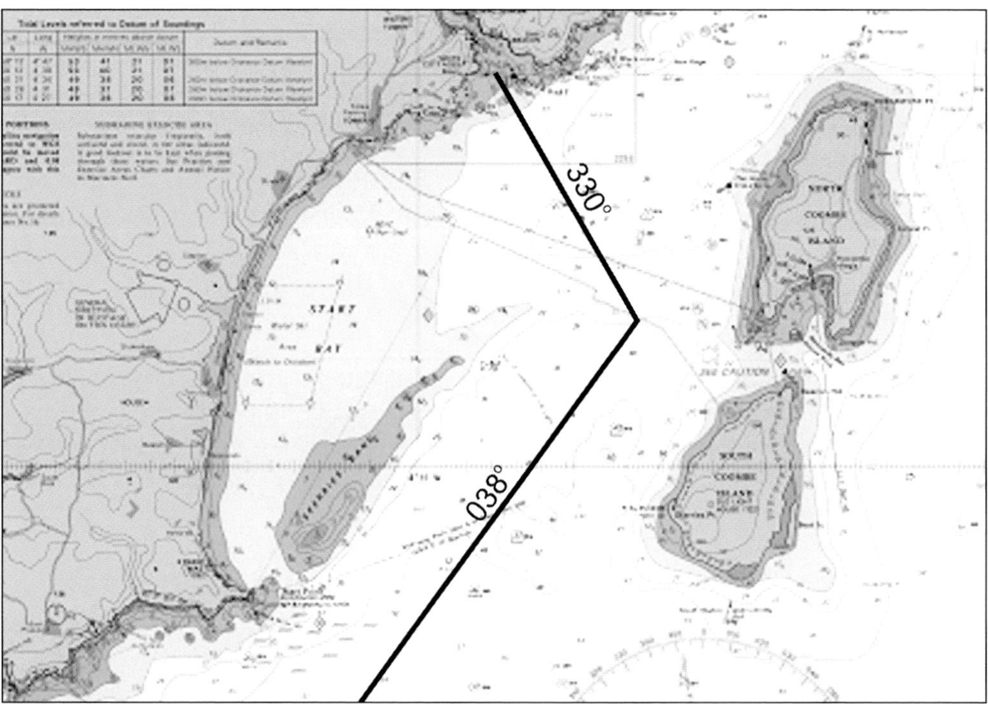


**Fig 11.14**

***Stage Two*** Select radar conspicuous points in the vicinity of the planned tracks. Radar conspicuous points are those which are readily obvious on a radar screen but that may not necessarily be so obvious to the naked eye. Piers, jetties, cliffs, in fact anything with a good vertical reflective surface will be radar conspicuous. Often objects that are obvious to the naked eye like church spires and tall buildings are not necessarily radar conspicuous. Having predicted the radar conspicuous points, draw a line parallel to the planned track passing through the edge of the chosen object (Figure 11.15).

***Stage Three*** Measure the perpendicular offset distances for each line and annotate it on the chart (Figure 11.16). These offset lines are called *parallel index lines* or *parallel indexes* (PI).

These parallel indexes are then noted and recorded in a Navigation Notebook before drawing the PI lines onto the radar screen.

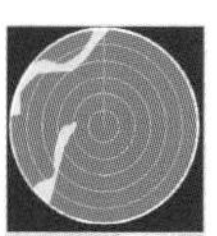

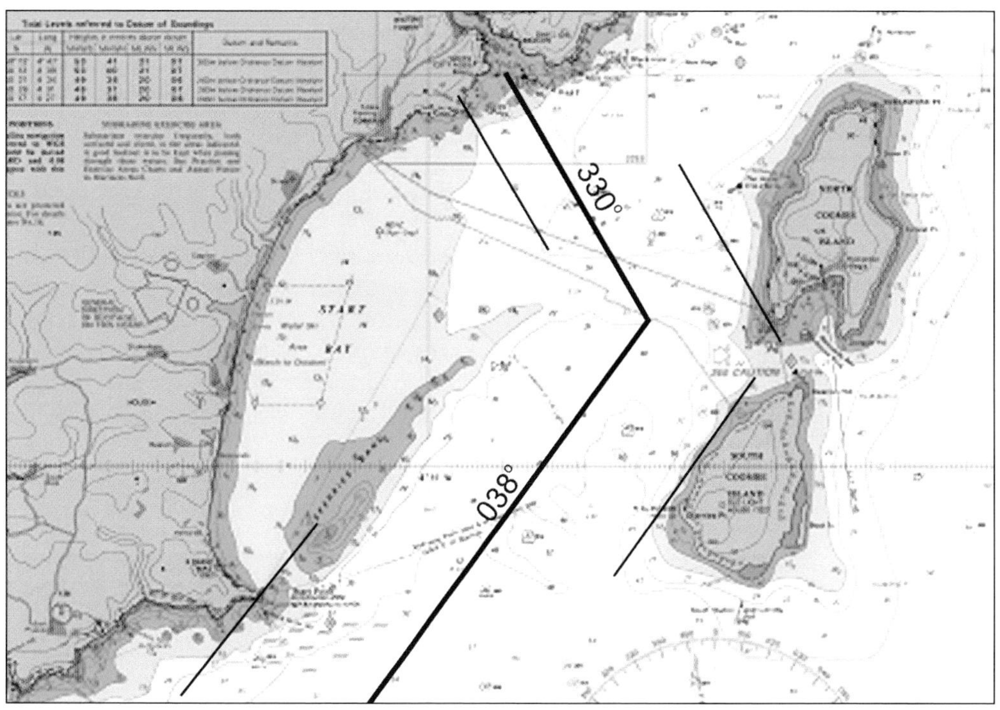


Fig 11.15

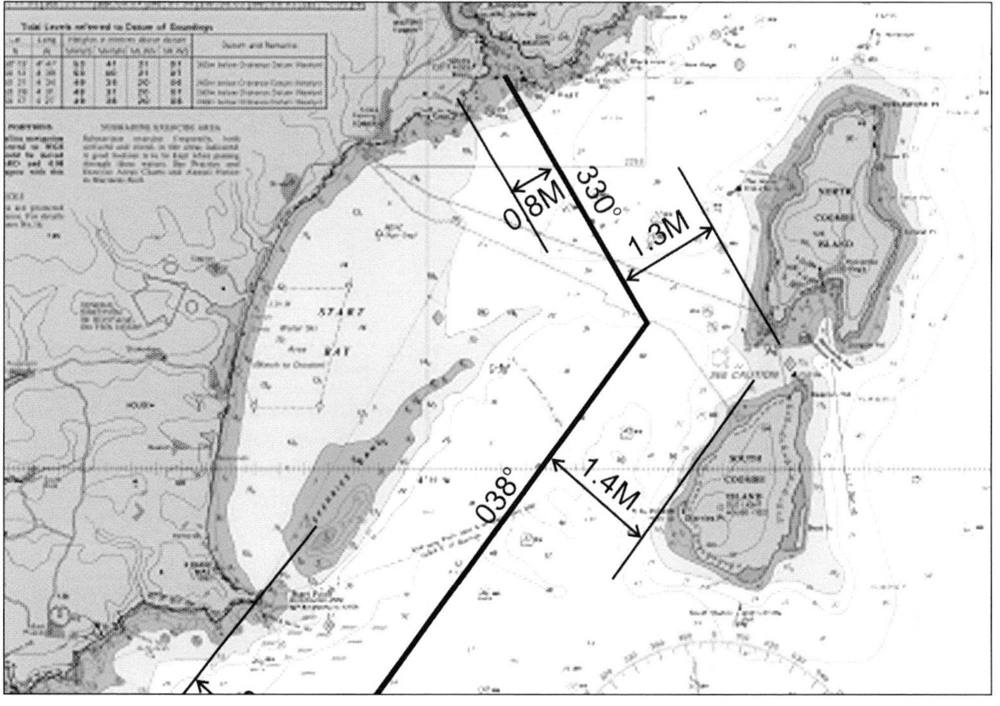


Fig 11.16

The bridge watchkeeper's skill is then to manoeuvre the vessel so that the first radar conspicuous point comes onto the PI and continue to manoeuvre so that it remains on the line. If the radar point starts to move too close to the vessel, manoeuvre away and vice versa.

This may seem difficult on paper but once it has been practised a few times, you will wonder how you managed before you encountered the 'black art' of parallel indexing.

There are many advantages in using parallel indexing, not least of which is the speed that it can be done.

Providing you manoeuvre so that the radar conspicuous point is on the PI line which you have drawn on the radar image, you can be sure that you are on your planned track and this will override the effects of tide and wind. This technique can usefully be employed by sailing vessels as a clearing line for knowing when to tack. Alterations of course become clear as, just before the next radar conspicuous point moves onto its PI, it is time to wheel-over. The wheel-over point can be worked accurately using turning data for the vessel and a second hatched PI can be drawn for more precise navigation.

In Figure 11.17, this particular radar draws a pair of parallel index lines for each bearing selected. In this case it is the line on the port side which is being used.

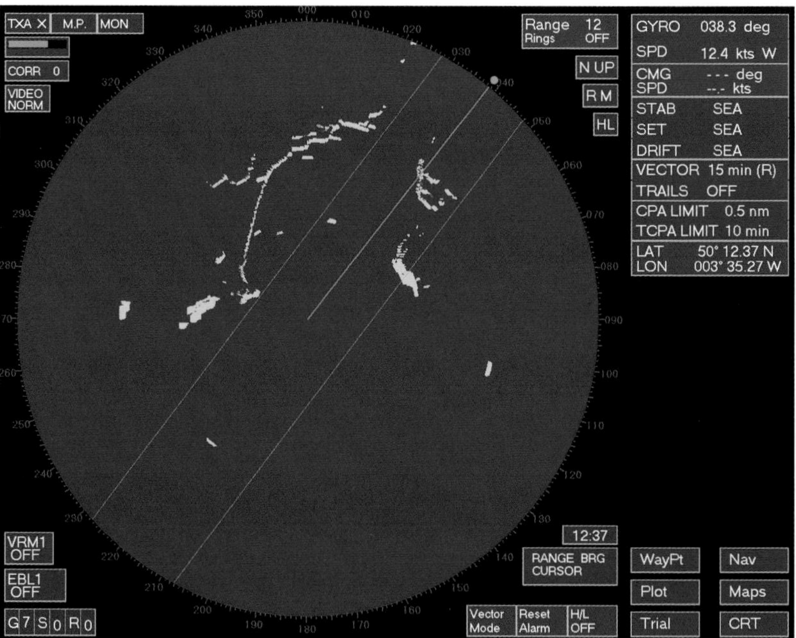


**Fig 11.17**
Parallel index.

# 12 Radar Plotting

**THE RADAR USED IN RELATIVE MOTION** is a simple and effective way of determining whether a risk of collision exists.

In good visibility, a steady compass bearing with decreasing range gives a good indication of the likelihood of a close-quarters situation developing and in poor visibility the radar can establish similar information by plotting. Plotting can be done in a number of ways. The paper plot was the original means of tracking contacts and before the arrival of the automatic radar plotting aid (ARPA) became the norm, it was the primary way of establishing whether a risk of collision existed. It was also the only way a mariner using radar could correctly interpret whether his vessel was overtaking and thus correctly interpret Rule 19 of the COLREGS. By plotting a succession of ranges and bearings it was possible to establish the course and speed of another vessel and confidently determine whether or not he was overtaking without relying on scanty information.

In order to plot another vessel you need to know your own course and speed through the water.

Start by plotting your Own Course (O) on the plotting sheet (Figure 12.1).

**TOP TIP**

*Do not, under any circumstances, use your course over the ground or speed over the ground in radar plotting as this will distort the aspect of the other vessel.*

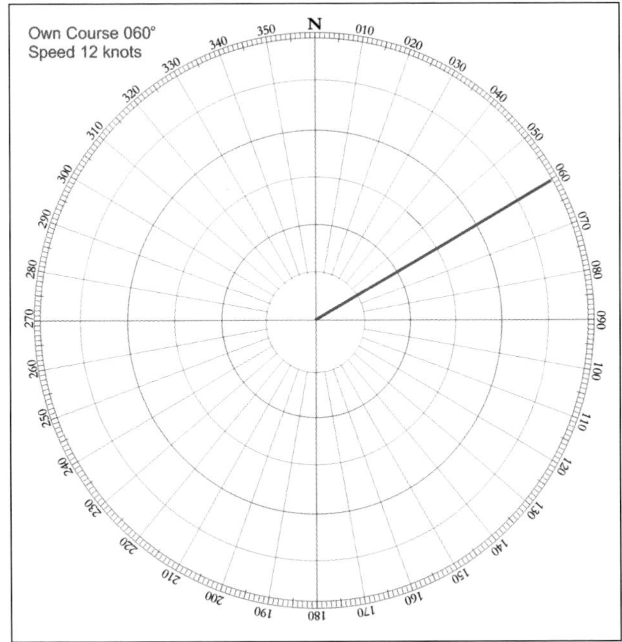


Fig 12.1

Measure time, range and bearing of each radar contact at regular (3, 6 or 12 minute) intervals (minimum of 3 times, bearings and ranges before plotting).

**Example**

1st Time: 06′ Bearing: 090°(T) Range: 6.0M

2nd Time: 12′ Bearing: 085°(T) Range: 4.5M

3rd Time: 18′ Bearing: 076°(T) Range: 3.2M

Plot the positions on the plotting sheet (Figure 12.2).

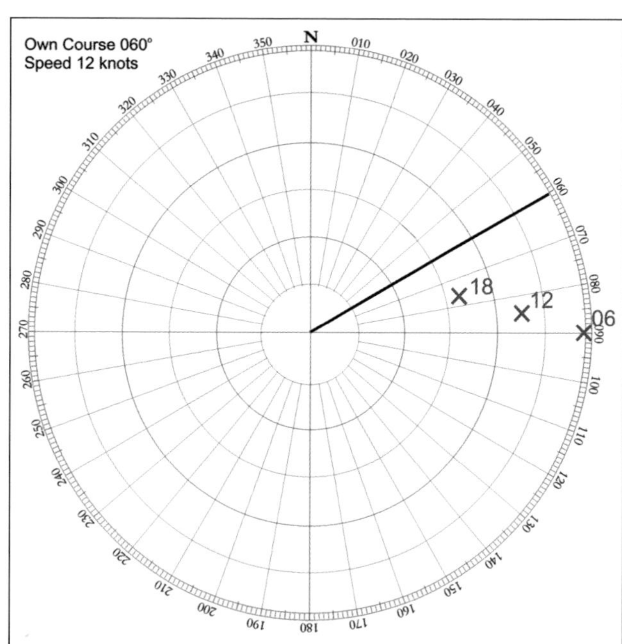


Fig 12.2

A radar set is one of the most important navigational safety aids to be installed on the bridge.

Join the plots which will be in a straight line, providing neither vessel has changed her course or speed, and extend it past the centre of the sheet.

The length of the line at right angles to that line passing through the centre is known as the CPA (Closest Point of Approach). This is the distance that will interest your Master most in the first instance (Figure 12.3).

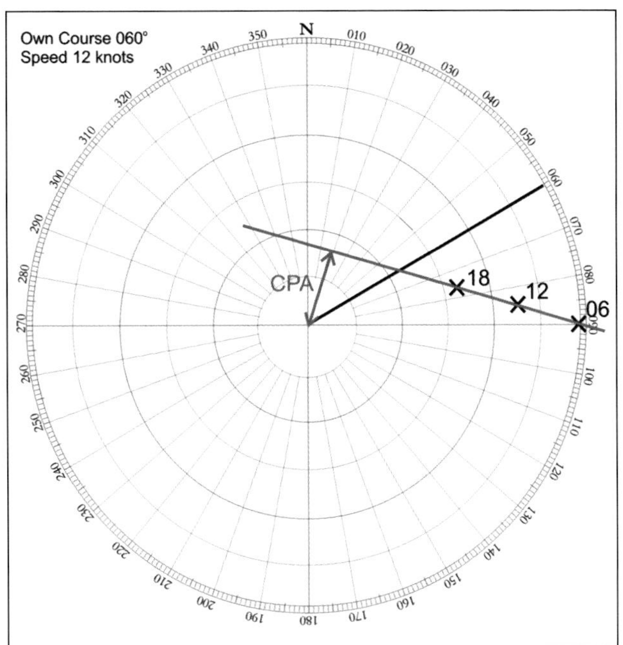


Fig 12.3

Time of CPA (TCPA) can be calculated using the time period between the first and last plots, related to the *relative* distances 'B' (between plots) and 'A' (from last plot to CPA position) (Figure 12.4).

Relative distance 'B' was covered in 12 minutes. Therefore, the time taken to travel along the relative distance 'A' which will give the number of minutes to the CPA will be:

(A ÷ B) × no of minutes of the original plotting period

$$3 \div 2.9 \times 12$$
$$= 11.6 \text{ minutes (say 12)}$$

Therefore TCPA = 12 minutes or at minute '30' (18+12)

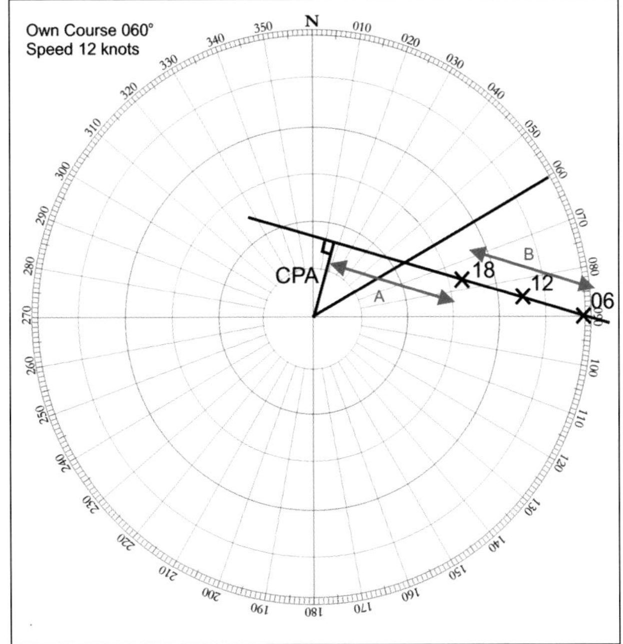


Fig 12.4

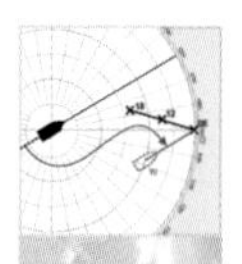



To calculate the course and speed of the other vessel which we shall call 'A'nother, we need to know where we were *relatively* at minute 06 when we first plotted 'A'nother.

Imagine we had dropped a fender overboard at minute 06. Where would it be relatively at minute 18?

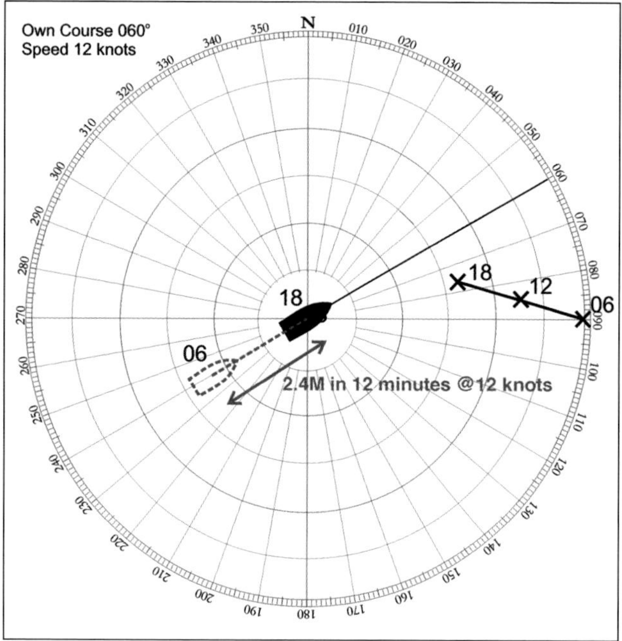


Fig 12.5

This line then gives the 'W'ay of our 'O'wn vessel for the plotting period (known as WO).

Transfer the 'Own' course and speed through the water line (WO) to join the first plot, maintaining its heading and length (speed in the plotting period). 'O' must align with the first plot taken (Figure 12.6).

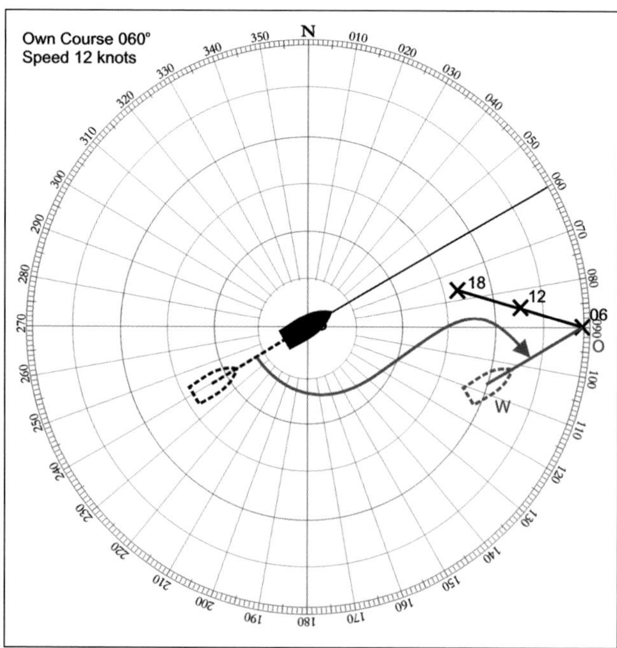


Fig 12.6

Having established 'WO', the position of the last plot is marked 'A', completing the 'WOA' triangle (Figure 12.7).

'OA' is the *relative* motion of the other vessel
'WO' is the 'Way of Own' – our own course
'WA' is the 'Way of Another' – the other vessel's course

These are marked with directional arrows to avoid confusion. The 'OA' directional arrow has a circle around it to remind you that it is relative speed and direction whereas the others are true speeds and directions.

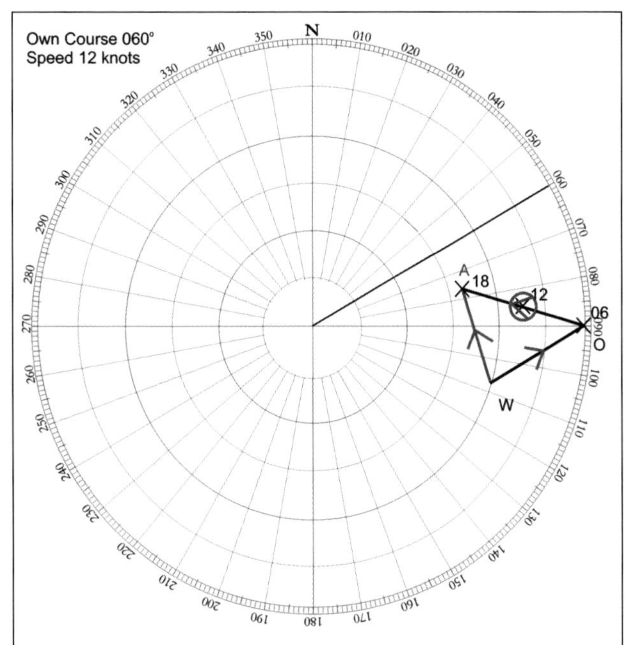


Fig 12.7

To measure the other vessel's heading, transfer the line 'WA' to run through the centre of the plotting sheet and read off the bearing on the outer edge. In this case 345°(T) (Figure 12.8).

If the length 'WO' was the distance *we* travelled in the plotting period, then the length of 'WA' is the distance the *other vessel* has travelled in the same plotting period.

2.2M in 12 minutes = 11 knots

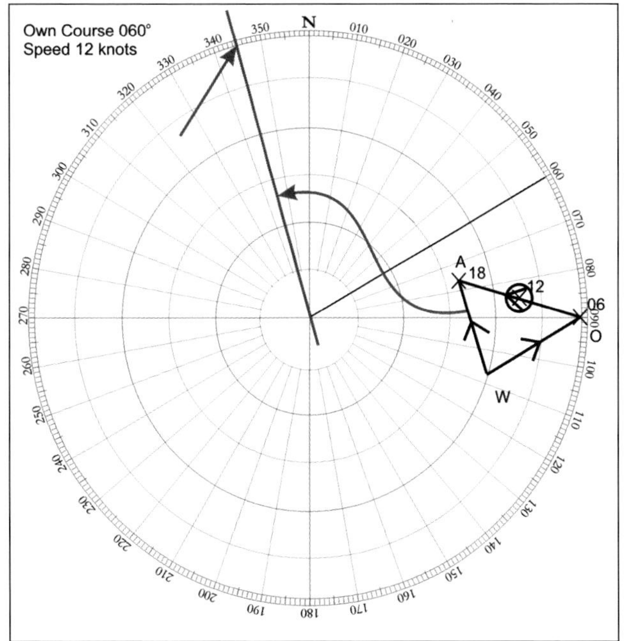


Fig 12.8

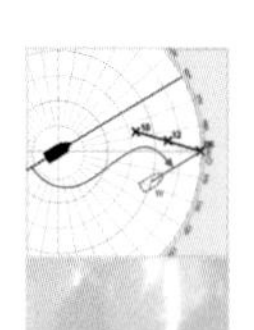

By extending the line 'WA', the angle between 'A'nother's heading and a line through the centre of the plotting sheet gives the aspect of the other vessel (Figure 12.9).

This is useful in interpreting Rule 19 of the COLREGS as to whether or not we are overtaking 'A'nother.

She sees us at '89° on her port bow' or at 'Red 89' and therefore we are not overtaking.

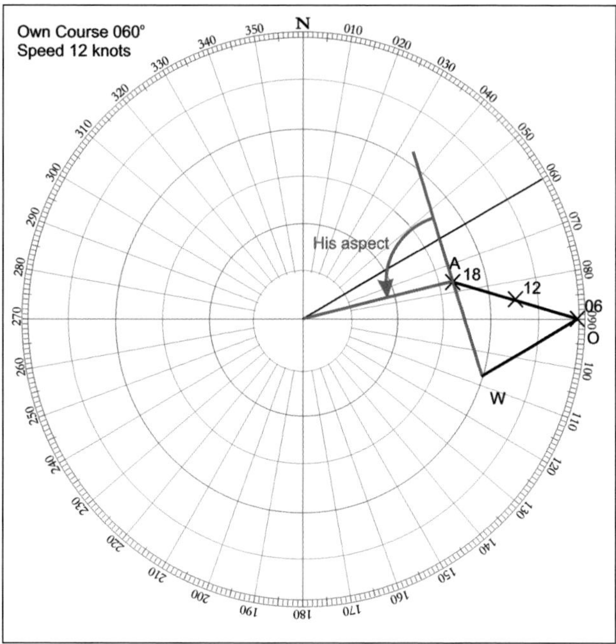


Fig 12.9

Now let's look at what happens if our own vessel alters 60° to starboard (Figure 12.10).

'WO' is the vector indicating our own course and speed. If we change our heading but maintain our speed, 'WO' remains fixed in length (because we haven't changed speed) but the course alteration changes the direction of 'WO' by 60° right to 'O¹'. It is important that 'W' remains in a fixed position.

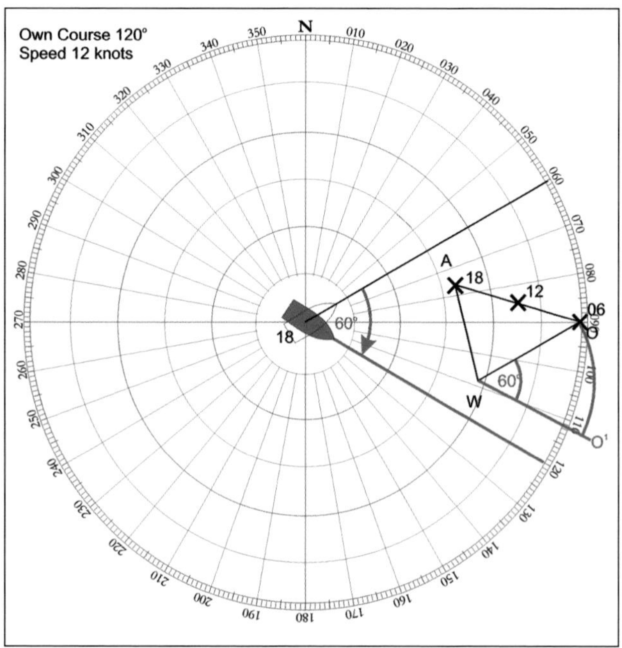


Fig 12.10

'O¹A' now gives the revised CPA following the course alteration = 3.0M (Figure 12.11).

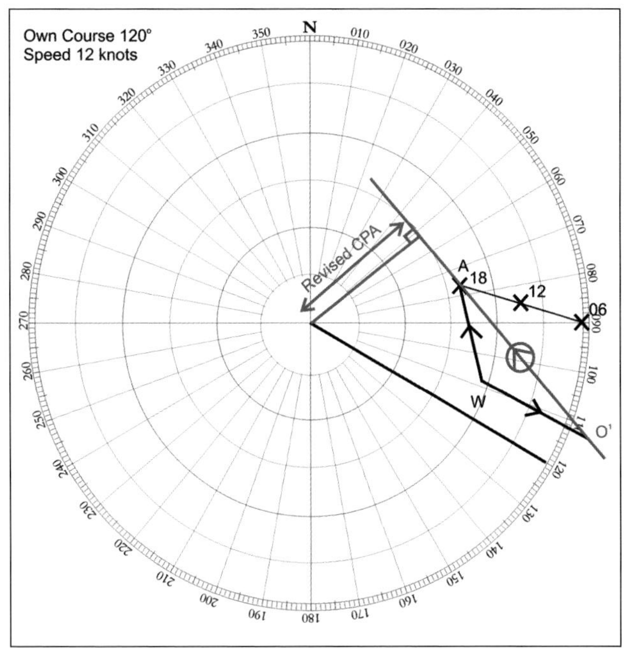


Fig 12.11

This also changes the TCPA.

As before TCPA
= A ÷ B x minutes.

Use the same number of minutes as before ie 12

Measure 'A' = 1.5M
Measure 'B' = 4.0M

Revised TCPA = 1.5 ÷ 4 × 12
= 4.5 minutes after minute 18
= minute 22.5
(see Figure 12.12).

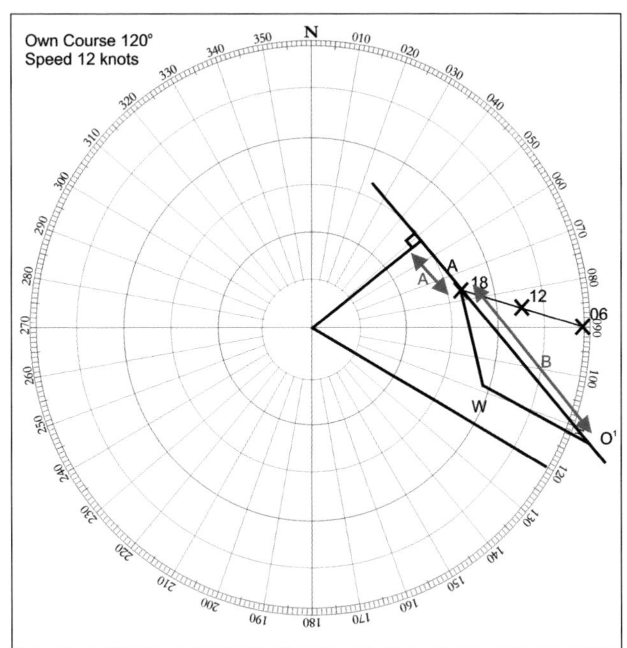


Fig 12.12

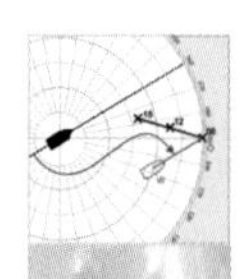



Let's now go back to the position before we altered course (Figure 12.13).

What happens if we change speed? Say, a reduction from 12 knots to 6 knots.

'WO' is 'W'ay of 'O'wn which was originally 2.4M long on the basis that at 12 knots we will travel 1.2M in 6 minutes and therefore 2.4M in 12 minutes.

Therefore to show a reduction in speed, the length of 'WO' should be reduced to the distance we shall travel in 12 minutes at 6 knots. This point is called 'WO[1]' and is now the distance travelled at 6 knots in 12 minutes ie 1.2M.

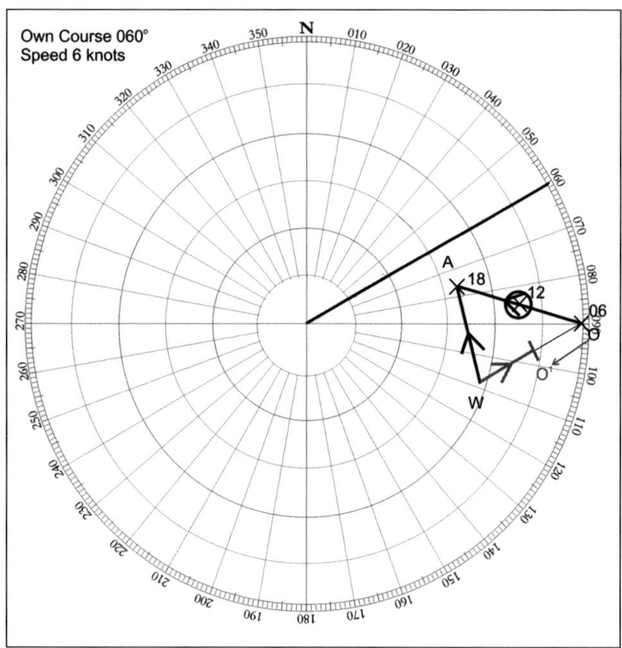


Fig 12.13

'O[1]A' extended gives the revised CPA at 2.6M (Figure 12.14).

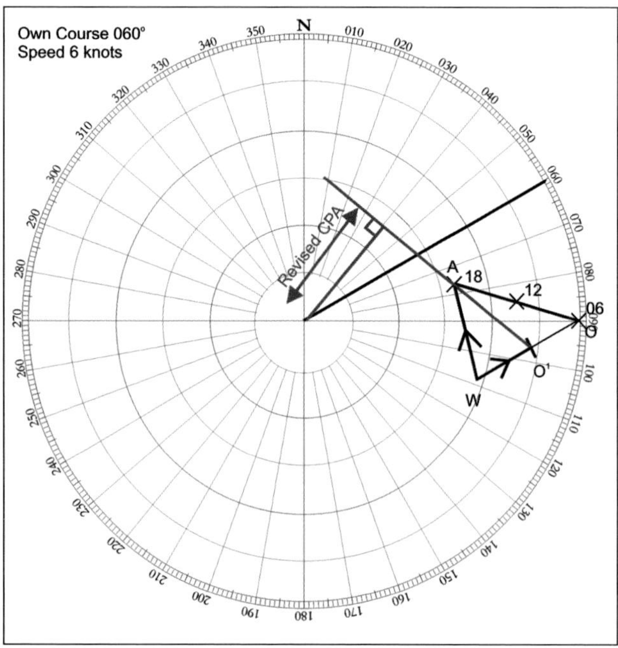


Fig 12.14

Now it is possible that when you plot an object that is in a fixed position such as a buoy or other navigation mark, you may be surprised to find from its vector that it appears to be moving. This is quite normal when your ARPA is set to 'sea stabilised'. This is when your heading and speed information is fed from a gyro or fluxgate and your ship's log rather than your GPS.

The fixed object will appear to move in the opposite direction to, but at the same rate as, the combined effects of the wind and tide or current on your own vessel. This can be a useful way of checking the effects of tidal stream or current and wind on your vessel (Figure 12.15). In this case the tidal stream or current would be going in the direction AW, and not WA.

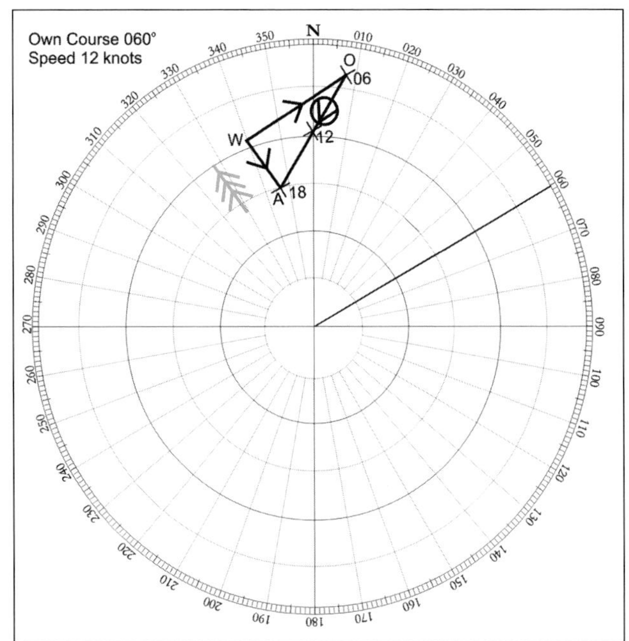


Fig 12.15

If your ARPA is 'ground stabilised' and you stop your vessel in the water – land, buoys and fixed navigation marks will appear to be stopped but your vessel will appear to be moving with the combined effects of wind, tide or current. This is a useful way of checking from where your ARPA is getting its information if you are in doubt.

# 13 Automatic Radar Plotting Aids (ARPA)

**WE HAVE ALREADY LOOKED AT HOW IT WAS POSSIBLE** to calculate the course and speed of another vessel using a series of (at least) three radar plots together with information about our own vessel's course and speed through the water. This manual plotting technique is relatively easy to computerise to avoid the laborious paper trail caused by paper plotting of several contacts simultaneously and is now included as a standard facility on all but the most basic yacht radar sets. However there are varying degrees of plotting aids available ranging from manual acquisition with no tracking of a small number of targets up to manual and automatic acquisition and tracking equipment which can follow more than 20 targets.

The IMO requirements for the carriage of radar and ARPA are detailed in the SOLAS Convention, Chapter 5, Regulation 19 and Annex 16.

In summary, every vessel over 300gt (gross tonnage) and under 3,000gt is required to be fitted with a minimum of one 9GHz 3cm X-band radar.

### Electronic Plotting Aid (EPA)

Vessels of 300gt–499gt are additionally required to have an electronic plotting aid capable of the manual acquisition and electronic plotting of at least ten targets but without automatic tracking.

### Automatic Tracking Aid (ATA)

Vessels over 499gt and under 3,000gt are also required to carry an automatic tracking aid enabling manual acquisition and automatic tracking of at least ten targets.

### Automatic Radar Plotting Aid (ARPA)

A full ARPA facility with manual or automatic acquisition of at least 20 targets and a trial manoeuvre option is not required on vessels under 10,000gt. Having said that, the majority of radar sets fitted in superyachts do have a full ARPA facility on one or more radar sets.

## How does ARPA work?

Heading and speed information are fed to the radar plotting aid and, by monitoring the relative movement of a selected target on a second to second basis, this is computed with your own vessel's heading and speed enabling the plotting aid to calculate the closest point of approach

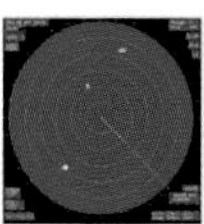

(CPA), time to the closest point of approach (TCPA), the true heading and speed of the target. Additionally, the bow crossing range (BCR) and bow crossing time (BCT) may also be calculated and displayed. This information is continually updated and, providing that the information from your own vessel's heading and speed inputs remain reliable, the target information produced can prove a most useful aid to the navigator in determining the risk of collision. It cannot be emphasised enough that this is an aid to navigation and navigators must not rely only on one source of information to the detriment of all others.

## Contact information example

| *Target 5* | *Updated 0.1 minutes ago* |
|---|---|
| BEARING | 089°(T) |
| RANGE | 9.1nm |
| COURSE | 223.8°(T) |
| SPEED | 15.3 knots |
| CPA | 6.7nm |
| TCPA | 25.4 minutes |

Each target manually or automatically selected will be provided with an indication of the target's motion trend within a minute of being selected and must, within three minutes provide a continuously updated indication of the target's predicted motion. This is shown as a *relative vector* (the default setting) from which it is possible to determine whether or not there is a risk of collision.

The direction of a vector is self-explanatory, however its length is determined by the operator according to a chosen time period. So vectors are displayed based upon 3, 6, 9,12,15 or whatever time period is selected by the operator. Ideally they need to be long enough to be able to determine direction but not so long that the end disappears off the screen otherwise their use in determining motion in time periods is lost. Navigators are generally fond of six-minute periods as speeds, whether relative or true, are easily calculated.

It is important to understand the significance of the different types of vector displayed in an ARPA radar.

### Relative vectors

The default setting of any ARPA radar is *relative vectors.* (Figure 13.1 page 175) This is the setting from which you can determine the risk (or not) of collision providing that your heading information is supplied from a gyro/fluxgate compass and your speed information is supplied from a 'water speed' log. I mention this specifically because if you have a Doppler log it can be set to provide water or ground speed.

**TOP TIP**

*Remember, input from a GPS or other electronic positioning system cannot be used to provide speed through the water.*

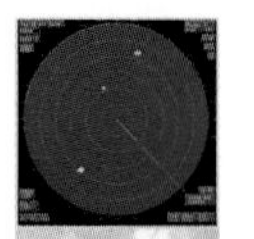



## True vectors

To the uninitiated, the whole concept of being able to see the true heading and speed in the form of a vector from another vessel may seem attractive. It may help to explain the true picture in terms of which way other contacts are really heading and give an idea as to their true speed – but be wary. This is not the information that a prudent navigator requires. He is primarily interested in determining whether a risk of collision exists and it is not possible to determine this with any certainty when using ARPA set to true vectors. Some ARPA sets give warning of the use of true vectors by outlining the vector box on the screen in red (Figure 13.2 opposite), others will not remain in true vector mode for more than a short period before reverting to relative vectors. It is imperative to know what sort of vectors you are looking at and, as a ready check, your own ship will also have its own vector when true vectors are displayed. Accidents have happened when bridge watchkeepers have thought that they were looking at relative vectors when in fact they were looking at true vectors. Some Masters will not allow their radar to be used in other than relative mode with relative vectors and this is not a bad policy amongst those who are inexperienced. It is not good policy to allow the radar settings to be changed according to the whim of each watchkeeper as, in the case of an emergency, it is all too easy for one setting to be mistaken for another.

We have looked so far at our own ship's movement information being supplied from a gyro/fluxgate and water speed log. This is not the only input which can be supplied and it is important to understand the differences about information input.

## Sea stabilised

If heading information is provided by a gyro or fluxgate compass, and the speed is measured as speed through the water as from a log, then the radar and ARPA is said to be 'sea stabilised'. That is to say the effects of tide (and wind) on your own vessel are not accounted for and any free-floating stationary or moving targets will be shown with their true heading and speed through the water calculated by the ARPA. This is important in determining the risk of collision and assessing aspect. It is the true heading and water speed together with aspect that is required to confidently assess the risk of collision.

If the wind and tide are not taken into the calculation, what happens to the apparent motion of a vessel at anchor or a navigation mark in a tideway? The tide will have the same effect on our vessel as it has on other free-floating or moving vessels in the locality, so whilst their heading and speed information is good for assessing risk of collision, what apparent motion does an anchored vessel or navigation mark, or land have? It appears to move in the opposite direction and at the speed of the combined forces of wind and tide on your own vessel.

So with 'sea stabilised' input:

1 Moving vessels have their water track and water speed calculated by the ARPA.
2 Stationary free-floating objects appear stopped.
3 Anchored vessels, navigation marks and land appear to move in the opposite direction of the combined effect of the tide or current and wind on your vessel at the same speed as the combined effect on your own vessel of tide and wind.

**TOP TIP**

*Always check that your ARPA is set to 'sea stabilised' before using it for collision avoidance.*

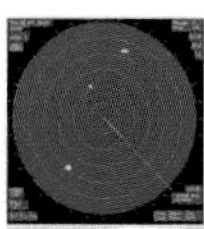

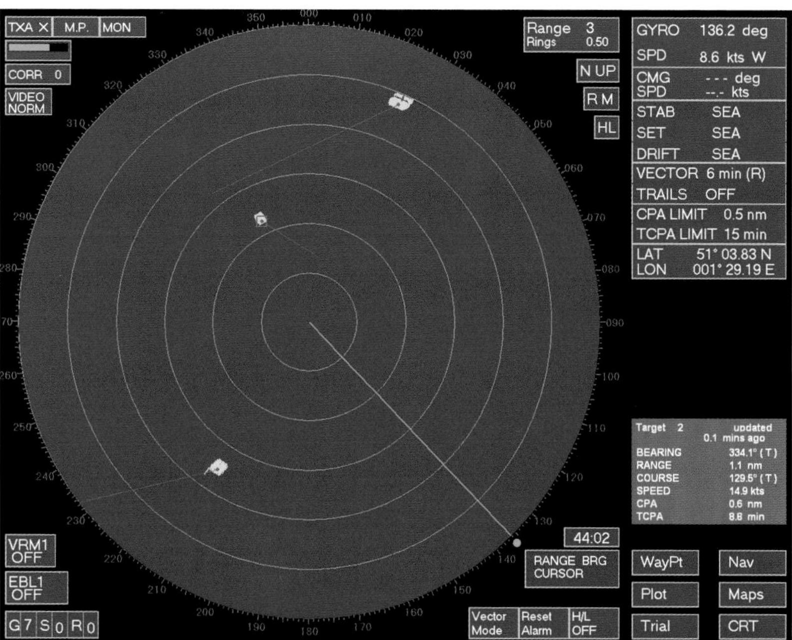


**Fig 13.1** Relative ARPA vectors.

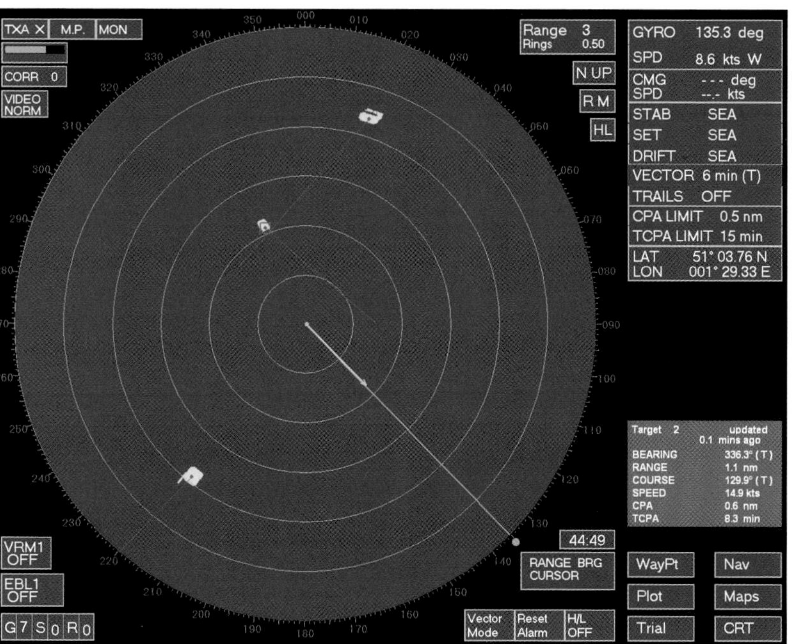


**Fig 13.2** True ARPA vectors.

This is the correct setting for determining whether a risk of collision exists. It will also calculate the accurate aspect of the radar contact so that correct action can be taken in a potentially close-quarters situation.

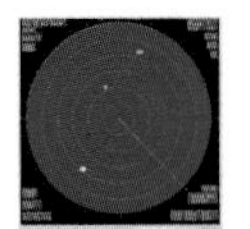



## Ground stabilised

If the heading and speed information supplied to the ARPA is obtained from a GPS, Loran 'C' or other electronic positioning system or from a Doppler Log set to output speed over the ground, the output image can be significantly different. Because the ARPA makes its calculations using your course and speed over the ground, the answers it generates will be the courses and speeds of all other contacts over the ground. Whereas in 'sea stabilised' input, fixed objects appear to move; in 'ground stabilised' mode they appear stationary.

So with 'ground stabilised' input:

1 Moving vessels have their ground track and ground speed calculated by the ARPA.
2 Stationary free-floating objects appear to move in the direction of the tide (and wind).
3 Anchored vessels, navigation marks and land appear to be stationary.

This setting is often used by commercial pilots in pilotage situations as it enables them to monitor progression along a planned track better than when 'sea stabilised'. However it can very easily be misinterpreted if used to assess the risk of collision.

**TOP TIP**

*Do not use your ARPA for anti-collision decisions if it is set to 'ground stabilised'.*

## CPA/TCPA limits

The operator can set alarm limits for the closest point of approach of any tracked target together with the time at which the alarm should be indicated. So an alarm could be set for any tracked target to be sounded if the CPA is less than, say 1nm and when the TCPA is, say 15 minutes. This will give the bridge watchkeeper adequate warning of a close encounter, but only if the target is already being tracked. Therefore small targets which may only appear at a relatively close range could easily be missed and these alarms can only be treated as yet another aid to the bridge watchkeeper.

## Guard zones

Together with ARPA, the radar will have the facility to set up a guard zone or zones to give audible warning of any contact entering a specified area on the screen. This can be another useful aid to the bridge watchkeeper but be aware that small contacts which are not detected within the range of the guard zone, and appear subsequently, will not trigger the alarm. This is yet another useful aid to navigation but it is far from infallible. (Figure 13.3 opposite.)

## Tracking history

The ARPA must be capable of displaying, on demand, the tracking history of each target for at least four equally spaced periods. These are usually at two minute intervals. This makes it easy for the bridge watchkeeper to keep track of a number of targets and keep a visual record of alterations of course or speed by other vessels and may help to be able to predict, with some success, the future intentions of targets. The history can either be set to relative or true tracks. It is shown in Figure 13.4 (opposite) as relative tracks.

## Trial manoeuvre

The ARPA should be capable of demonstrating a 'what if' manoeuvre by one's own vessel. This enables the bridge watchkeeper to try out a manoeuvre to see if it will work before committing

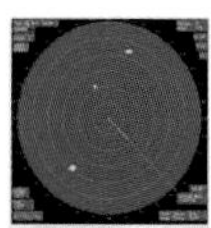

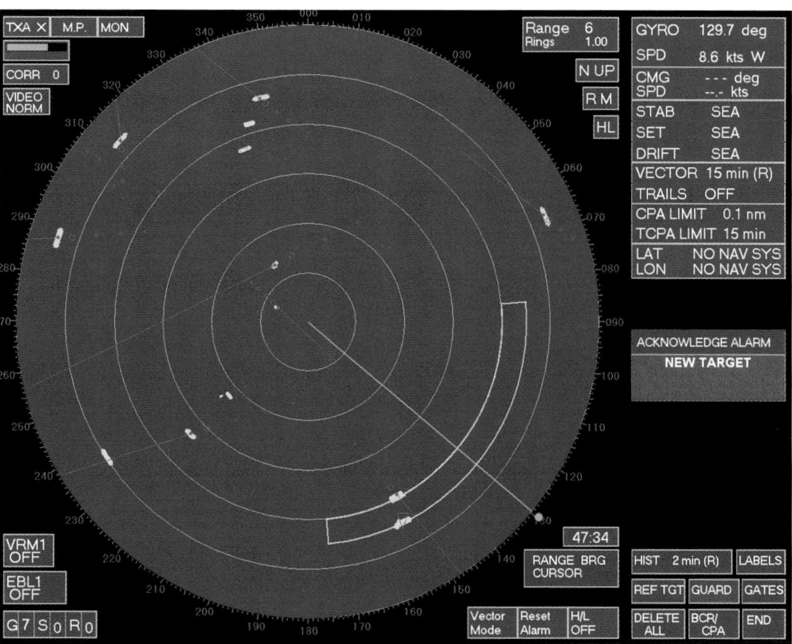


**Fig 13.3**
Guard zone.

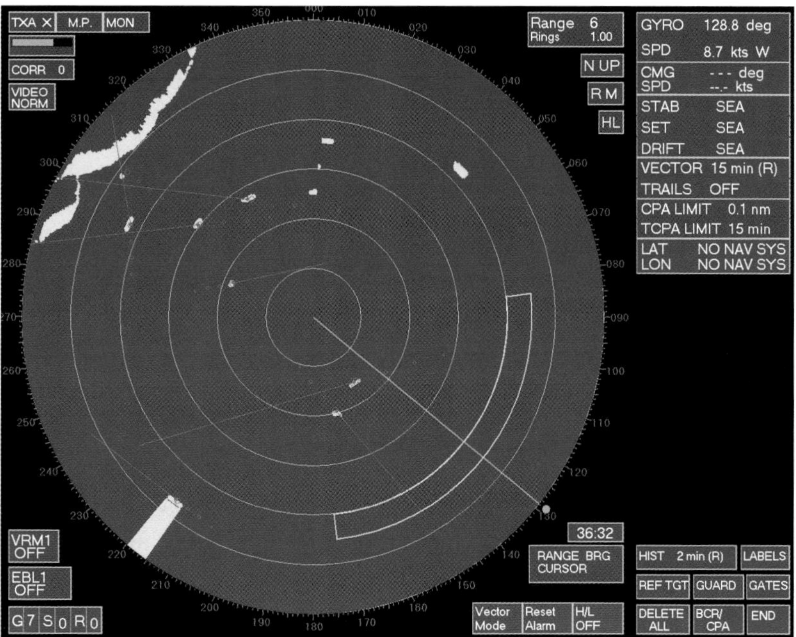


**Fig 13.4**
Tracking history.

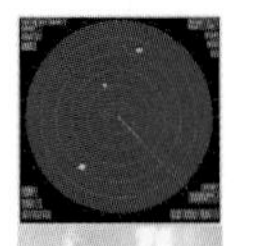



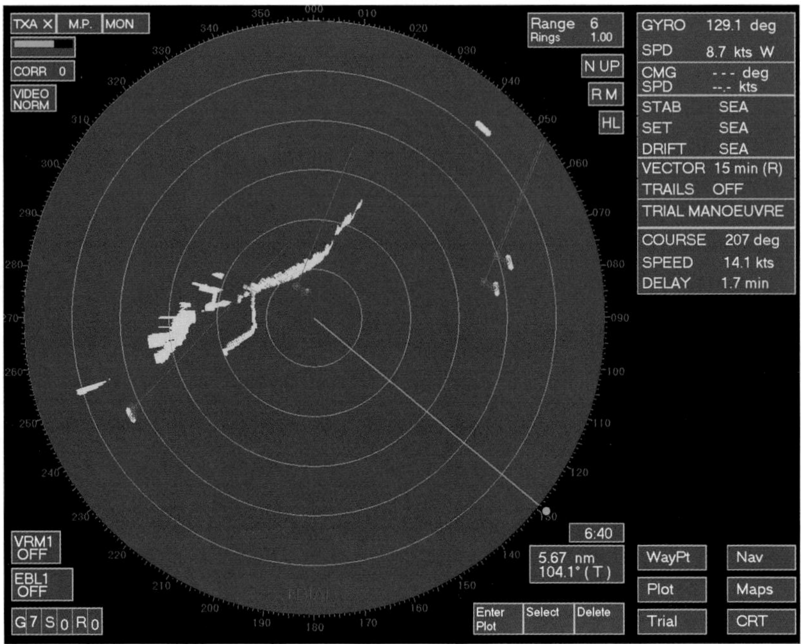


**Fig 13.5**
Trial manoeuvre.

himself/herself to it. It is important to ensure that the displayed vectors are showing relative motion as it would be easy to be misled by determining a manoeuvre based upon true vectors which will not give an indication of revised CPA. The operator sets the new course, new speed and any time delay before it is executed and the display (clearly marked 'TRIAL' 'SIM' or 'T') shows the predicted result of a manoeuvre. (Figure 13.5.)

# Inaccuracies

## Gyro or fluxgate compass error

In setting up a radar with an automatic plotting facility, it is imperative that the information fed to the computer is as accurate as possible. Inaccurate heading information will produce equally inaccurate ARPA information so it is imperative that the heading input is as precise as possible. Every degree that your own ship's heading is out will be reflected in the heading calculation of every other tracked target. The IMO required specification of a gyro input is to be within 0.75° of the true direction. Provided this remains constant, then its effect is not significant. However if the gyro is susceptible to irregular random errors, then even small random errors can cause a significant error to the ARPA's calculations.

## Log error

If the ship's log proves inaccurate, it is possible to input speed manually so this aspect can be overridden but having done so it is important not to forget to adjust the speed input at every change of speed. If the ARPA loses the log input altogether, it will display a message 'LOG ERROR' but this must not be misread as meaning that the log is inaccurate. The ARPA has no

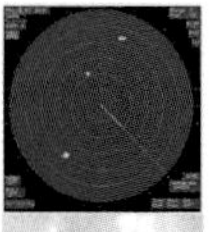

way of determining whether log input is accurate or not. All it can determine is whether it has an input or not.

## Vector inaccuracies

Inaccuracies in heading or speed input will not affect relative vectors as the calculation is based on the relative change in a target's position, however any information about its true heading or true speed will be affected. If the gyro has a fixed error and the radar image is stabilised, the picture will be slewed around but the CPA and TCPA information will not be affected.

If true vectors are used with inaccurate heading and/or speed input, the resulting target information will be incorrect and could lead to a bridge watchkeeper making an incorrect decision, possibly leading to a dangerous situation. It cannot be emphasised enough just how important accurate input is to the safe operation of ARPA.

If the accuracy of the input fluctuates, this is most likely due to log errors rather than the heading errors. A Doppler log, which relies upon bouncing sound off water layers, can become confused in heavy weather when the water through which the transducer is passing becomes aerated, causing a false layer which in turn leads to false speed readings. Sailing vessels whose speed can vary enormously in light winds have difficulty in supplying a steady speed output which in turn affects the reliability output of true vector information.

## Lost target

If the ARPA loses a target, it will initially widen the 'target gate' to make sure that the loss has not been caused by an unexpected change of course or speed of the target. If the strength of a target is such that the ARPA can no longer track it, a screen notification 'LOST TARGET' and audible alarm will sound.

## Target swap

It is possible that if two radar targets, which have been selected for automatic plotting, pass very close to each other, the ARPA vectors may switch from one target to the other and 'target swap'. Although the performance standards issued by the IMO specifically mention that target swap is to be minimised in the design of ARPA radar, it can still happen. Each selected target has a 'target gate' which is the area in which the radar searches for a contact located on the previous sweep. This 'target gate' is relatively large when the target is first acquired and as the ARPA tracks the target and is better able to predict its movement, it reduces the size of the gate to avoid target swap.

If the 'target gate' is too large it is easy for the ARPA to select another target within the parameters of the gate and continue tracking the wrong target. The target gate therefore has to reduce in size enough to minimise the chance of target swap and yet still remain sensitive enough not to be diverted by radio noise or sea clutter. The alert bridge watchkeeper will recognise target swap without difficulty.

## Missed targets

It is possible when using ARPA in its automatic acquisition mode that targets may be missed altogether. This is particularly possible with small targets which may not start to show on the display until less than three miles, by which time the operator may consider the area to be clear of contacts. It is also possible that a target visible on the display is actually so weak that the acquision parameters are not met and it is ignored.

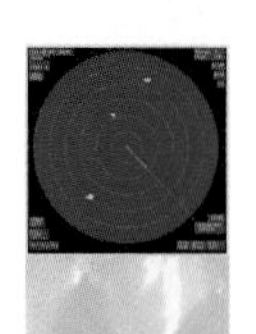



### Operator error

Perhaps the most dangerous scenario when using ARPA is the operator mistaking a true vector for a relative one and using the extension of the true vector to give a CPA. This is not as unlikely as it may seem and reinforces the argument for either restricting inexperienced watchkeepers to relative vectors only or to ensuring that the ARPA is a type which returns automatically to relative vectors after a fixed period of time. Either way if the watchkeeper is desperate to establish a vessel's true course and speed it is possible to use the selected target information box on the radar screen.

# 14 Electronic Chart Display and Information Systems (ECDIS)

**MARINE ELECTRONIC CHARTING SYSTEMS** have been around since the mid-1990s and I suspect that the view at that time was that the demise of paper charts would be well underway before the end of the 20th century. However navigators are cautious souls and the UK Hydrographer of the Navy still has very healthy sales of paper charts as well as an increasing demand for electronic charts.

The advantages of the electronic chart are well-known and include the advantage of having a 'live' record of the ship's position against a graphical representation of a paper chart, automatic selection of the correct chart scale, easy updating, fast route planning, interrogation of information from the chart and ability to obtain access to additional charts virtually instantaneously over the internet or telephone.

However, despite the huge attraction of ECDIS there are still very few ships relying totally on electronic charting and to some extent the very careful wording of the requirements of SOLAS V has tended to slow down the total acceptance of electronic charts.

### Nautical publication requirements

SOLAS Chapter V regulation 19.2.1.4 states that all ships shall have:

*'Nautical charts and nautical publications to plan and display the ship's route for the intended voyage and to plot and monitor positions throughout the voyage; an ECDIS may be accepted as meeting the carriage requirements of this sub-paragraph.'*

In order to meet this requirement an ECDIS must:

1 Meet the requirement of **Resolution A.817(19)** adopted by the IMO on 23 November 1995 – *Performance Standards for Electronic Chart Display and Information Systems (ECDIS).*

2 Be Type Approved against **IEC 61174** (Second Edition Oct 2001) – *the International Standard for ECDIS – operational and performance requirements, methods of testing and required test results.*

3 Be fitted with an approved backup in accordance with **Appendix 6 to Resolution A.817(19)**.

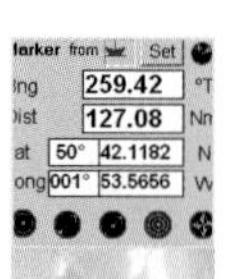



4 Be used with official electronic navigation charts (ENCs) for the entire voyage.
5 Be used with the latest weekly chart updates.

Unless all the above can be met, paper charts must be used to meet carriage requirements. The following points are important from a practical viewpoint:

1 It is not just the ECDIS software that must be Type Approved but the entire system – processor, display, housing (console), all of which must satisfy ergonomic requirements and meet IMO and IEC standards.
2 For a paperless bridge, the backup requirement is a second independently-powered, Type Approved ECDIS which must be acceptable to the ship's flag state authority.
3 Adequate ENC coverage is becoming available for European waters but is patchy elsewhere. Where ENCs are not available, the Raster Chart Display System (RCDS) may be used using raster navigational charts (RNCs). Where RNCs are used, an appropriate backup folio of paper charts (approved by the flag state authority) must be carried even if two ECDIS systems are carried. The UK Admiralty ARCS charts are RNCs.

The main factor that has limited the take-up of Type Approved ECDIS is the lack of global Electronic Navigation Chart (ENC) data. It is worth emphasising that the ENC required as part of ECDIS must be issued by or under the authority of a national hydrographic office – and not by private chart manufacturers (eg C-Map or Transas) who produce data in similar formats.

# ECDIS equipment

The hardware of the ECDIS is generally computer based with graphics capability, a high performance PC or a graphics workstation installed in a console linked with other items of ship's equipment. Thus, ECDIS obtains the ship's heading from the gyro or fluxgate compass and the ship's speed through water from the ship's log. Alternatively, the speed and course over the ground (SOG and COG) can be supplied from a GPS. Radar images can be superimposed over the chart which some navigators find helpful in confirming radar contacts against charted objects.

The publishers of official data for the electronic nautical charts are the national Hydrographic Offices (HOs) of the maritime nations, as is the case for the paper nautical charts. Hydrographic Offices can be themselves the producers of the data or they may commission private companies to produce data and then verify and certify the results.

Non-certified data from private suppliers is not permitted for navigational purposes and is allowed only to be used as a supplement to official navigational charts.

At present, data supply is the weak point of ECDIS. The hydrographic services are switching from production of paper nautical charts to digital ECDIS data. At present, only part of the Earth's surface has been covered digitally with official data. Since other services, such as regular updating, nautical publications, etc, also have to be converted to a digital format, it will be some time before an up-to-date digital global database is available for navigational purposes.

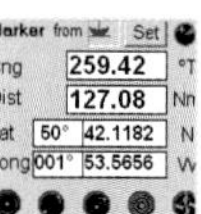

# Horizontal datums *(not to be confused with Chart Datum)*

The cartographer produces charts using a specific horizontal datum. There are over 100 different horizontal datums used throughout the world and whilst there is a move in Europe to convert all charts to WGS-84, it is important that the datum setting in the ECDIS matches the horizontal datum to which the raster electronic charts have been constructed.

# Electronic charts

There are two basic types of electronic charts. These charts can be divided into two generic types: the raster chart (RNC) used in a Raster Chart Display System (RCDS) and a vector chart (ENC) or S-57 format chart:

## Raster charts

A raster navigational chart (RNC) is a visual scan of a paper chart. It cannot be interrogated for further information and zooming in simply makes each individual chart larger; it does not increase the amount of information available. The ARCS range of charts supplied by the UK Hydrographic Office are raster charts (Figure 14.1).

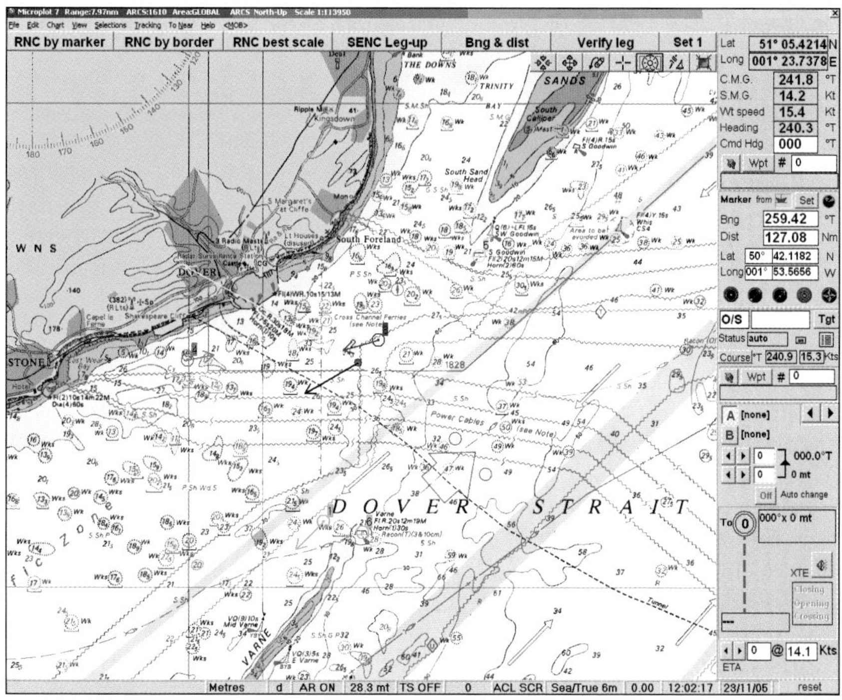


**Fig 14.1** UKHO ARCS or raster chart. By courtesy of UKHO.

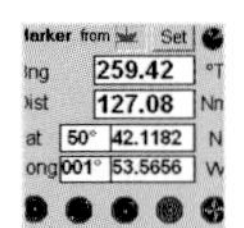



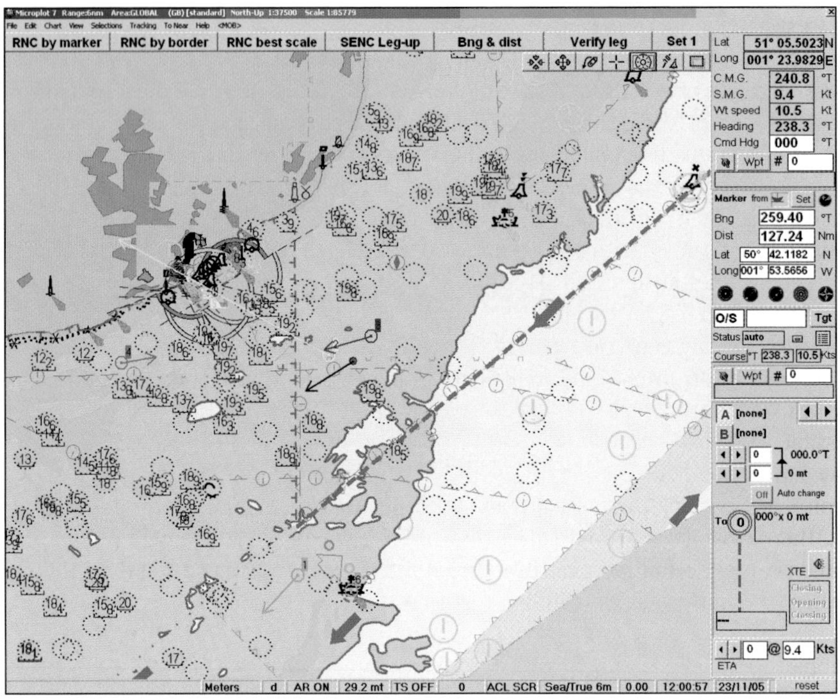


**Fig 14.2** UKHO S-57 vector chart.

## Vector charts

A vector chart, also described as 'S-57 format', is more complex. It is composed of layers of information. Each individual point on the chart is digitally mapped, allowing the information to be used in a more sophisticated way. By clicking on a feature the details of that feature are displayed. The user has the option of selecting which layers are displayed and, as the chart is zoomed-in, more and more information is displayed. 'S-52 format' refers to the specification given by the IMO for the display of each individual object on an S-57 electronic chart. It covers the design and colour of the symbols used (Figure 14.2).

## Differences between a raster chart display system (RCDS) and vector charts

- Unlike vector charts where there are no chart boundaries, RCDS is a chart-based system similar to a portfolio of paper charts. Raster navigational chart (RNC) data, itself, will not trigger automatic alarms (eg anti-grounding). However, some alarms can be generated by the RCDS from user-inserted information. These can include:

1. Clearing lines
2. Ship safety depth contour lines
3. Isolated dangers
4. Danger areas

- Horizontal datums and chart projections may differ between raster navigational charts. Mariners should understand how the chart horizontal datum relates to the datum of the

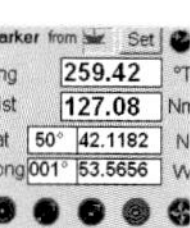

position fixing system. In some instances, this may appear as a shift in position. This difference may be most noticeable at grid intersections and during route monitoring. Vector charts will all be drawn to the same horizontal datum.

- Raster navigational chart features cannot be simplified or removed in order to suit a particular navigational circumstance or task at hand. This may affect the superimposition of radar/ARPA.
- Without selecting different scale charts, the look-ahead capability of raster charts may be somewhat limited. This may lead to some inconvenience when determining range and bearing or the identity of distant objects.
- Orientation of the RCDS display to other than Chart Up, may affect the readability of chart text and symbols (eg, Course Up, Route Up).
- It will not be possible to interrogate RNC features to gain additional information about charted objects.
- It is not possible to display a ship's safety contour or safety depth and highlight it on the RCDS display, unless these features are manually entered during route planning.
- Depending on the source of the RNC, different colours may be used to show similar chart information. There may also be differences in colours used during day and night time.
- An RNC should be displayed at the scale of the paper chart. Excessive zooming in or zooming out can seriously degrade RCDS capability, for example by degrading the legibility of the chart image.
- Mariners should be aware that in confined waters, the accuracy of chart data (ie, paper charts, ENC or RNC data) may be less than that of the position-fixing system in use. This may be the case when using differential GNSS. ECDIS provides an indication in the ENC which allows a determination of the quality of the data.

Electronic chart presentation is only one aspect of ECDIS. ECDIS is also a comprehensive information system. It enables the user to call up information on any item displayed in addition to the graphics presentation. For example, a lighthouse will appear on the chart as a tower symbol. The system can give further information on this object; the fact that the tower may have horizontal red/white stripes, is a 28m high steel structure on a masonry base and is called 'Adlard Light', and that it used to be manned but is no longer operational and is now preserved as a monument. The data may make it possible to call up a further text presenting a detailed history of the lighthouse and it may also be possible to view a digitised photo of this lighthouse. The amount and quality of the information available on the individual objects depends on how up-to-date, accurate and well maintained the database is.

For the user, ECDIS is only one item of equipment among many on the bridge of a modern ship. Operating the ECDIS is thus not the main duty of a ship's officer. Rather, the system replaces the conventional chart table and is intended to permit all types of work traditionally connected with the paper nautical chart and to make these activities easier, more precise and faster. These include route planning, entry of observations, instructions and notes, position determination and, last but not least, updating charts with the aid of electronic *Notices to Mariners*.

As long as there is no complete coverage with ECDIS data, RNC data may serve as a practical alternative. Each ECDIS will also be able to read and display this raster data, although such a functionality is not included in the ECDIS specification. The scanned paper charts, however, provide no real alternative to ECDIS data.

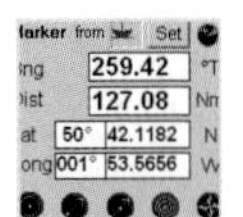




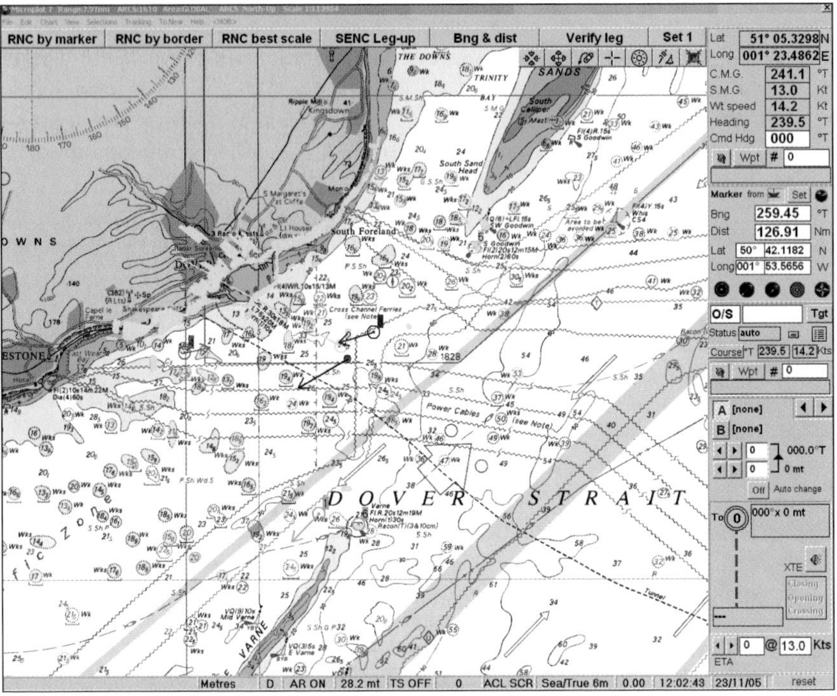


**Fig 14.3** S-57 chart showing radar overlay in yellow.

To sum it up, an ECDIS must offer the following characteristics:

- Reading ENC data (S-57 format) and transferring it to SENC
- Presentation of objects and their characteristics according to presentation library (S-52 format)
- Anti-grounding function
- Warning of obstructions to shipping
- Updating
- Various types of chartwork must be possible, eg:
  - Entering fixed position
  - Route planning
  - Entering notes and observations
  - Sounding, measuring of distances

Only an ECDIS that has been officially certified may be used in navigation as an adequate replacement for the paper nautical charts. It goes without saying that in a certified ECDIS only certified 'official' data may be used for navigation purposes. There is, however, also the possibility of permitting the use of a system that does not strictly meet all the requirements, the so-called Electronic Chart System (ECS), which can be utilised like an ECDIS but may not be employed as the sole item of navigation equipment.

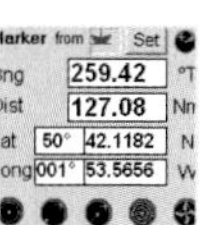


# What are the advantages of ECDIS?

An ECDIS satisfying all the requirements is not only an adequate replacement for the paper nautical chart but also a system containing all information important for navigation that can be called up at any time and without delay. Today, this information is still scattered about in various publications, and manual search procedures are laborious and time consuming. ECDIS also offers the possibility of automatic anti-grounding alarm, which is not possible with any other navigation aid.

As an experienced captain once remarked, 'With ECDIS, a navigator knows for the first time in the history of seafaring not where his ship was, but pretty much where she is!'

A further advantage of ECDIS compared to all other navigation aids is the individual adaptation of the chart picture to the particular requirements. This is possible because the chart picture is produced only during operation. It is possible to show only the relevant shallow water contour for a super tanker with a draught of 25m or for a ferry with a draught of only 5m. The presentation library controls this via adjustment of the safety depth/safety contours.

Automatic updating is much faster, easier and also less prone to error than chart adjustment currently laboriously carried out manually with a considerable time lag. Updating can even be called up on a digital telephone or via satellite, and incorporated instantaneously. ECDIS makes the navigational aspects of seafaring easier and, if carried out diligently, also safer.

The facility to overlay the radar picture on the ECDIS screen is regularly used by some and scorned by others, but if used conscientiously, it certainly has its merits.

# What are the disadvantages of ECDIS?

As with all equipment, rubbish in is rubbish out. If for any reason, your position-fixing equipment 'loses the plot' literally, and it has been known for GPS to talk rubbish from time to time, then the position information displayed on the ECDIS will not be reliable. It is therefore most important that the navigator does not rely exclusively on any one source of information.

As the user is able to specify the layers of information to be displayed using vector (S-57) charts, it would be possible to exclude layers of very pertinent information thus lulling the user into a false sense of security and possibly danger. It is most important that bridge watch keepers use ECDIS information responsibly. (Figures 14.4 and 14.5 below and Figures 14.6 and 14.7 overleaf.)

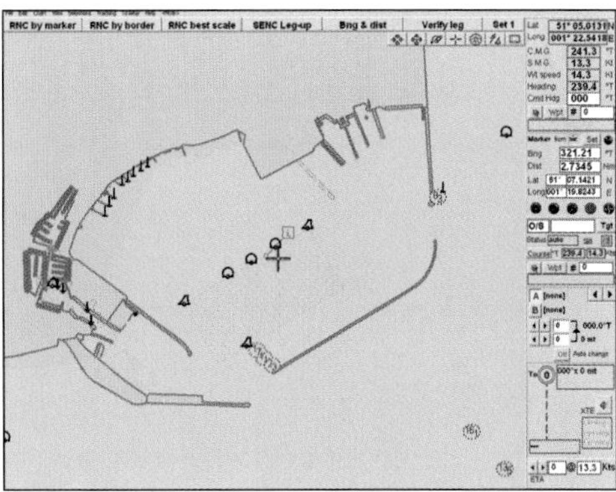


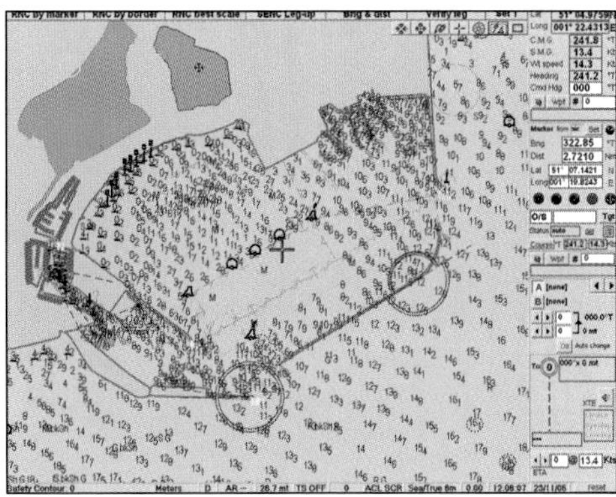

**Figs 14.4, 14.5** S-57 charts of Dover harbour showing (left) too little information and (right) too much.

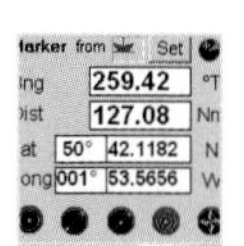

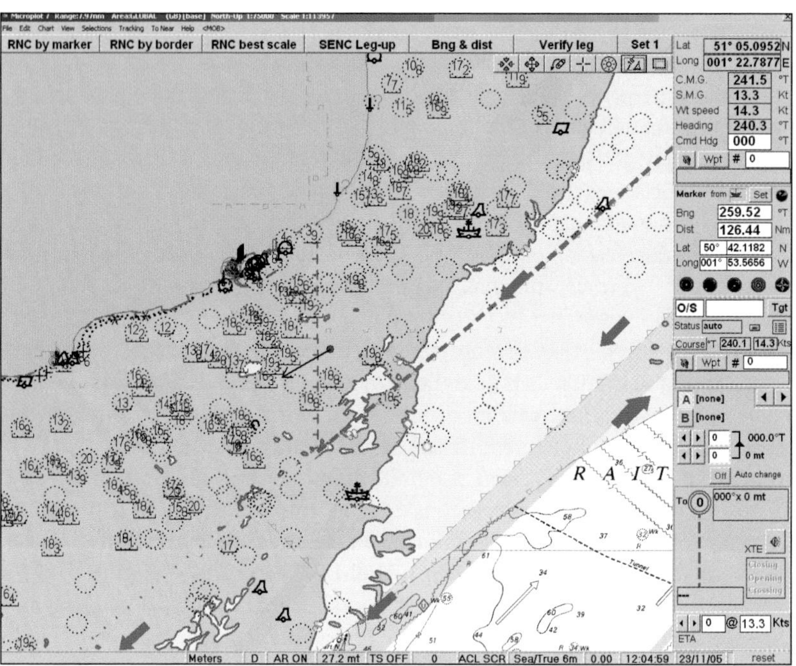


**Fig 14.6** A S-57 vector chart that is a little lacking in chart information.

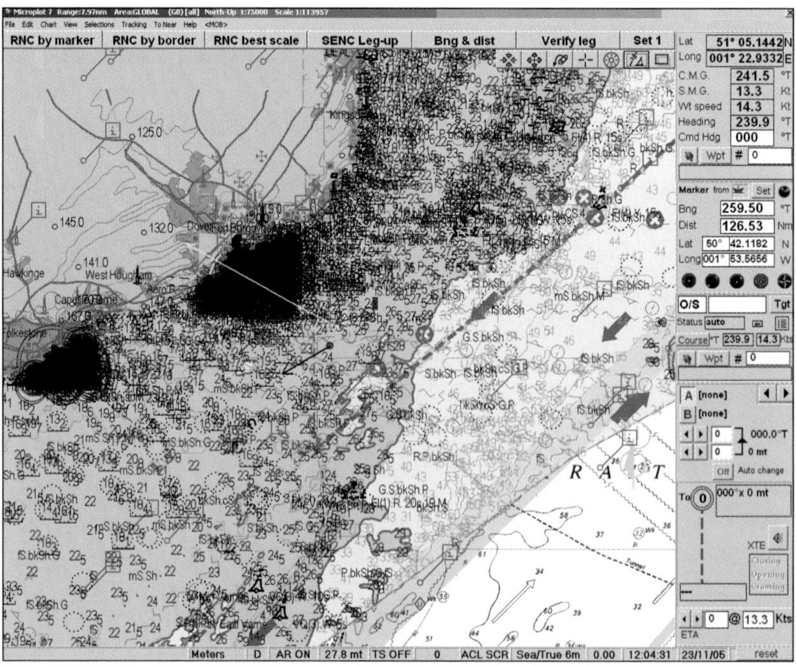


**Fig 14.7** A S-57 vector chart with far too much chart information.

# 15 Voyage Planning

**THE IMO'S GUIDELINES FOR VOYAGE PLANNING**, should be followed on all vessels. The key elements of the voyage plan are:

APPRAISAL of all relevant information
PLANNING the intended voyage
EXECUTION of the plan taking account of prevailing conditions
MONITORING the vessel's progress against the plan continuously.

**TOP TIP**

*Make sure you have got your head around these four stages of passage planning before attempting any deck exam. They could save you an enormous amount of time and grief.*

Investigations show that human error contributes to 80% of navigational accidents and that in many cases essential information that could have prevented the accident was available to but not used by those responsible for the navigation of the vessels concerned. Most accidents happen because of simple mistakes in use of navigational equipment and interpretation of the available information, rather than any deficiency in basic navigational skills or ability to use equipment.

Masters, skippers and watch keepers should therefore adhere to the IMO Guidelines taking the following measures to ensure that they appreciate and reduce the risks to which they are exposed:

1 Ensure that all the vessel's navigation is planned in adequate detail with contingency plans where appropriate;
2 Ensure that there is a systematic bridge organisation that provides for:
  (a) comprehensive briefing of all concerned with the navigation of the vessel;
  (b) close and continuous monitoring of the vessel's position ensuring as far as possible that different methods of determining the position are used to check against error in any one system;
  (c) cross-checking of individual human decisions so that errors can be detected and corrected as early as possible;
  (d) information available from plots of other traffic is used carefully to ensure against over-confidence, bearing in mind that other vessels may alter course and/or speed;
3 Ensure that optimum and systematic use is made of all appropriate information that becomes available to the navigational staff; and ensuring that the intentions of a pilot are fully understood and acceptable to the vessel's navigational staff.

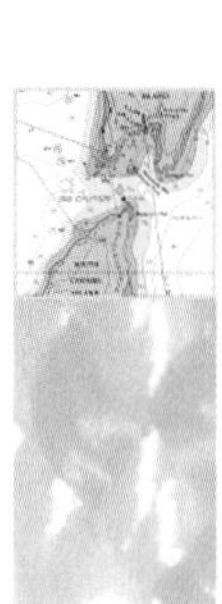



# Responsibility for voyage planning

In most deep-sea vessels the master delegates the initial responsibility for preparing the plan for a voyage to the officer responsible for navigational equipment and publications (usually known as the navigating officer.) On smaller vessels, including fishing vessels, the Master or skipper may have the responsibility of the navigating officer for voyage-planning purposes. Prior to departure, the navigating officer will prepare the detailed voyage plan from berth to berth in accordance with the IMO Guidelines and to the Master's requirements. If the port of destination is not known, or is subsequently altered, the navigating officer must extend or amend the original plan as appropriate.

# Principles of voyage planning

The four stages of Appraisal, Planning, Execution and Monitoring logically follow each other. An appraisal of all information available must be made before detailed plans can be drawn up and a plan must be in existence before tactics for its execution can be decided upon. Once the plan and the manner in which it is to be executed have been decided, monitoring must be carried out to ensure that the plan is followed.

## Appraisal

Appraisal is the process of gathering all information relevant to the proposed voyage, including ascertaining risks and assessing its critical areas. The IMO Guidelines list the items that should be taken into account. An overall assessment of the intended voyage should be made by the Master, in consultation with the navigating officer and other deck officers who will be involved, after all relevant information has been gathered. This appraisal will provide the Master and his bridge team with a clear and precise indication of all areas of danger, and delineate the areas in which it will be possible to navigate safely taking into account the calculated draught of the vessel and planned under-keel clearance. Bearing in mind the condition of the vessel, her equipment and any other circumstances, a balanced judgement of the margins of safety which must be allowed in the various sections of the intended voyage can now be made, agreed and understood by all concerned.

## Planning

Once a full appraisal has been carried out, the navigating officer implements the planning process, acting on the Master's instructions. The detailed plan should cover the whole voyage, from berth to berth, and include all waters where a pilot will be on board. The plan should be completed and include all the relevant factors listed in the Guidelines.

The appropriate charts should be clearly marked showing the areas of danger and the intended track, taking into account the margins of allowable error. Where appropriate, due regard should be paid to the need for advanced warning to be given on one chart of the existence of a navigational hazard immediately on transfer to the next. The planned track should be plotted to clear hazards at as safe a distance as circumstances allow. A longer route should always be accepted in preference to a shorter more hazardous route. The possibility of main engine or steering gear breakdown at a critical moment must not be overlooked.

Additional information which should be marked on the charts include:

- All radar-conspicuous objects and RACONs, which may be used in radar position fixing.
- Any transit marks, clearing bearings or clearing ranges which may be used. It is sometimes possible to use two conspicuous clearing marks where a line drawn through them runs clear of natural dangers with the appropriate margin of safety; if the vessel proceeds on the safe side of this transit she will be clear of the danger. If no clearing marks are available, a line or lines of bearing from a single object may be drawn at a desired safe distance from the danger; provided the vessel remains in the safe segment, it will be clear of the danger. Parallel index lines should also be drawn on the radar where appropriate.

If an electronic chart system is used to assist voyage planning, the plan should also be drawn up on the paper charts. Where official (ENC) vector data is available, an ECDIS provided with fully compliant ENC data for the vessel's voyage may be used instead of paper charts. Raster Chart Display Systems (RCDS) using official and up-to-date raster charts can be used in conjunction with paper charts to assist voyage planning and route monitoring. Hazards should be marked on the RCDS as well as on the paper chart. Systems that use unofficial chart data should not be used for voyage planning or navigation.

Depending on circumstances, the main details of the plan should be marked in appropriate and prominent places on the charts to be used during the voyage. They should also be programmed and stored electronically on an ECDIS or RCDS where fitted. The main details of the voyage plan should also be recorded in a bridge notebook used specially for this purpose to allow reference to details of the plan at the conning position without the need to consult the chart. Supporting information relative to the voyage, such as times of high and low water, or sunrise or sunset, should also be recorded in this notebook.

It is unlikely that every detail of a voyage will have been predicted, particularly in pilotage waters. Much of what will have been planned may have to be adjusted or changed after embarking the pilot. This in no way detracts from the real value of the plan, which is to mark out in advance, areas where the vessel must not go and the appropriate precautions which must be taken, and to give initial warning that the vessel is standing into danger.

**TOP TIP**

*Remember, there's no such thing as a poor navigator, it's much more likely to be a poor navigational plan.*

## Execution

The finalised voyage plan should be carried out, taking into account the factors listed in the Guidelines. The Master should take into account any special circumstances which may arise, such as changes in weather, which may require the plan to be reviewed or altered.

## Monitoring

The vessel's progress along the pre-planned track is continuously monitored. The officer of the watch, whenever in any doubt as to the position of the vessel or the manner in which the voyage is proceeding, should immediately call the Master and, if necessary, take appropriate action for the safety of the vessel.

The performance of navigational equipment should be checked prior to sailing, prior to entering restricted or hazardous waters and at regular and frequent intervals throughout the voyage.

Advantage should be taken of all the navigational equipment with which the vessel is fitted for position monitoring, bearing in mind the following points:

- Positions obtained by electronic positioning systems must be checked regularly by visual bearings and transits whenever available.
- Visual fixes should, if possible, be based on at least three position lines.
- Transit marks, clearing bearings and clearing ranges (radar) can be of great assistance.
- It is dangerous to rely solely on the output from a single positioning system.
- The echo sounder provides a valuable check of depth at the plotted position.
- Buoys should not be used for position fixing but may be used for guidance when shore marks are difficult to distinguish visually; in these circumstances their positions should first be checked by other means.
- The charted positions of offshore installations should be checked against the most recent navigational notices.
- The functioning and correct reading of the instruments used should be checked.
- Account must be taken of any system errors and the predicted accuracy of positions displayed by electronic position fixing systems.
- The frequency at which the position is to be fixed should be determined for each section of the voyage.

Each time the vessel's position is fixed and marked on the chart, the estimated position at a convenient interval of time in advance should be projected and plotted. With ECDIS or RCDS care should be taken to ensure that the display shows sufficient 'look-ahead' distance and that the next chart can be readily accessed.

Radar can be used to advantage in monitoring the position of the vessel by the use of parallel indexing. This is a simple and most effective way of continuously monitoring that a vessel is maintaining its track in restricted coastal waters. Parallel indexing can be used in any situation where a radar-conspicuous navigation mark is available and it is practicable to monitor continuously the vessel's position relative to such an object. It also serves as a valuable check on the vessel's progress when using an electronic chart.

# Pilotage

The plan covers the voyage from berth to berth and therefore includes the pilotage stage. The IMO Guidelines do not give specific advice on this important stage, therefore the following notes should be taken into consideration when planning and executing the pilotage stages.

Pilots make a significant contribution to the safety of navigation in the confined waters and port approaches of which they have up-to-date knowledge, but it must be stressed that the responsibilities of the vessel's navigational team and the officer of the watch do not transfer to the pilot. After boarding the vessel, in addition to being advised by the Master of the manoeuvring characteristics and basic details of the vessel for its present condition, the pilot should be clearly consulted on the voyage plan to be followed. The general aim of the Master should be to ensure that the expertise of the pilot is fully supported by the vessel's bridge team.

Attention is drawn to the following extract from IMO Resolution A.285 (VIII):

*'Despite the duties and obligations of a pilot, his presence on board does not relieve the officer of the watch from his duties and obligation for the safety of the vessel. He should co-operate closely with the pilot and maintain an accurate check on the vessel's position and movements. If he is in any doubt as to the pilot's actions or intentions, he should seek clarification from the pilot and if doubt still exists he should notify the Master immediately and take whatever action is necessary before the Master arrives.'*

# Other publications

In addition to the IMO Guidelines, it is highly recommended that you also refer to the following publications which contain valuable advice on bridge watchkeeping in general and voyage planning in particular:

- *Bridge Team Management – A practical guide* published by the Nautical Institute
- *Bridge Procedures – A Guide for Watchkeepers of Large Yachts under Sail or Power* published by Adlard Coles Nautical
- *Bridge Procedures Guide* published by the International Chamber of Shipping

# Keeping a navigational record

- Key navigational activities to be logged.
- A complete record of the voyage must be able to be restored. The IMO states:

*'All ships engaged on international voyages shall keep on board a record of navigational activities and incidents which are of importance to safety of navigation and which must contain sufficient detail to restore a complete record of the voyage, taking into account the recommendations adopted by the Organisation. When such information is not maintained in the ship's log-book, it shall be maintained in another form approved by the Administration.'*

**TOP TIP**

*Don't be too enthusiastic about cleaning off charts until the voyage is satisfactorily completed.*

It must be possible to reconstruct the ship's track throughout the voyage. The IMO Guidelines state that navigational records (whether paper, electronic or mechanical) should be retained on board for a period of not less than 12 months. The MCA's interpretation of this requirement is that records retained for 12 months should provide sufficient detail to reconstruct any voyage during that period. The MCA recognises that it is impractical to retain voyage details on paper charts for longer than the duration of the voyage. Therefore sufficient details of waypoints, courses, times of alteration of course and or speed and other relevant details must be entered in the deck log book and courses and positions on all navigational charts should be retained until the voyage is completed.

# 16 Search and Rescue

**SEARCH AND RESCUE** is the activity of locating and recovering persons either in distress, potential distress or missing and delivering them to a place of safety. The Search and Rescue Services provide a comprehensive search and rescue service for those reported in trouble either on land, on water or in the air and for those reported missing. The fully integrated organisation of search and rescue co-ordinators and search and rescue units using a comprehensive communications infrastructure provides a well-developed search and rescue model.

SOLAS Chapter 5 Safety of Navigation states in Regulation 7 on Search and Rescue Services:

> *'Each Contracting Government undertakes to ensure that necessary arrangements are made for distress communication and co-ordination in their area of responsibility and for the rescue of persons in distress at sea around its coasts. These arrangements shall include the establishment, operation and maintenance of such search and rescue facilities as are deemed practicable and necessary, having regard to the density of the seagoing traffic and the navigational dangers and shall, so far as possible, provide adequate means of locating and rescuing such persons.'*

Today, the Global Maritime Distress and Safety System (GMDSS), together with the provisions of the International Convention on Maritime Search and Rescue (SAR), should ensure the successful rescue of persons in distress at sea.

Although the obligation of ships to assist vessels in distress was enshrined both in tradition and in international treaties (such as SOLAS), until the adoption of the 1979 SAR Convention, there was no international system covering search and rescue operations. In some countries there was a well-established organisation able to provide assistance promptly and efficiently but in others there was nothing to speak of.

Of those who took an interest, the co-ordination and control of search and rescue operations was organised on an individual country basis in accordance with its own requirements and as dictated by its own resources. As a result, national organisational plans were developed along different lines. The dissimilarity of such plans and lack of agreed and standardised procedures on a worldwide basis gave rise to difficulties, particularly in the initial stages of the alert. In some cases, this resulted in an uneconomical use of search and rescue facilities or an unnecessary duplication of effort.

In l978, the Maritime Safety Committee (MSC), IMO's senior technical body, had adopted the IMO Search and Rescue Manual (IMOSAR) to help governments to implement the International Convention on Maritime Search and Rescue, which complemented the 1971 Merchant Ship Search and Rescue Manual (MERSAR). The IMOSAR manual provided guidelines rather than

requirements for a common maritime search and rescue policy, encouraging all coastal states to develop their organisations on similar lines and enabling adjacent states to co-operate and provide mutual assistance. It was updated in 1992.

The IMOSAR and MERSAR manuals have since been replaced with the International Aeronautical and Maritime Search and Rescue (IAMSAR) Manual, developed jointly by IMO and the International Civil Aviation Organization (ICAO) and published in three volumes covering Organization and Management; Mission Co-ordination; and Mobile Facilities.

The SAR Convention was designed to provide the framework for search and rescue operations. It and the two associated manuals, together with other resolutions and recommendations adopted at the l979 Conference, was designed to ensure that such operations are conducted with maximum speed and efficiency, no matter where the distress incident occurs. But its effectiveness depends almost entirely on how well it is implemented and this depends in turn on the action taken by Parties to the Convention.

The Convention imposes considerable obligations on Parties – such as setting up the shore installations required – and in 1998 IMO adopted a revised Annex to the Convention which clarifies the responsibilities of governments and puts greater emphasis on the regional approach and co-ordination between maritime and aeronautical SAR operations. The aim of the revision was to overcome any difficulties that countries had with implementing the original convention. The revised Annex entered into force in 2000.

By mid-2003, the SAR Convention had been ratified by 75 countries representing just over 51% of world merchant shipping tonnage.

Following the adoption of the 1979 SAR Convention, the MSC divided the world's oceans into 13 search and rescue areas; in each of which the countries concerned have delimited search and rescue regions for which they are responsible

Provisional search and rescue plans for all of these areas were agreed during a series of regional conferences held around the world, and they were completed when plans for the Indian Ocean were finalised at a conference held in Fremantle, Western Australia, in September 1998.

Work is ongoing on clarifying boundaries and developing on-shore facilities and SAR services, including the establishment of an electronic database for the global SAR plan and the GMDSS (Global Maritime Distress and Safety System) Master Plan. The GMDSS system is a crucial component of the SAR system.

## GMDSS

The Global Maritime Distress and Safety System – which became fully effective on 1 February 1999 – is essentially a worldwide network of automated emergency communications for ships at sea. It means that all ocean-going passenger ships and cargo ships of 300 gross tonnage and upwards must be equipped with radio equipment that conforms to international standards as set out in the system. The basic concept is that search and rescue authorities ashore, as well as shipping in the immediate vicinity of the ship in distress, will be rapidly alerted through satellite and terrestrial communication techniques to a distress incident so that they can assist in a co-ordinated SAR operation with the minimum of delay.

# Key functions of search and rescue

The key functions of SAR are to co-ordinate:

1. Maritime SAR in offshore, inshore and shoreline areas
2. Aeronautical SAR over land and sea
3. Inland SAR

These functions are undertaken through the ability of the various authorities and organisations to:

1. Receive details of persons, vessels and aircraft in distress
2. Communicate between SAR units and the co-ordinating authority
3. Communicate between SAR units
4. Communicate between co-ordinating authorities
5. Maintain declared SAR units as appropriate to:
   (a) provide assistance to persons, vessels and aircraft in distress
   (b) deliver survivors to a place of safety or where further assistance can be rendered

# IAMSAR manual

SOLAS Chapter V Safety of Navigation requires ships to carry an up-to-date copy of Volume III of the International Aeronautical and Maritime Search and Rescue (IAMSAR) Manual. Jointly published by IMO and the International Civil Aviation Organization (ICAO), the three-volume IAMSAR Manual provides guidelines for a common aviation and maritime approach to organising and providing search and rescue (SAR) services. Each volume (available separately in loose-leaf form, binder included) can be used as a stand-alone document or, in conjunction with the other two volumes, as a means to attain a full view of the SAR system.

The IAMSAR manual's three volumes are as follows:

*Volume I: Organisation and Management.*

*Volume II: Mission Co-ordination* (assists personnel who plan and co-ordinate SAR operations and exercises).

*Volume III: Mobile Facilities* (intended to be carried aboard rescue units, aircraft and vessels to help with performance of a search, rescue or on-scene co-ordinator function, and with aspects of SAR that pertain to their own emergencies).

*Volume III* is of interest to and should be carried by all ships at sea and covers:

1. An overview of SAR
2. Rendering assistance
3. On-scene co-ordination
4. On-board emergencies

# Distress

Distress is described as a threat of grave and imminent danger to a vessel, a person, an aircraft or a vehicle.

# Master's obligation

The Master of a ship at sea, which is in a position to provide assistance on receiving a distress signal from another vessel in distress at sea, is bound to proceed at best speed to their assistance and to inform them and the search and rescue service that they are doing so. If the ship receiving the distress alert is unable or, in the special circumstances of the case, considers it unreasonable or unnecessary to proceed to their assistance, the Master must enter in his Official Log Book (OLB) the reason for failing to proceed to the assistance of the persons or vessel in distress and inform the appropriate search and rescue services accordingly.

The Master of a ship in distress or the search and rescue services concerned have the right to requisition ships that they consider are best able to render assistance and there is an obligation on the Master of the ship requisitioned to comply with the requisition by continuing to proceed at best speed to the assistance of vessel or persons in distress.

Masters of ships in the vicinity may be released from this obligation once it is clear that their ships have not been requisitioned and that one or more other ships have been requisitioned and are heading in the direction of the casualty.

# Distress procedures

## Rescue Co-ordination Centre

Worldwide, national Rescue Co-ordination Centres (RCCs) are responsible for the co-ordination of both maritime and aviation search and rescue. They are also responsible for the management and operation of the ground segment of the Cospas-Sarsat distress beacon detection system used by Electronic Position Indicating Radio Beacons (EPIRBs). The RCCs are staffed by highly trained SAR specialists who usually have a naval, merchant navy, air force, civil aviation or police service background. They also co-ordinate medical evacuations and broadcast maritime safety information.

## SAR procedure

On receiving a distress signal or being notified of a missing civil aircraft or seagoing vessel, the RCC will take action to establish the safety of the aircraft, vessel or source of the signal. This action may include:

(a) Co-ordinating a search and rescue with assistance from organisations as appropriate, such as the defence forces, trained aviation organisations (Civil SAR Units), emergency medical helicopters, state police services, state emergency services, the Australian Communications Authority (ACA), airlines, the general aviation industry, volunteer marine rescue groups, the Bureau of Meteorology, the shipping industry and fishing co-operatives.

(b) Passing co-ordination to the appropriate regional police organisation to conduct search and rescue operations within their jurisdiction.

## Distress alerts

Traditionally SAR authorities have been alerted to emergency incidents through radio distress calls ('Maydays'), flare sightings, calls from worried friends or relatives, or the more formal overdue ship/aircraft reports. This in turn has usually required a painstaking evaluation of many variables such as aircraft endurance, terrain, weather in the area, wind, currents, survival gear carried, and of course, the skipper's experience and likely intentions. Naturally these sorts of considerations remain very important whenever a search and rescue operation is being mounted.

## Satellite system

Today's technology takes most of the search out of search and rescue through the utilisation of satellites and modern radio distress beacons. Aviators call their radio distress beacons ELTs (Emergency Locator Transmitters, mounted permanently in the aircraft) or PLBs (Personal Locator Beacons, which are portable and carried on the person).

Mariners call their beacons EPIRBs – Emergency Position Indicating Radio Beacons – and the main difference being that an EPIRB, unlike an ELT, is designed to float upright in water with its antenna pointing upright.

Under the COSPAS-SARSAT international satellite aided tracking system, polar orbiting satellites are able to detect distress signals from radio beacons. As the satellites pass overhead, signals are detected and relayed back to an RCC through ground receiver stations. So advanced is the technology that the location of the ship or aircraft in trouble can be pinpointed to within about 20km – often within one or two hours, depending on the positions of the satellites and the beacon at the time.

Radio distress beacons operate on frequencies of 121.5MHz and 406MHz beacon, which can indicate a position to within 6km anywhere on the Earth's surface. They can relay much more information than simply the distress location. For example a 406MHz beacon can be programmed to provide the RCC with information such as the registration details of the aircraft or vessel. This may allow further information to be gathered relating to the type of craft, survival gear carried and the number of people on board etc. After defining the search area, aircraft or other rescue craft rely on homing equipment to locate the beacon's exact position. It is important that once a beacon is switched on in a distress situation, you should not switch it off until rescue has been affected or you are advised to by the rescue authority.

## Types of rescue beacon

For fishing boats, yachts and other recreational craft, requirement and type of beacon used depends primarily on where the vessel operates. If you are an ocean-going craft capable of going more than 30–50 miles offshore (out of VHF range), a 406MHz beacon is recommended and may be insisted upon if the vessel is operating commercially. These beacons must be registered with the national radio licensing authority as part of the radio equipment certificate.

An enhanced type of EPIRB (often referred to as a 'GPIRB') incorporates Global Positioning System (GPS) technology and thereby combines accurate location determination and near instantaneous distress alerting though geostationary satellites. Once activated, the internal GPS finds its own position and the GPIRB broadcasts its identity and position to within an accuracy of about 100m. This capability shortens the time required to get an accurate fix on the beacon position, thus enhancing the speed and effectiveness of search and rescue operations.

*Note: It is planned that 121.5MHz distress beacons will cease to operate from February 2009 when only 406MHz beacons will be detected by the satellite system.*

## Inadvertent EPIRB activation

Where a beacon has been activated inadvertently, the nearest Rescue Co-ordination Centre (RCC) should be advised immediately and the EPIRB should be left turned on until the RCC has correctly identified its signal and given specific instructions to turn it off. There is currently no penalty for reporting inadvertent activations. Testing of EPIRBs should be done monthly and a record made in the GMDSS Log. There is a switch which allows a test without making a distress transmission. Batteries must also be kept current.

While satellites and satellite-compatible distress beacons have significantly improved the effectiveness of SAR operations, the system is NOT a substitute for carrying appropriate marine band radio. Your initial distress alert should still be made by DSC radio if possible. You should activate your distress beacon only if radio contact cannot be made (or if radio contact is lost) or when told to do so by a rescue authority.

## On-scene co-ordinator (OSC)

It is quite likely that the Search and Rescue Mission Co-ordinator (SMC) will pass responsibility for on-scene co-ordination to a suitably equipped and crewed vessel at the scene of the incident. Until an OSC has been designated, the first facility arriving at the scene should assume the duties of the OSC. When deciding how much responsibility to delegate to the OSC, the Search and Rescue Mission Co-ordinator normally considers the communications and personnel capabilities of the facilities involved. The poorer the communications, the more authority the OSC will need to initiate actions. The duties of the on scene co-ordinator (OSC) are detailed in Section 3 of Volume III of the IAMSAR Manual and include:

1. Co-ordination of operations of all SAR facilities on-scene.
2. Receive the search action plan or rescue plan from the SMC or plan the search or rescue operation, if no plan is otherwise available.
3. In consultation with the SMC when practicable, modify the search action or rescue action plan as the situation on-scene dictates, keeping the SMC advised.
4. Co-ordinate on-scene communications.
5. Monitor the performance of other participating facilities.
6. Ensure operations are conducted safely, paying particular attention to maintaining safe separations among all facilities, both surface and air.
7. Make periodic situation reports (SITREPs) to the SMC. SITREPs should include but not be limited to:
   (a) Weather and sea conditions
   (b) The results of search to date
   (c) Any actions taken
   (d) Any future plans or recommendations.
8. Maintain a detailed record of the operation:

(a) On-scene arrival and departure times of SAR facilities, other vessels and aircraft engaged in the operation
(b) Areas searched
(c) Track spacing used
(d) Sightings and leads reported
(e) Actions taken
(f) Results obtained.

9 Advise the SMC to release facilities no longer required.
10 Report the number and names of survivors to the SMC.
11 Provide the SMC with the names and designations of facilities with survivors aboard.
12 Report which survivors are in each facility.
13 Request additional SMC assistance when necessary (for example, medical evacuation of seriously injured survivors).

### SAR SITREPs

Normally the SMC will designate the SAR-dedicated frequencies to be used by the OSC. It is important that regular reporting in the form of SITREPs is made to the SMC. Each SITREP should be prefixed with a reference number ie SAR SITREP 001, SAR SITREP 002 etc so that the SMC can ensure that none are missed. Full details of the information required in SAR SITREPs are available in Appendix D of IAMSAR Volume III.

## Planning the search

It is necessary to establish a datum (not to be confused with Chart Datum or horizontal datum). The datum is a starting point from which the search is commenced. Factors to be taken into account include:

1 Reported time and position of the casualty.
2 Any sightings.
3 Any time delays between the reported time and the arrival time of the SAR facilities.
4 Estimated tide/current and leeway.

## Search patterns

There are a number of approved search patterns detailed in Section 3 of IAMSAR Volume III suitable for surface craft as well as aircraft. These have been calculated based upon the size of the casualty and the type, speed and number of SAR assisting facilities which are expected on-scene.

Because it is an international requirement for IAMSAR Volume III to be carried aboard all vessels and SAR aircraft, instructions for search patterns can be easily passed from the OSC to the assisting craft by using the page number and description which is detailed in Section 3 of IAMSAR Volume III.

# Annex A

# Navigation and Radar Module Syllabi for OOW and Master (Yacht)

*Extracts from the MCA Course Syllabi.*

## Officer of the Watch (yacht) less than 3000gt

### Navigation and Radar (OOW, Yachts)

*Duration*
This module must be conducted over a minimum period of ten days.

*Content*
The module will consist of sections on basic chart work, navigation aids, basic radar operation and plotting.

*Assessment*
There will be practical in-course assessment throughout and satisfactory completion of this assessment will allow the student entry to the final written examination at the end of the course.

The in-course assessment will include demonstrating competence in:

*Basic chartwork and position fixing, including:*
- Running fix with tides and leeway
- Compass bearings and conversion from compass to true bearings
- Horizontal angles
- Clearing bearings and transits

*Operation and setting up of electronic navigation aids including:*
- GPS
- Loran C
- Electronic chart systems

- Echo sounders and logs
- Basic operation and setting up of Radar and use of PI's
- Operation of AIS (Automatic Identification System)
- Knowledge of chart symbols and abbreviations
- The IALA system of buoyage: both A and B and the Cardinal system

The written examination will consist of a 2½ hour theory paper in two parts:

*Part 1* will consist of 3 questions – 1 each on chartwork, secondary port tidal calculation and radar plotting.

*Part 2* will consist of 4 questions carrying equal marks to test 'under pinning knowledge' of which the candidate must answer 3.

Candidates must achieve a minimum of 60% in both parts.

The practical part of the course must occupy at least half of the course period (a minimum of five days).

## TOPIC 1 • COMPASS WORK

**1 Magnetic compass**

1 Understands basic magnetism;
2 Draws a diagram of the Earth's magnetic field;
3 Understands the difference between magnetic and geographic poles;
4 Understands the magnetic meridian;
5 Explains the reason for magnetic variation;
6 Recognises the method of obtaining local magnetic variation from the chart.

**2 Understands deviation of the magnetic compass**

1 Understands the reasons for the change in deviation of the magnetic compass with changes in the ships head;
2 A basic knowledge of induced magnetism;
3 Has a basic knowledge of the methods of correcting a compass for deviation by use of magnets and soft iron correctors.

**3 Shows correct application of deviation and variation to compass courses and bearings**

1 Converts compass course to true and true to compass;
2 Converts compass bearings to true bearings and true bearings to compass bearings.

**4 Understands the need for regular checks of the compass error**

1 Demonstrates the ability to calculate compass error using transits;
2 Applies compass error correctly.

## TOPIC 2 • GYRO COMPASS

**1 Understands the practical application of the gyro compass**

1 Understands the need to regularly check the accuracy of the gyro compass;
2 Calculates gyro error using transits;
3 Applies latitude and speed correction correctly.

## TOPIC 3 • CHARTWORK

**1 Demonstrates ability to interpret information on Admiralty charts**

1 Knows chart symbols and abbreviations;
2 Understands the significance of the notes, warnings and chart datum;

**2 Different chart projections; gnomonic, mercator and port plans**

**3 Position line, circle of position and transferred position lines**

1 Understands differences of position and position lines;
2 States the definition of DR, EP and fix;
3 Plots ships position using compass and speed log;
4 Plots running fix with tide and leeway.

**4 Understands the difference between ground and water track**

**5 Fixes position by:**

1 Compass bearings;
2 Running fix;
3 Ranges and bearings
4 Dipping distances;
5 Calculates distance off by vertical angle.

**6 Understands the use of danger angles and danger circles**

1 Calculates the correct danger angle allowing for height of tide.

**7 Fix ships position using echo sounder**

1 Use of line of soundings combined with range or bearing.

## TOPIC 4 • CHART CORRECTING

**1 Understands the importance of up to date charts**

1 Recognise the latest correction on a chart;
2 Understands how to check that a chart is up to date.

**2 Understands information contained in the *Weekly Notices to Mariners (N to M)* and cumulative lists of chart corrections**
   1 Demonstrates ability to correct charts accurately;
   2 Demonstrates ability to correct other publications including ALL, ALRS, pilot books etc.

## TOPIC 5 • NOTICES TO MARINERS

**1 Understands the importance of up to date information**
   1 Uses NAVTEX and radio to obtain latest information before and during voyage.

**2 Understands importance of Ts and Ps**

**3 Has knowledge of the contents of the *Annual Summary of N to M***

## TOPIC 6 • TIDES AND TIDAL CALCULATIONS

**1 Tides and calculations**
   1 Understands basic reasons for tides;
   2 Differentiates between spring and neap tides;
   3 Understands relationship between Chart Datum, LATS, MHWS etc;
   4 Understands information contained in the Admiralty Tide Tables;
   5 Calculates height and range of tide at standard ports;
   6 Calculates times and heights of tide at secondary European ports;
   7 Calculates height of tide for a given time at standard and secondary ports;
   8 Calculates the time for a given height of tide at standard and secondary ports.

## TOPIC 7 • INTERNATIONAL REGULATIONS FOR PREVENTING COLLISIONS AT SEA (COLREGS)

**1 COLREGS**
   1 Full knowledge of the COLREGS.

## TOPIC 8 • BUOYAGE SYSTEM

**1 Demonstrates a full knowledge of the IALA system A and B**

## TOPIC 9 • NAVIGATION AIDS

**1 Hyperbolic navigation systems**
   1 Understands the propagation of electromagnetic waves with particular reference to:
      - Frequency and wavelength;

- Ground wave, sky wave;
- Ionospheric affects;

2 Loran-C system:
- Understands the relationship between master and slave stations in a Loran chain;
- Understands the methods used to differentiate between master and slave stations;
- Explains the method of differentiating between chains;
- Time difference;
- Understands the basic principle of the Loran-C system;
- Understands the errors and limitations of the Loran-C system;
- Day/night effect;
- Propagation effect;
- Additional secondary factors;
- Demonstrates ability to fix position using Loran-C receiver.

**2 Satellite navigation systems (GPS)**

1 States the principle of satellite navigation systems;
2 Aware of the errors of GPS system and their causes;
3 Demonstrate an understanding of the terms DOPS etc;
4 Aware of the problems associated with datum correction;
5 An outline knowledge of differential GPS.

**3 Echo sounders**

1 Understand the echo-ranging principles;
2 Use of echo-ranging for depth calculation;
3 Time base measurement;
4 Understand the operation of a simple echo sounder;
5 Demonstrates the correct setting up procedures:
- Correct range;
- Alarms;
- Correct gain;
- Correct datum (depth below keel);

6 Understands the errors of the echo sounders:
- Effect of water density;
- Effect of shallow water;
- Aeration;
- Cavitation;
- Multiple returns (second trace);

7 Dangers and correct use of phased scales.

**4 Speed logs**

1 Basic knowledge of measuring speed and distance through the water;
2 Towed and rotating logs;
3 Doppler logs:
- Knowledge of Doppler shift principle;
- Explains the method used in Doppler log to measure ship speed;
- States that speed can be measured in all directions;

- Understands the errors of a Doppler log system;
- Understands the dangers associated with Doppler logs for speed input into true motion radar and ARPA;

4 Electromagnetic logs:
- Knowledge of the principle of electromagnetic log;
- Understand that electromagnetic logs read speed through the water;
- Understands the errors of the electromagnetic log.

**5 Electronic Chart Display and Information Systems**

1 Understands the difference between ECS and ECDIS;
2 Understands the types of chart available:
- Raster charts with reference to ARCS;
- Vector charts;
- Be aware of S-52 and S57 IMO approved standard formats;
- Be aware of the significance of ENC and their use with ECDIS.

**6 Understands the methods of fixing the ships position on ECS**

1 DGPS and Loran-C etc;
2 Understands the potential errors due to incorrect chart datum;
3 Understands the limitations of accuracy;
4 Understands the method of making corrections to electronic charts;
5 Appreciates the need for accurate records of corrections;
6 Explain the use and operation of radar overlays and the associated dangers.

**7 Understands the proper use of AIS**

1 Understands the principles of AIS;
2 arious modes of AIS operation are understood;
3 Limitations of AIS are identified;
4 Information obtained by AIS are interpreted and used correctly.

## TOPIC 10 • RADAR

**1 Principles of radar**

1 Understands echo-ranging principle;
2 Describes the function of the scanners and associated aerial system;
3 Describes bearing determination by azimuth of scanner;
4 Appreciates the effect beam width has on beam distortion and bearing error;
5 Describes the formation of side lobes and multiple echoes;
6 Appreciates the importance of vertical beam width;
7 Understands factors affecting minimum range and discrimination:
- Pulse repetition frequency (PRF);
- Pulse length;
- Target aspect;
- Height of scanner;

8 Understands the factors affecting target size and quality:
- Aspect of target;
- Material;

9 Understands the errors in radar information and identifies false targets:
- Multiple echoes;
- Side lobes;
- Shadow and blind sectors;
- Second trace echoes;
- Meteorological effects.

**2 Operation of radar**

1 Understands correct setting up procedure;
2 Understands the action of each of the following controls:
- Brilliance, gain, tuning, pulse length, range;
- Clutter, sea and rain;
- Auto clutter controls;

3 Understands the use of the heading marker;
4 Understands the dangers of incorrectly aligned heading marker;
5 Uses the heading marker switch correctly during watch keeping;
6 Takes ranges and bearings using the electronic bearing line and variable range markers;
7 Understands the errors in range and bearing;
8 Understands parallel indexing techniques;
9 Understands the methods of parallel indexing using index lines;
10 Sets up index lines correctly;
11 Correctly interprets the information supplied by the radar;
12 Interprets relative and true tracks correctly.

**3 Radar plotting**

1 Understands the method of laying out a paper plot:
- OAW triangle;
- Understands CPA;
- TCPA and method of calculating course and speed;

2 Interprets plotted information correctly and acts according to IRCPS;
3 Knowledge of COLREGS Rule 19;
4 Understands the effects of alteration of course and/or speed of own ship.

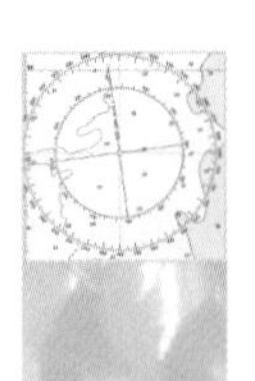



# Master (Yacht) Less than 500gt Navigation, Radar and ARPA Simulator

### *Duration*

This module must be conducted over a minimum period of ten days (60 hours).

### *Content*

This module to be split into sections: Navigation, Radar, ARPA and Simulation. The structure of this module must incorporate at least five days use of an MCA type-approved radar simulator or any other system approved by the MCA to be suitable for this course. A minimum of three days must be devoted to tuition in the practical use and aspects of ARPA.

### *Assessment*

The assessment shall be in two parts:

(a) *In-course practical assessment.*
Candidates MUST satisfactorily complete the in-course assessment before they are eligible to take the written exam. The in-course assessment will consist of:
 1 Preparing a comprehensive passage plan for a voyage of over 50 miles or three hours passage, which ever is the greatest. If possible, this should be one of the passages run as a simulator exercise.
 2 Successful completion of a series of simulated exercises, demonstrating competence in the use of electronic navigational aids (including radar/ARPA operation), general navigation and an understanding of the International Regulations for Preventing Collisions at Sea (COLREGS).

(b) A written 2½ hour 'under pinning knowledge' theory exam. The written paper will consist of six questions and candidates should attempt all questions.

To achieve a pass the candidates must achieve at least 60% in both parts.

## TOPIC 1 • PASSAGE PLANNING

**1 Appraisal and planning – identify most suitable route**
 1 Set courses on charts between points of departure and destination;
 2 Assess and allow suitable margins of safety from dangers;
 3 Identify and highlight dangers on the charts.

**2 Consult all relevant documentation**
 1 Weather throughout route, including TRS storms, winds, potential fog, ice and any other aspect that could restrict passage;
 2 Prevailing currents and tides (heights and directions) in relevant places;
 3 Pilot book information: shallow patches, restricted areas, conspicuous landmasses;
 4 Reporting areas, VTS and other communication requirements;
 5 Pilotage areas requirements.

**3 Determine all aspects affecting navigation**

1 Determine changes in compass errors by variation chart or similar;
2 Identify position fixing arrangements;
3 Identify transit bearings and other means of determining the compass error;
4 Determine suitable parallel indexing and identify index ranges;
5 Define contingency arrangements;
6 Identify Traffic Separation areas;
7 Identify fishing areas;
8 Identify any other special areas and restrictions, which may affect the safe navigation.

**4 Pre-sailing briefing**

1 Understand the importance of pre-sailing briefing;
2 Identify information to be discussed at pre-sailing briefing.

**5 Use of ECDIS with passage planning**

1 Plan and save a route using ECDIS, adding text and warnings, where necessary;
2 Set appropriate alarm parameters ie cross track error, safety depths, safety contour, guard rings;
3 Determine the availability of appropriate charts and their coverage;
4 Understand the limitations and potential dangers of over-reliance on ECDIS.

**6 Fuel consumption and range**

1 Determine total distance to travel and fuel consumption;
2 Determine a safe fuel reserve required;
3 Determine fuel required at departure port.

**7 Execution and monitoring**

1 Fixes vessel's position by visual and/or radar fixes;
2 Fix vessel's position by electronic navigational aids;
3 Determine course to steer to make good a desired course;
4 Effectively monitor the vessel's progress on an electronic chart;
5 Compare positions obtained by different methods;
6 Activate 'contingency arrangements' when proven necessary due to steering, engine breakdowns, etc;
7 Maintain the vessel in a safe position;
8 Monitor other vessels in the vicinity by radar/ARPA;
9 Comply correctly with the COLREGS.

**8 Conduct arrival briefing**

1 Understand the importance of arrival briefings;
2 Identify the information to be discussed at an arrival briefing.

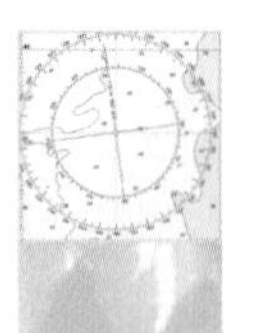



## TOPIC 2 • KNOWLEDGE OF COLREGS

**1 Application of the COLREGS – conduct exercises on an approved simulator**

1. Appreciate the need for early and substantial action and dangers of assumptions made on inadequate information;
2. Understand the importance of using radar in clear visibility to appreciate its capabilities and limitations;
3. Take suitable action within the Rules to avoid close-quarter situation with vessels in sight of one another.
4. Take action to avoid close-quarter situation with vessels detected by radar alone, but not observed visually;
5. Determine a safe speed taking into account all prevailing conditions;
6. Whilst conducting a simulated passage, analyse potential collision risks with multi-vessel encounter, determine and execute best action to avoid a close-quarter situation with all the vessels. The target vessels should be approaching own ship from all directions including overtaking;
7. Conduct a pre-planned coastal passage on the simulator in clear and/or reduced visibility to test navigation and chartwork skills.

## TOPIC 3 • SEARCH AND RESCUE

**1 Principles of search and rescue – practical application of search and rescue**

1. Understand the basic contents and use of International Aeronautical and Marine Search and Rescue (IAMSAR) Manual;
2. Conduct a simulated multiple ship SAR exercise to include at least three ships;
3. Appoint OSC (On Scene Co-ordinator) for exercise clear of coastal control;
4. Delegate responsibilities;
5. Establish a datum;
6. Conduct full communications and instructions;
7. Initiate multiple ship search patterns;
8. Establish inter-ship communications to prepare for recovery;
9. Understand how the use of ECDIS can aid the search patterns;
10. Follow standard international SAR procedures;
11. This exercise should reflect the implications of GMDSS and other additional facilities available to assist SAR.

## TOPIC 4 • RADAR AND ARPA

**1 Radar display – setting up radar display**

1. Setting up the display;
2. Demonstrate effective use of brilliance and gain on a raster scan display;
3. Demonstrate the correct use of tuning (manual & AFC);
4. Align correct heading and test accuracy;
5. Select correct range, speed, display mode;

6 Understand the importance of selecting correct pulse length;
7 Understand correct use of enhance and anti-rain clutter controls;
8 Understand and manipulate anti-sea clutter control, auto and manual;
9 Adjust for optimum setting of all other controls.

**2 Understand the significance of video processing**
1 Understand use and limitations of correlation;
2 Understand use and limitations of interference rejection.

**3 Understand modes of operation**
1 TM and RM, North Up, Head Up and Course Up;
2 Understand the significance and advantages of ground and sea stabilised.

**4 General radar knowledge**
1 Understand the minimum required range and bearing discrimination;
2 Understand the effects of PRF and pulse length and their effects on the display;
3 Comprehend the maximum and minimum range of the standard marine radar;
4 Understand the effects of the position of scanner;
5 Understand the factors effecting target responses to radar;
6 Realise the significance of spot size of targets and target identification;
7 Analyse the factors effecting radar echo responses;
8 Understand the different wavelength of transmission and their significance;
9 Analyse the significance of target trails.

**5 Use of radar in navigation**
1 Obtain radar bearings and ranges to fix the vessel's position by use of fixed and variable range markers;
2 Appreciate the accuracy of the bearing marker and the use of bearings;
3 Understand the effects of heading marker misalignment;
4 Appreciate need for regular cross-referencing bearing and range markers;
5 Use the radar with parallel indexing for different index ranges;
6 Understand the importance of cross-checking the accuracy of radar against other means of navigation;
7 Operate ARPA radar interfaced with an ECDIS;
8 Transfer target information from ARPA to ECDIS and know its limitations;
9 Understand the principle and limitations of overlaying radar picture onto ECDIS.

**6 Radar performance and false echoes**
1 Understand the use of performance monitors and PM aids;
2 Understand the effects of precipitation on the radar display;
3 Understand the effects of other meteorological conditions on detection and display;
4 False echoes and how to reduce their effects:
- Reflected echoes;
- Multiple echoes;
- Second trace returns;
- Side lobes effects;

- Radar to radar interference;
- Blind/shadow sectors;
- Overhead cables and their effect on range and detection.

**7 Safety precautions with radar equipment**

1 Dangers working in the vicinity of the radar scanner;
2 Dangers of high voltages within the transceiver;
3 Code of Safe Working Practices for Merchant Seamen with reference to working on radar equipment.

**8 Practical radar plotting**

1 Perform paper and real-time simulator relative plotting of more than one target;
2 Interpret target movements and comply with collision avoidance under COLREGS;
3 Understand the effects of changes of course and/or speed of a target vessel;
4 Appreciate the hazards of small changes compared with substantial changes of course or speed;
5 Understand the effects of inaccuracies of course and speed inputs into a plot and to a true motion and relative motion display;
6 Understand the effects of changes in course or speed or both by own ship on the tracks of other vessels on the display;
7 Appreciate the relationship of speed to the frequency of observations;
8 Plots to include alterations of course and speed.

## TOPIC 5 • ARPA

### Introduction

*The ARPA content of this course must follow the contents of the MCA approved ARPA course, the syllabus and structure being clearly defined.*

### Aim

The aim of the course is to provide training in the fundamentals and operation of ARPA radar equipment and in the interpretation and analysis of information obtained from this equipment. To comply with IMO and statutory requirements, the ARPA radar must be under the control of a person qualified in the operational use of ARPA.

### Objectives

At the end of the course the officer should be capable of effectively using ARPA equipment as a safe aid to navigation and collision avoidance through the ability to:

- Follow procedures for operating the equipment and maintaining the display;
- Obtain and analyse the data provided;
- Take action as required for the safe conduct of navigation based on correct interpretation and analysis of ARPA data.

**Format of the course**

To achieve the objectives of the course and to cover the syllabus topics, the course shall consist of demonstrations, instruction and intensive simulator exercises on the use of ARPA. Practical real time exercises followed by a de-brief and discussion of actions taken during the exercises are an essential feature to enable the student to acquire and demonstrate proficiency in the operation of the equipment.

Due attention must be given to:

1 The need to act at all times in accordance with the provisions of the COLREGS and the Basic Principles and Operational Guidance for the Keeping a Safe Navigational Watch.
2 The dangers inherent in over-reliance on ARPA data.
3 The capabilities and limitations of the system and those factors which can affect the system's performance and accuracy.
4 Real time plotting, associated with collision avoidance manoeuvring, using a simulator as an essential part of this section of the course.

**Design of exercises**

The exercises should require the participants to illustrate the principles of keeping a safe navigational watch, chartwork and collision avoidance. The design and conduct of the exercises should be progressive and the later exercises designed to stretch the ability of the participants.

**Student numbers**

In order to satisfactorily achieve the objectives there should never be more than two active participants to each ARPA workstation on the simulator.

**Automatic radar plotting aids**

The theoretical and practical content of the course will incorporate the following:

**1 Understand the possible risks of over-reliance on ARPA**

1 The importance of keeping a visual lookout;
2 The limitations of the equipment;
3 The need to retain the principles and guidance of keeping navigation watch.

**2 Principle types of ARPA systems and their display characteristics**

1 The use of ground and sea stabilised displays;
2 The dangers of ground stabilised displays when using the ARPA for anti-collision purposes;
3 Appreciate the minimum IMO performance standards for ARPA.

**3 Understand the factors affecting system performance and accuracy**

1 The effects of inaccurate or failure of speed or course inputs;
2 Factors which influence true and relative vector accuracy;
3 The use and accuracy of ground and sea stabilised vectors;
4 Appreciate tracking capabilities and limitations;
5 Understand the possibility of target swap and its effects;
6 Appreciate the processing delays on an ARPA;
7 Understand the operational warnings (tests and alarms), their benefits and limitations.

**4 Manual and automatic acquisition of targets**

1 Demonstrate an ability to acquire targets manually;
2 Acquire targets using auto-acquisition;
3 Explain clearly the difference between true and relative vectors;
4 Understand the use of true and relative vectors, graphical representation of target information and danger areas;
5 Use of information on past positions of targets tracked.

**5 Setting up and maintaining displays**

1 Explain the dangers and effects of incorrectly adjusted controls;
2 Discuss the factors affecting the selection of speed input (ground/sea stabilising);
3 Discuss the use of common system operational tests eg performance monitors.

**6 Obtaining information from the ARPA display**

1 Demonstrate an ability to identify critical echoes;
2 Demonstrate an ability to determine the relative and true course and speed of targets;
3 Demonstrate an ability to determine CPA and TCPA of targets;
4 Detection of velocity alterations of targets and its limitations;
5 Effects of own ship alterations, use of trial manoeuvre facility.

**7 Application of the COLREGS**

1 Understand the correct application of the COLREGS with simulated exercises.

**8 Appreciate the factors involved in decision-making based on ARPA and other navigational information**

1 Apply the COLREGS correctly based on ARPA information.

**9 Introduction to mapping**

1 Understand the basic ideas of mapping;
2 Appreciate the alternative methods provided to lock the map and the inherent dangers associated with each method;
3 Appreciate the potential dangers of the use of ARPA mapping facility.

**10 Interfacing ARPA with other systems**

1 Understand the ability to transfer data between navigational aids and their limitations, ie ARPA to ECDIS, GPS to ARPA and ECDIS;
2 Appreciate the dangers and limitations of data transfer between equipment.

# Annex B
## Radar Requirements

Radar and associated equipment required by Regulation 19 of SOLAS V comprises:

- **Radar unit – 9GHz 3cm 'X' band**
- **Radar unit – 3GHz 10cm 'S' band**
- **Electronic Plotting Aid (EPA)**
  EPA equipment enables electronic plotting of at least ten targets, but without automatic tracking.
  *Note* The wording of the Regulation in the case of EPA includes '...or other means to plot electronically the range and bearing of targets to determine collision risk.' Therefore manual plotting equipment is no longer acceptable except for existing vessels still complying with SOLAS V/74.
- **Automatic Tracking Aid (ATA)**
  ATA equipment enables manual acquisition and automatic tracking and display of at least ten targets.
- **Automatic Radar Plotting Aid (ARPA)**
  ARPA equipment provides for manual or automatic acquisition of targets and the automatic tracking and display of all relevant target information for at least 20 targets for anti-collision decision making. It also enables trial manoeuvres to be executed.

## Carriage requirements

**9GHz 3cm 'X' band Radar** is required on any vessel of 300gt and over.
**3GHz 10cm 'S' band Radar** is to be fitted as the second radar, which is required on ships of 3,000gt and over unless the Administration considers it appropriate to carry a second 9GHz radar. The two radars must be functionally independent of each other. The MCA will require a reasoned case for why a 3GHz radar cannot be carried.
**EPA** is to be incorporated in radar equipment on ships of 300gt and over, but less than 500gt.
**ATA** is to be incorporated in radar equipment on ships of 500gt and over (replacing the requirement for an EPA). On ships of 3,000gt and over the second radar must also be equipped with an ATA. The two ATAs must be functionally independent of each other.
**ARPA** is to be incorporated in one radar equipment on ships of 10,000gt and over. The second unit must incorporate ATA if not ARPA.

| Summary of minimum radar requirements | | | | | |
|---|---|---|---|---|---|
| GROSS TONNAGE | 9GHz RADAR | 3GHz RADAR* | EPA | ATA | ARPA |
| 300–499 | 1 | | 1 | | |
| 500–2,999 | 1 | | | 1 | |
| 3,000–10,000 | 1 | 1 | | 2 | |
| 10,000 + | 1 | 1 | | 1** | 1 |

**Administration may approve a second 9GHz radar instead*
*** Or second ARPA*

*NB: The Performance Standards and associated testing standards for radar equipment are listed in ANNEX 9 – IMO Performance Standards for navigational equipment.*

# Index